*The Best Guide to*

*Eastern Philosophy*

*and Religion*

To

Prof. Paul Bateman

On the occasion of your

90th birthday

With warm regards,

Krishna Alladi

Mar 2009

# The Best Guide to Eastern Philosophy and Religion

*Diane Morgan*

RENAISSANCE BOOKS

*New York*

*For Liza Gregory with love*

www.stmartins.com

*Design by Lisa-Theresa Lenthall and Tanya Maiboroday*
*Illustrations by Amanda Tan*

Note: In this book, eras will be denoted with the designations B.C.E. (Before the Common Era) and C.E. (Common Era) rather than the equivalent (and Christian) B.C and A.D.

Library of Congress Cataloging-in-Publication Data

Morgan, Diane.
    The best guide to eastern philosophy and religion / Diane Morgan.
       p. cm.
    ISBN 1-58063-197-5
    1. Asia—Religion. 2. Philosophy, Asian. I. Title.

  BL1082.M67 2001
  200'.95—dc21
  2001018576

First Edition: August 2001

10  9  8  7  6  5

## ACKNOWLEDGMENTS

I'd like to thank everyone who helped make this book possible—from Agni to Zoroaster. But I owe my most heartfelt thanks to my good friend, the enlightened (and enlightening) Amanda Pisani. Her perspicacity, generosity, insight, and unbounded good humor make her a joy to work with.

# CONTENTS

# *Introduction*

*A*ll religion, whether Western or Eastern, is a nexus. It forms a bridge between the absolute and the relative, between the apparently real, and the truly real, between what we perceive as secular and what we know as holy.

How that absolute, holy, truly real realm exists, by what power, and for what purpose, is differently conceived by the two great traditions. Most Western traditions, such as Judaism, Christianity, and Islam, see the absolute as transcendent, beyond, and other. Most Eastern traditions, on the other hand, envision it as immanent, within, and ultimately identical with the seeker.

Western religion conceives the ultimate as God, and the goal of most people practicing the Western tradition is to know God, obey God, and form a loving and vital relationship with God. God is a person. Eastern thought tends to be nontheistic. It sees the ultimate as something transpersonal, and the goals of its practitioners are awareness and unity. Although many Eastern religions have a place for gods in their scheme of things, they see ultimate reality as something that is both beyond the gods yet, at the same time, locked within the heart of every being. So it might be accurate to say that while in Western thought the divine is a person, in Eastern thought, every person is ultimately divine.

The concept of time marks another telling difference between Eastern and Western thought. In the West, time is often compared to a swift-running river. It flows in one direction—toward eternity. This viewpoint makes us look at eternity in a one-sided way. Eternity lies in the future; it's something that awaits us. (The title of James Jones's great novel of World War II, *From Here to Eternity*, captures completely this Western attitude.) We don't care where the river springs from; we're not much interested in our past. Although many Westerners spend a considerable amount of time contemplating a life after death, life before birth is left out of the equation. We don't know, and we don't care. The classic Rinzai Zen koan, "What was your face before you were born?" doesn't have much meaning for us. In the East, however, time is more aptly compared to a great primeval ocean, always existing, totally surrounding us. It's our source and our destination. Eternity doesn't await us, for we are present in it right now.

For the West, time means history, and history has meaning. Western religions depend upon historical events to give significance to their most precious beliefs. God acts through history to teach lessons, redeem, or punish. The Exodus, the Crucifixion, and the Night of Power stand as formative events in Judaism, Christianity, and Islam. This concept is entirely absent from Eastern philosophy. Although it would be wrong to say that history is meaningless to Buddhists or Hindus or Taoists, it would be better to say that history is a reflection of human rather than divine action. It results from our acts, not God's plan.

Because of its different perspective, Eastern religious thought has always fascinated, and often confused, the Western mind. It emphasizes values the West has forgotten. It celebrates the self, and yet it's the opposite of selfishness. It shows us a reality that goes beyond our world, yet it is not otherworldly. Far from being impractical, disengaged, and indifferent (charges commonly made against them), Eastern religions offer the physical, mental, and spiritual tools to enable a person to live life more fully and deeply. They lead the way not off into some weird, indefinable ether, but a path deep down into the truest self. Call it absolute. Call it Brahman. Call it Tao. Or speak of it in silence.

Many people see some Eastern traditions, notably Confucianism and Theravada Buddhism, as philosophies rather than religions.

This is a false distinction. In the East, lines blur between religion and philosophy. The sacred is not distinct from the profane. All branches of knowledge are seen as aspects of one truth. To Westerners, who tend to think in terms of categorization, definitions, and labels, this is a strange, even annoying, state of affairs. The Hindu convention of discussing the absolute, unconditioned reality only in terms of negatives, *neti neti* ("not this, not this"), seems calculated to drive Occidental students insane. Only when the West stops insisting the East use a Western perspective can Westerners hope to understand the Eastern religions.

Each Eastern tradition opens a window on a different aspect of life, from breathing techniques, through sexuality, manners, meditation, metaphysics, worship, art, and ethics. And each tradition has produced a variety of sacred literature to reflect the diverse concerns of its practitioners. The Rig Veda sings glorious songs of praise. The Bhagavad Gita draws the paradoxical connection between action and detachment. The Tao Te Ching teaches us to live following the example of nature, while the Confucian Classics show us how to make a civilization. The Upanishads speak philosophically about the nature of the ultimate and the human relationship to it. The great sutras of Mahayana Buddhism teach worship, wisdom, and compassion. Not least, the Tibetan Book of the Dead shows us how to die.

A few general remarks: In every religious tradition, there is a difference between popular belief and scholarly formulation. To complicate matters still more, popular customs differ from place to place, and scholarly attitudes are far from monolithic. And both change over time, sometimes radically. Other complexities emerge. Religion that has been exported to a different culture assimilates some of the attitudes and folkways of that culture. Hinduism in Bali and Buddhism in Japan or America are radically different from their Indian roots. Does this make them less authentic—or only less Indian, less "localized"?

Most troubling, however, is the inevitable gulf, often vast, between the ideals of any religious tradition and the way it is actually practiced. Too often, when comparing religions, we are inclined to value our own religion by its ideals, while denigrating other religions based on the habits of their practitioners. For example, Christians may hold up their own religion as a religion of peace and point accusing fingers at the wars fought between Muslims and Jews, while conveniently forgetting the bloody battles Christians have fought throughout the ages—and still do. This is tremendously unfair, of course. The truth is that few individuals of any faith live up to the noble concepts espoused by their religious heritage. This is in the nature of things. The great world religions have this one thing in common: They give us something to strive for. Religions are not for perfect people. Perfect people don't need a religion; they need worshippers.

Most of us aren't perfect, however, and we aren't living the ideal life. Why is this? Each spiritual tradition I'll be looking at in this book offers a different explanation as to what obstacles separate us from the ideal life we should be living. For the Hindus it's ignorance; for the Buddhists it's suffering; for Taoists it's unnaturalness; for Confucians it's lack of reciprocity. Each tradition offers us a way past or through or over the obstacles and presents us a guide to a life more rich, more joyful, more wise.

# *Hinduism—*

# *The Luminous Self*

Ask somebody what comes to mind when you mention the word *Hinduism*. Here's what you'll hear: sacred cows, karma, caste system. Yoga, reincarnation, Mahatma Gandhi. Image worship. Beds of nails. Gurus. The Kama Sutra. Perhaps someone will mention "suttee." Others may talk about avatars or even the Bhagavad Gita. Some of these words do describe certain elements of Hinduism, but none of them comes close to touching its heart.

Yet the heart of Hinduism is vast. It has given birth to traditions as diverse as Buddhism, Jainism, Transcendental Meditation, and the philosophy of health guru Deepak Chopra. It's given us yoga and Tantra and meditation. It has a religious philosophy that is more sophisticated than anything the West has yet produced and a philosophical religion that is eerily close to particle theory and quantum mechanics.

*Shiva, as Lord of the Dance*
*India, c. 950–1000 C.E. (copper alloy)*

Hinduism is unique among the major religions of the world. It has no founder. It has no dogma. It has no central authority, no pope, and no ecclesiastical council to decide what Hindus must or must not believe. The result is a bewildering, glorious medley of competing philosophies, disparate religious practices, and divergent lifestyles. It's a religion that seems uniquely able to accommodate the individual seeker. Like an amoeba, Hinduism constantly varies its shape.

A devout Hindu can be a monotheist, a polytheist, or a nontheist. He can worship at shrines or worship at home. Or not worship at all. He can renounce the world or conquer it. He can give up sex or raise a large family. There is no creed to recite, only paths to follow. The choice of those paths is completely up to the seeker. In Hinduism, the road to freedom begins with freedom.

# *A  L a n d s c a p e ,   a   P e o p l e ,*
# *a n d   a   F a i t h*

*D*efining *Hinduism* is difficult. (One source I consulted passed the buck by saying that Hinduism is a religion practiced by Indians who aren't Muslim, Buddhist, Jain, Sikh, or Christian.) To complicate matters even further, Hinduism varies greatly from place to place. A Hindu from Bali practices a very different sort of Hinduism than do Hindus from India, and Hindu customs in northern India differ markedly from those in the south.

The word *Hindu* has no ideological connotation like Protestant, Unitarian, Baptist, or Seventh Day Adventist. Hinduism isn't named after a founder like Christianity, Buddhism, or Confucianism. It doesn't assign itself a name intended to describe what its adherents believe about it, like Islam, which means "surrender," or "Catholic," which means "universal." Only Judaism defines itself precisely the way Hinduism is defined by Westerners. Just as Judaism is the religion of the Jews, so Hinduism is the religion of the Hindus.

But Hindus themselves don't call their religion "Hinduism." They may use the word *darshana*, which is often translated as "philosophy," but really means "seeing" or "experience." Or they may refer to their faith as the *Sanatana Dharma*, the eternal way of truth.

One thing that separates so-called "axial religions" like Hinduism, Christianity, and Buddhism, from aboriginal, traditional ones is their attitude toward life. Traditional African, Australian, Native American, and early European religions celebrate life for what it is. Beginning several thousand years ago, however, someone came up with the idea that human existence was flawed in some basic, essential way. In other words, something was wrong with the way life was lived. The idea of "sin" developed and troubling questions emerged. Why did some people suffer, through apparently no fault of their own? Why do evil people prosper? What happens after death or before birth? What is the relationship, if any, between gods and human beings? Is there a connection between worship and ethics?

---

**A NONBINDING TRADITION**

*Early Hindus didn't think about differentiating their religious beliefs and practices from those of others. There is no word in any Indian language that precisely matches what Westerners mean by religion, a word whose Latin root means "to bind." Hinduism is a nonbinding tradition. It regards all sincere attempts to find divine truth as valid.*

---

## BASIC HINDU BELIEFS

Although Hindus don't have a creed to adhere to, or a catechism to follow, nearly all Hindus assent to certain general principles or articles of faith. (There's no penalty if you don't agree with all of them, although people might look at you funny.) Here's the short list of what Hindus believe:

"'Ekam sad vipra behudha vadanti.' Truth is one, but it is called by different names."

—The Vedas

- They believe that their sacred scriptures, the Vedas, are divine works that manifest the glorious primal energy of both creation and eternity.

- They believe in a supreme Ground of Being, the Brahman, who is uncreated, unborn, changeless, incorruptible, and utterly holy.

- They believe that each person has divinity within him or her.

- They believe that the universe exists through endless cycles, and that individual souls pass through incarnation after incarnation.

- They believe in karma (that our lot in this life is a result of past deeds in other incarnations, and that our future happiness depends on how we live here and now).

- They believe that all life is holy and that eventually every single soul, including the souls of animals, will achieve liberation, peace, and freedom in the knowledge of the Brahman.

- They believe that all religions, rightly understood, can bring their followers to salvation.

As alien as these beliefs seem, it's this last point that is the real stumbling block to outsiders. Our Western passion for categorizing has made religious truth seem like an exclusive property. If one path is "true," according to Occidental reasoning, then other paths must be "false" to the degree they diverge from the true path. Hindus have a different view. Only Westerners, with their "one life to live" attitude, get hung up on taking the "right road." "Two roads diverged in a yellow wood, And sorry I could not travel both and be one traveler," lamented Robert Frost.

Hindus aren't troubled by divergent paths. Unlike Frost, they have time to take as many roads as they choose, if not in this life, then in another one. And as we shall see, time doesn't matter much for Hindus—they know there's a lot of it.

### The Hindu Concept of Time

To understand Hinduism it is essential to understand the Hindu notion of time. Here's a famous parable. Once every thousand years a raven flies over the top of the world's highest peak, carrying in his bill a silken, fringed scarf. The mountain is so high that the raven can just barely make the pass, especially because he's dragging a scarf, no easy task even for a pretty strong raven. (This is probably why he attempts it only once in a thousand years.) At any rate, as the raven flies over the summit, the very edge of one fringe brushes the top of the mountain. When the entire mountain has been worn away by the fringe of the passing scarf, one moment in the life of this cosmos has passed.

## THE TRUE REALITY

Hinduism attempts to release us from the false reality into the true reality. This is a tough job, because there's plenty of pleasure and satisfaction in this illusory world: food, sex, wealth, fame, social action, or personal achievements. None of these are bad things; but they don't last. And what doesn't last can't ultimately be real. The pleasures of this life are also habit-forming; they keep us coming back to them over and over, lifetime after lifetime. And habits, no matter how pleasant, are fetters on our liberty. Unless we break these habits, we'll never find freedom or truth. Hinduism wants to show us the way there. It gives us a lot of options. It gives us philosophy to stretch the mind, yoga to expand the spirit, and devotional paths to stir the heart. It has a complex and symbolic mythology that is part religious text, part high literature, and part entertainment.

Hinduism was the first major world religion to suspect a profound difference between the world of appearances and ultimate reality. It was the first to suggest that behind the multiplicity of entities in the universe—trees, stones, horses, perceptions, thoughts, gods, and demons—there was a single, undying unity behind it all. It was the first religion to try to find that unity. The search continues.

## THE HOLY LAND OF HINDUISM

To the Hindus, an invisible thread connects every aspect of nature to every other. And so, it makes perfect sense that the landscape itself has a divine quality.

### Sacred Rivers

India has seven sacred rivers, but the holiest of them all is the Mother Ganges. The Ganges herself is a river goddess; her ultimate origin is the "merciful foot" of the god Vishnu. The river is thus a celestial one, flowing across the heavens, then pouring over the head of the god Shiva before tumbling to earth. Sometimes Mother Ganges is shown as a water nymph in Shiva's hair. That's because the stories say that in olden days the Ganges was so powerful she threatened to drown India. Shiva saved the day by having

**SEVEN SACRED RIVERS**

*The seven sacred rivers of India are the Ganges, the Sindhu (Indus), Sarasvati, Yamuna (now Jumna), Narmada, Godavari, and Kaveri. Don't bother trying to locate the Sarasvati. It's fictional.*

her flow through his matted hair, which was apparently a good water-soaker-upper.

The Hindu sacred rivers are said to flow with the waters of immortality. (The very term *Hindu* is derived from the Indus River.)

### Sacred Cities

Located on the Ganges is India's most holy city, Benares (now called Varanasi). It is called the "luminous," or city of light, and for a millennium and a half it was sacred to Buddhists and Jains as well as to Hindus. (The Buddha preached his first sermon here.)

For Hindus, Benares is the city of the great god Shiva, who, they say, will save it even as he destroys the rest of the universe. In fact, it is so holy that those who manage to die by the river in Benares will achieve spiritual liberation. Even meditation at Benares is more auspicious than elsewhere, especially if performed at one of the city's many cremation sites. To smear one's body with the crematory ashes is most auspicious of all.

## A HINDU HISTORY

Scholars believe that Hinduism is a cross-fertilization of two cultures: the indigenous Indus Valley Civilization and the invading Aryan culture.

### The Indus Valley Civilization

The first civilization that we know anything about in India is the Indus Valley Civilization. This famous, albeit mysterious culture was rediscovered in 1917 by an Indian archaeologist who found an ancient knife sticking out of the ground. Since then, it has been excavated in about twenty-five sites along the Indus and Ghaghar Rivers. Altogether, it may have consisted of more than 150 towns and cities, of which the two most important were Mohenjo-Daro (The Mound of the Dead) and Harappa. The whole complex of places is located in the Larkana Valley of modern Pakistan, but Pakistan used to be part of India and that's what's important.

The Indus Valley Civilization flourished from about 2500 to 1500 B.C.E., and no one really knows why it declined, although certainly enough theories have been proposed. (Its writing system is still

**SEVEN SACRED CITIES**

*All together, India has seven sacred cities. Besides Benares, these are: Ayodha, Mathura, Hardvar, Kanci, Ujjain, and Dvaraka.*

undeciphered, which doesn't help matters any.) Scholars have been impressed with what they term as the strongly religious nature of the Indus Valley people, but suspect that the inhabitants were pretty much like modern-day folk; some were religious and some weren't. Their religion seems to have been goddess-centered, although there are also indications of a complementary phallic-worship, symbolized by bulls and some rather interesting phallic-shaped objects scattered here and there. There are also some figures who look for all the world like seated yogins (or yogis, if you prefer).

**YOGI OR YOGIN**

*Although many English speakers prefer the word yogi, yogin is an equally correct term.*

The Indus Valley Civilization is generally identified with the dark-skinned Dravidian people. Although originally considered as hicks living in a cultural backwash, it turns out that in fact the Dravidians were considerably more civilized than their eventual conquerors. They grew cotton, wheat, barley, and had an excellent system of brick drains. In fact, the Indus Valley people seemed as obsessed by plumbing as we are today. They had indoor latrines, bathing rooms, and running water. The Indus Valley folk were also expert metalsmiths, but unfortunately for them, hadn't mastered the use of iron. This proved to be their undoing.

## The Coming of the Aryans

The light-skinned Aryans, who *were* skilled in the use of iron weaponry and chariots, showed up in the Punjab region around 1500 B.C.E. No one knows where they came from originally—one good guess is southeast Europe. Some settled in Iran. (Iran and Ayran are cognates.)

**WHAT IS AN ARYAN?**

*Thanks to its misuse by Adolf Hitler and his friends, the word* Aryan *has acquired negative associations in the West. (Hitler was under the impression that there was such a thing as an Aryan race and that he belonged to it.) The word* Aryan *actually means "noble" in the ancient Indo-European language the original Aryans spoke. That language is the mother tongue to Sanskrit, Greek, and Latin (from which come Spanish, French, and Italian), among others.*

The Aryans didn't arrive in one fell swoop. They probably dribbled in, over a period of about a thousand years or so. It's possible that the Indus Valley people didn't even know the Aryans were there until it was too late, although some historians contend that the arrival of the warlike Aryans brought the peaceful Indus

Valley Civilization to a screeching halt. The Aryans were a polytheistic, class-oriented people whose religious pantheon bore a remarkable resemblance to that of the Greeks and Romans. They worshipped male sky gods, chief of whom was Dyaus, the shining god of heaven. (The English word *day* is linked to *Dyaus*.) Their main religious rituals apparently involved fire and sacrifice. Religious ideals that we associate with classical Hinduism, such as asceticism and renouncing the world are *not* Aryan at all and may have belonged to the indigenous population. Or they may be a later development.

At any rate, modern Hinduism derives from both Aryan and Dravidian culture, although traditionally, the Aryans have been considered the founders of most Hindu religious concepts and traditions. The blending of the cultures was a slow process, and certain aspects of modern life reflect the lively tension between them.

## HINDUS TODAY

The Hindu people comprise many ethnic groups and dozens of cultures. More than a billion people live in India today, and 40 percent of them are under the age of fourteen. Besides Hindus, about 80 million Muslims and 15 million Sikhs currently dwell in India.

Although most Hindus live in India (about 700 million of them), another 60 million are scattered across the globe. More than 2 million Hindus live in the United States, and hundreds of thousands more live in what one might think are rather unlikely places: Trinidad, Guyana, and Surinam have almost half a million Hindus each, a large minority population. South Africa alone has 1.5 million Hindus, and millions more live in Indonesia, Bangladesh, Bhutan, Afghanistan, Singapore, Sri Lanka, Pakistan, France, Germany, the Gulf States, Mauritius, Reunion, Malaysia, Nepal, and Canada. Only seven Hindus are reported in Iceland, but one might perhaps expect no more.

Hindus come in many styles. Just as a Christian can be a Methodist or a Catholic or a Jehovah's Witness, so a Hindu can be a Shaivite, a Vaisnavite, or a Sakti. They can't be Jains or Sikhs or Buddhists, however. Even Hinduism has its limits.

**THE INDIAN PEOPLE**

*With one billion inhabitants India is, next to China, the world's most populous country (and it has only one-third the land mass of China). The people of India speak 745 different languages among them. Fourteen of those languages are "official" (including English), but the most commonly spoken language in India is Hindi.*

## CHAPTER RECAP

- Hinduism is the oldest world religion, but has no single human founder.

- Hindus believe that each person has divinity within her- or himself.

- Hindus believe that all religions will eventually lead their followers to salvation.

- Hinduism is a blend of the ancient Indus Valley Civilization and the nomadic Aryan culture.

- There are about 800 million Hindus in the world.

*Recommended Reading*

Basham, A. L. *The Wonder that Was India.* Sidgwick & Jackson, 1954.

Embree, Ainslee T. ed. *The Hindu Tradition.* The Modern Library, 1961.

Hopkins., Thomas J. *The Hindu Religious Tradition,* 1971.

Pelikan, Jaroslav, ed. *Sacred Writings,* Vol 5: The Rig Veda. Motalil Banarsidass Publishers Pvt. Ltd., 1992.

Sen, K. M. *Hinduism: The World's Oldest Faith.* Penguin Books, 1961.

Wheeler, Sir Mortimer. *Civilizations of the Indus Valley and Beyond.* McGraw-Hill, 1966

# *Aryan and Vedic*

# *Religious Tradition*

*T*he Aryans were a rather strange bunch, religiously speaking. Although they were a polytheistic people, they had no idols of their gods. They had no temples and worshipped under the open sky. They had no cult and no dogma. They had something better, though: they had poetry.

## THE VEDAS

The Vedas are the world's most ancient scripture. To the uninitiated, they look like a collection of hymns and directions for sacrifice, but for the devout Hindu they represent not only the highest spiritual discipline, but also the very means by which the universe is sustained. For the Hindus, the Vedas are "uncreated" scripture. They have no beginning in time. This means that they are not the work of human beings or even of God. They are the very truth, life, and essence of the cosmos.

### Oral and Written Words

The earliest written Vedas date to about 1400 B.C.E., but the songs they capture in letters are a great deal older, although no one can say by how much. They are very old. They are called *shruti* scriptures in Sanskrit, meaning that they were "heard." That makes them holy.

Like all ancient peoples, the Aryans regarded oral knowledge as more sacred than written lore, and the most secret teachings were never written down, where just anyone might find them. What is oral is spoken, of course, and what is spoken contains the sacred breath of life. That's another reason why oral knowledge is considered more holy than what is written. In addition, oral knowledge is knowledge enshrined on the heart—memorized (not read), and so is part of the living being who recites it.

The Vedic texts are written in a kind of sacred code. The text is plain for all to read—but its deepest meaning is for the initiated only. Even today, studying the Vedas means studying with a master, because no one gets very far into the truth on his own. For Hindus, the Vedas are the foundation scriptures upon which all other sacred works must be based.

## THE SACRED LANGUAGE

The language of the Vedas is Sanskrit, a language so holy that the very word *Sanskrit* means "perfect." It is one of the oldest languages on earth. Hindu scholars believe that every word in Sanskrit has both literal and symbolic significance, and the ancient Aryans thought that language had power over the physical universe.

As a spoken tongue, Sanskrit disappeared around 500 B.C.E. As a sacred instrument for religious purposes, however, it is still used for rituals and texts, even in religious movements that developed long after Sanskrit ceased to be spoken. (However, many texts of Bhakti Hinduism are written in Tamil, a pre-Aryan, Dravidian tongue.)

The original written Vedas are four in number: The Rig Veda, the Sama Veda, the Yajur Veda, and the Atharva Veda, each with its own special power. Each Veda has four layers: a collection of hymns *(Samhitas)*, directions about sacrifice *(Brahmanas)*, the "forest songs" *(Aranyaka)*, and the brilliant, visionary, and beautiful Upanishads, which search for the meaning behind it all. These parts are pretty much successive, meaning that the *Samhitas* are earliest, then the *Brahmanas*, and so on, although there is some overlap—but the Vedas are more than mere literature. For Hindus, the ultimate reality of the universe, the Brahman, is in some way identical with them. They are *shruti*, the breath of the eternal.

Other religious writings are considered *smriti*, or that which is only "remembered," as opposed to *shruti*, that which is heard directly. These *smriti* include the great Indian epics, the laws of Manu, the Puranas, or stories of the gods, and the Tantras. These texts do not have quite the religious authority of the Vedas, although some, like the Bhagavad Gita, are greatly beloved by the Indian people. In fact, the purpose of *smriti* is not to add a revelation, but to explain the scholarly Vedas in a different way.

### The Rig Veda

The Rig Veda, with its rich and echoing images, brings poetic truth to the mystery of creation. It is the oldest and most important of all the Vedas, consisting of ten books and 1,028 hymns to the gods—the Shining Devas. There is no exact translation of the word *Deva*, but it refers to beings with special powers. The Vedas also include sacred mantras, ancient, powerful formulas meant to be chanted aloud by the *hotar*, the officiating priest.

### The Word and the Power

For Hindus, sound itself has power and the ability to purify the listener; it is also a specific attribute of space. And every sound has both an audible aspect and a spiritual, or subtle, unheard aspect. Most of the older mantras have real meanings, but more recent ones are simply abstract sounds. (The argument as to whether mantras are meaningful or meaningless is a lively one in Hindu circles.) Mantras are still used in Bhakti Hinduism today.

Most mantras end in a nasal "m" sound, although some end in "k" or "t." A true mantra contains the

**STUDYING THE VEDAS**

*Although all orthodox Hindus accept the authority of the Vedas, they insist that the Vedas do not teach anything that cannot be learned through one's own experience. Still, the Vedas aren't for everybody. Even the goddess Parvati got bored and fell asleep while her husband Shiva was explaining them to her.*

---

THE BRAHMAN'S SONG

*According to the Vedas, the Brahman actually sang the world into existence. This may be hard for you to reconcile with the Hindu concept of time, which is circular rather than linear. In a philosophic sense, Hinduism does not ascribe to the idea of "creation" at all. The universe has no real beginning and no real ending. Apparent "creations" are just the beginning of another cycle.*

---

real name of divinity, or, in some traditions, a hidden "seed" of that name.

In the classic Hindu tradition, mantras are special formulas—not panaceas handed out to anyone who wants one. Only a select few were empowered to chant sacred mantras. Among the requirements were ritual and moral criteria (including utter sincerity). The chosen were also masters of necessary practical skills. (Mantras must be chanted in a particular way, at a specific volume, and with the right kind of controlled breathing.) Certified mantra-chanters also had to have the essential intellectual background and have attained a certain status in an esoteric tradition. This is a far cry from the practice of modern "gurus" who hand out mantras upon request (or payment) from a devotee.

One of the most holy mantras is the Savitri, composed in an ancient poetic meter called Gayatri. This verse forms part of the crepuscular (twilight and dawn) meditations of high caste Hindus. When correctly transmitted, the verse confers the power that bestows "second birth" and leads the student from the darkness of ignorance to the light of knowledge. In English the mantra reads: "Aum! Earth, mid-world, heaven! Let us meditate on that most excellent light of the divine Sun, that it may illumine our minds." In Sanskrit: *"Om bhur bhuvah svah!/Tat savitur varenyam/Bhargo devasya dhimahi/Dhiyo yo nah prachodayat"* (Rig Veda: Book III, Hymn 62, Verse 10).

## The Vedic Gods

Most of the old Vedic deities were nature gods, representing the sun, fire, wind, and the like. Others symbolize abstract concepts such as space and speech. These gods are very ancient, and modern Hindus no longer worship most of them, at least under their present names. Some have survived into the present times, however, and many others have transmuted into more modern and familiar gods.

### Agni—The Fire God

The Rig Veda opens with hymns to Agni, god of fire and sacrifice. (The English word *ignite* is a cognate to *Agni.*) Almost two hundred Rig Vedic hymns are directed to this critical god. As fire goes from earth to heaven, the early Aryans considered Agni, the carrier of the sacrifice, to be a kind of messenger god between earth and sky, or a priest who presides over the sacrifice.

Every morning Agni was born again: from the earth, from the water, and in the sky. In fact, whenever a fire was lit, Agni was born again. After the fire died down, the ashes were called "the seed" of

Agni, and it was believed that the god would arise again from the ashes. (More poetically, Agni is considered the divine spark within every human being.) Because fire is not only the vehicle of divine sacrifice, but the cooker of food, the creator of warmth, and the dis- patcher of darkness, it is suitable indeed that the Vedas open with hymns to him, although he was not the most important of the Vedic gods. "Worthy is Agni of greatest praise— by the living man as by the ancient sages" (Rig Veda: Book I, Hymn 1). Agni was considered lord of the

> ### MANY GODS IN ONE
>
> *One thing that is confusing to non-Hindus is the idea that there can be many gods, yet only one Brahman. Brahman is not just a super-God, one superior to the others. It's better to think of the other gods as humanly conceived aspects of the Brahman. Thus, modern Hinduism, properly understood, is not a polytheistic religion, as is often charged. The early Vedic religion is more like classic polytheism, but even here we see a hint of the idea that all gods are really one.*

house, father, and honored guest, all at once. He was also an absolutely benevolent and trustworthy guide for human beings and had no dark side. He represented the divine will.

Agni had seven tongues and seven arms (or rays). His blazing head faced all directions at once. Most interestingly, his back was made of butter.

In some respects, Agni is still alive in India. A special ritual reminiscent of his worship is performed even today, the *agnihotra* rite. Two or three times daily, the head of the house, reciting mantras, offers clarified butter *(ghee)*, milk, barley, or rice to the god. Only members of the three upper castes are allowed to perform this rite.

High caste weddings are still celebrated with the bride and groom sitting before the sacred fire, which symbolizes both love and sacrifice.

### Indra—The Thunder God

Indra is the long-haired, thunder-wielding sky god (much like the Greek god Zeus). He is the lord of storms and of the monsoon, and god of a hundred sacrifices. He gave life to the sun and discovered the use of (or stole) the magical intoxicant plant soma. In fact, it is said that soma is so powerful that only Indra could drink it undi- luted. Indra rides a white elephant named Airavata. Airavata has four tusks and doubles as a rain cloud. Indra wears golden armor and is often shown bearded, an anatomical detail that practically assures us of his outsider status. (The aboriginal Indians are seldom bearded.) The Rig Veda honors him with more than 250 hymns. One of the hymns declares that the devotee would not "sell Indra for a thousand or even ten thousand pieces [of gold, one presumes]." This is a good thing, since gods normally do not take kindly to being sold.

> ### THE TRUE MYTH OF MYTH
>
> *The word* myth *is often used today to denote something that isn't true. However, that is not what the word means, nor is it the sense in which I am using it. The word stems from the Greek* mythos *and means "story" or "communication." Mythology refers to a set of beliefs and narratives about gods or God. That's all.*

Most famously, Indra slew the demon-dragon Vritra, although in other versions, Vritra is slain by a cow. In either case, when the deed was done, the Seven Rivers of Being were released and we could attain the ultimate in truth and light, since the dark power of ignorance had been defeated. So far as I know, this is the only mythology extant in which a cow kills a dragon. At any rate, this heroic deed (if true) accounts for the great esteem in which Bossy is held throughout India.

Symbolically, Indra represents the illuminated mind or the power of pure existence. (One fairly late story about Indra recounts how the other gods turned him into a pig to punish him. This sort of thing never works. Indra enjoyed wallowing around in the mud so much that he refused to return to heaven. Eventually the other gods had to kill him to get him back. This is a parable, of course.)

### VISHNU IN THE VEDAS

*The Vedas also contain several hymns to far-striding Vishnu, who is one of the few Vedic gods to survive into modern times. In the Vedas, Vishnu is described as manifesting the threefold forms of light: fire, lightning, and sunlight. The whole world is gathered in the dust of Vishnu's footsteps.*

### Soma—The God of Delight

Soma is in some aspects more material than the other Gods: he is an intoxicating nectar, or something. Soma was also the chief plant used in sacrifices, at least if the Rig Veda may be believed. No one knows what the original soma plant was, although people have come up with a lot of guesses: a mushroom, barley, liquor, or some extinct plant. Marijuana aficionados like to point out that soma is also called "sacred grass." My favorite suggestion is that soma was made from rhubarb stalks.

Whatever it was, the plant's juice was supposedly pressed out between stones, which doesn't sound like any of the choices, except possibly the extinct plant. It was apparently drunk with water and milk. The Vedas refer to it as "ruddy" in color, which doesn't help. In various other places it's referred to as "brown," "tawny," or "clear."

According to scripture, soma grows in a lonely, windy place. We just don't know which lonely, windy place, perhaps Wuthering Heights.

The visionary, holy *rishis* of the Rig Veda purportedly drank soma to help them achieve the insightful ecstasy necessary for the singing of the immortal hymns. The

---

**THE SECRET FORMULA**

*There exist a group of sky gods, the Gandharva, who alone knew the secret of making soma. Since there are 6,333 of them, you'd have thought that somebody would have spilled the beans. But nobody did. When the Gandharvas weren't making soma, they taught singing and dancing.*

---

soma cult died out about 700 B.C.E., possibly because the plant became extinct. One wouldn't think it would be due to lack of interest. Nowadays, meditation and severe ascetic practices to some extent replace the use of soma, but no one claims they are as much fun.

### Varuna—The God Who Binds

Varuna is the Lord of Consciousness, who presides over air and water. He is a highly moral god and knows everything that is going on, both in heaven and on earth.

Varuna is the god to whom sinners pray for forgiveness. Often associated with him is Rita, the god of cosmic order. Rita controls sunrise, sunset, and all regularly occurring natural phenomena. Rita is what makes basset hounds produce more basset hounds instead of rottweilers. (Although Rita was originally considered a god, over time *rita* was thought of as a concept. The idea of *rita* was later supplanted by the Hindu notion of *dharma*.)

"Whenever two plot together, and think they are alone,/King Varuna is there, and all their plans are known."

—Rig Veda

### Rudra—The Roarer

Rudra is a loud-mouthed god who attacks anyone opposing divine power. The Aryans feared him greatly, and most of their hymns to him just ask him to leave them alone and not kill them. Later on in Hindu history, Rudra gets subsumed into the great god Shiva. More rarely, he is identified with Agni.

## Purusha—The Primordial Man

Purusha is the Cosmic Person, the living principle of consciousness. He is both finite and infinite, the one and the many. He is part of the Universal Brahman and also part of all creation.

This is a pretty good trick. But because he has a thousand heads and a thousand eyes, you shouldn't put much beyond him. He has a thousand feet, too. The sun was born from his eye (at least from one of them), and the moon from his mind. Indra and Agni were born from his mouth, and the wind from his breath. Space came out of his navel. All this activity makes Purusha the first sacrificer. Since there was nothing else, he sacrificed himself to make the world, and the whole universe, therefore, depends upon sacrifice. This story arguably conflicts with that of Brahman singing the world into existence, but to the Hindu mind, it's just another way of looking at things.

On a more practical note, the Rig Veda identifies Purusha as the first "person," so to speak. In the beginning the world was just one huge human-shaped body. This being looked around and said, "Here I am!" At first he was afraid, but then he reasoned, "Because I'm the only one here, I have nothing to be afraid of." People are never really afraid of being alone in the dark. They're afraid of not being alone.

### EQUINE SACRIFICE

*One source says that the original sacrifice was not of Purusha but of a horse. Horse sacrifices were all the rage among royal Aryans. The most important sacrifice was the Ashvamedha, usually celebrated in honor of a great victory. In the most exalted of these, one was supposed to offer 609 horses, but it's not clear that they were really all killed. One hopes not.*

One holy text, the Brihadarankara, says Purusha was the size and shape of a man and woman embracing. Then he got lonely, so he split into his component halves, male and female, and the human race was born. So were horses, donkeys, and cows.

## The One (Tad Ekam)—The Source of the Mystery

The here is one entity (I hesitate to use the word *divinity* here, though, because it is different from ordinary gods) that, although strange and hidden in the Vedas, emerges as the ultimate source of being. Thousands of years before Genesis was written, the Rig Veda sings a creation hymn *(Nasadiya)* of extraordinary profundity.

Then was neither Being nor Non-Being.
There was no kingdom of air—no heaven beyond.
What moved? What covered? What shielded?
Did water there stir, the deep, unfathomed depth of water?

Death was not then, nor immortality. No mark split day
    from night.
Only That One, breathless, yet breathed by its own nature:
Other than That—nothing. Nothing.

Darkness was cloaked in darkness.
This All was void. Was chaos.

Somehow by the great power of warmth was born that One.
Then. Then rose desire.
Desire, the primal seed. The birth of spirit.
Then the Wise Ones, the holy Rishis, searched with their heart.
They found the bond and the boundary between the Is and
    Is Not.

The cord stretched tight between them.
What was above, and what below?
There were the makers, the powers, the birth-force. But.

Who really knows? Who can here declare it?
Whence was it born, and whence comes this cosmos?
For the very gods come after the world's creation.

So who does know, how it first came into being?
Only He—the author of this creation,
Whether He formed it all or whether he formed none of it,
Whose limitless eye controls this universe,
Only He truly knows it,
Or perhaps he does not know.

**THE GOD OF LIGHT**

*Mitra is the god of light and love. He leads his devotees to the truth.*

These evocative words are far removed from the general run of religious literature. Far from claiming to know the precise time, method, or reason for the birth of the universe, it maintains a stance of wonder and awe. It recognizes the necessity for a creator, but the creator it envisions is too vast for human thought. The poem has more questions than answers and bears more resemblance to Job than to Genesis.

**SACRED KNOWLEDGE**

*The Vedas are simply (or not so simply, after all) "sacred knowledge." The English words* wisdom *and* vision *are both related to* Veda.

### The Sama Veda—Wisdom of Melody

As I mentioned, the Rig Veda is not the only Veda. The Sama Veda adopts mantras to a musical tradition, intended for Soma sacrifices. They are sung on a seven-note scale. Many of the songs are the same mantras as those in the Rig Veda.

### The Yajur Veda—The Knowledge of Sacrifice

The Yajur Veda is a collection of sacrificial mantras; it was written to accompany the Rig Veda. Items sacrificed *(yajna)* included grains, butter, goats, and once in a while, even horses. (To this day, goat sacrifices are performed in parts of India.) The most auspicious sacrifices were performed in the open air, preferably at the confluence of two rivers. These spots are still held holy by Hindus.

Sacrifice served a number of purposes: it was a communication to the gods; it was an offering of wealth; it was a sign of loyal obedience. Whatever the occasion, however, sacrifice was transformative. As the sacrifice was consumed by flames, it changed into an entirely different substance. This is symbolic. By sacrifice, we ourselves change into different (presumably better) people.

The Yajur Veda has more than sacrificial formulas; it also contains one of Hinduism's most beloved prayers, one that appears again and again in Hindu literature: "From unreality to Reality, from darkness to Light, from death to Immortality—Lead me."

### The Atharva Veda—Wisdom of the Fire Priests

The Atharva is a collection of 732 hymns, spells, magical formulas, and incantations for religious and healing purposes, including cures for snakebite and baldness. It reflects strong pre-Vedic, non-Aryan influences, including in some places an apparent disapproval of sacrifices. For this reason, the Atharva Veda has always been treated rather gingerly by orthodox sacrificial priests. The Atharva Veda also repeats some of the hymns found in the Rig Veda.

### The Brahmanas—The Sacred Words

The second part of the Vedas, the Brahmanas, are the earliest prose writings in the Hindu tradition. (The Samhitas are all poetry.) The Brahmanas were composed between 1000 and 700 B.C.E., but weren't written down until about 300 B.C.E.

Each Veda has at least one Brahmana attached to it as a commentary. (The Sama-Veda has eight of them.) The Brahmanas emphasize "practical matters." They contain, for instance, rules about sacrifice. The Brahmanas tell us that those who do not perform sacrifices correctly will become "the food of death" themselves. Some say that during the Brahmanas period, the sacrificial rituals became more important than the gods in whose honor they were performed, but perhaps this is an exaggeration. The Brahmanas also specify the norms of conduct: no murder, no theft, no adultery.

### Aranyakas—Forest Songs

The third layer of the Vedas, the Aranyakas, are somewhat later than the Brahmanas, dating from about 800 to 600 B.C.E. They contain mantras, commentaries, and instructions for particular rituals like the Brahmanas, however, the Aranyakas emphasize the symbolic, inner meaning of the sacrifices. The Aranyakas are intended for one who has reached the third stage of life, according to the Laws of Manu, and achieved the state of "forest dweller." The Hindu understanding of the stages of life are discussed in chapter 4.

### The Upanishads

The final layer of the Vedas is the Upanishads (800 to 500 B.C.E.), which take the form of a dialogue between teacher and student. They are so important to later Hindu philosophy and so influential in the West that I am reserving discussion of them for a later chapter.

**THE HUNDRED PATHS**

*Probably the most important of the Brahmanas is the Brahmana of the Hundred Paths, the title of which indicates some of the richness of the Hindu tradition.*

## KARMA AND SAMSARA

One of the most troubling of all philosophical questions is: Why do we suffer? For many it takes a more specific form: Why do

**THE SHEATHS
OF THE SOUL**

*Some Hindus believe that
the soul has four "coverings"
or sheaths. One is the physical body, a second is the
"breath" body, a third is the
instinctual body, and the
fourth is the cognitive body.
These sheaths all change
form and eventually perish.
Only the inmost soul, the
atman, is immortal.*

innocent people suffer? Or in the words of a recent bestseller, "Why do bad things happen to good people?" The premise behind all these questions is the same. The creator of the cosmos, the lord of worlds, must be just. (It's not really clear to me why this should be so, but it seems to be a pretty common assumption, so there must be something to it.) Yet injustice abounds throughout the universe. Babies are born deformed. Old people are brutalized. Children are neglected, animals abused. It doesn't seem as though this can be the work of a righteous god or a just principle. But to admit that the universe may be corrupt or unjust is too frightening to believe.

Hinduism has developed a unique answer to this question (which goes by the quirky theological title of "theodicy" or the justice of God). For Hindus, the answer is this. What appears unjust, is not really unjust—if we could see it through cosmic eyes on a cosmic scale. Of course, life is unjust on a small scale. But that's because we're only seeing a part of the picture. The soul is not born with the body nor does it die with the body. And the soul is the source of our actions. The body is merely the temporary home of an immortal spirit. The results of one's actions may not show up in this lifetime or the next. Certainly Hitler never got what was coming to him (at least, not in this life), but Hindus believe that this life is not the limit of all life.

A murder committed in one life may cause the murderer to be murdered himself in the next life. This is what is meant by karma. Karma means both one's actions and the fruit of one's actions, and we are responsible for our own karma. The life we live now is the result of our past (sometimes long past) actions. A life of selfishness, lechery, and debauchery may result in the next life being filled with privations and loneliness. A high caste person who does evil will find himself much lower on the social scale next time around. A low caste person is living out the consequences of his past actions.

It is commonly asserted that Hinduism doesn't have a system of ethics. Nothing could be further from the truth. Every ethical teaching in Hinduism is accompanied by the phrase "in thought, word, and deed," thus making ethics all-encompassing. The whole system of karma is based on ethics, an ethics that goes far beyond mere action, a system that looks into motive too.

The fact that one cannot recall one's evil actions from a past life doesn't negate the fact that they were performed. Every act leaves a kind of "karmic trail." For example, you may commit horrendous acts in a drunken state and not recall them the next day. Still, you are held accountable for your deeds. And you'll have a hangover too.

In the religious sphere, this means that those who live honorably in this life can expect to pass to a more fortunate birth in the next life. But if you live an evil life, you will be reborn to a life of misery.

The important thing to remember is that we ourselves are responsible for our present fate by our past actions. And the decisions we make now will make the difference in our future life. It's all a matter of evolving consciousness. Just as an acorn will eventually become an oak, so too the soul will finally achieve its own perfection (which of course is hidden deep within it all the time). According to the Mandikya Upanishad, there are actually three states of consciousness. The first is the normal waking state. The second is the dreaming state, and the third is the state of deep and dreamless sleep. But many Hindus speak of the Fourth State *(turiya)*. This is the ultimate, super-conscious, transcendental state also called *samadhi,* which requires special effort to obtain.

The word we translate as *reincarnation* or *transmigration* is the Sanskrit word *samsara,* which means "to wander." The soul wanders through eternity, undergoing successive birth and rebirth, death and re-death, until it finally attains liberation. Birth and rebirth are not random happenings, however; everything is connected by the chains of karma. Every action has a consequence, and some consequences are so far-reaching that they must be played out over several lifetimes.

This concept explains not only the apparent injustice of the universe, but it also solves a few other puzzles. It explains why some people seem so spiritually aware and others merely gross creatures of physical needs. Spiritually advanced people have worked hard for a long time, many lifetimes, to get where they are now. One life is not enough, in the Hindu view, to produce a

---

### NEW BEGINNINGS

*Some Hindus believe you might even be doomed to spend a few lifetimes as an animal, possibly a cockroach. A few Hindus believe that a really awful life might result in the person beginning over again as a plant. Worst of all, apparently, would be a return to life as an Untouchable.*

---

### KARMIC THEORY

*In Hinduism, karma can be good or bad. In Jainism, a heresy of Hinduism, all karma is bad.*

"Through pure deeds
one becomes pure.
Through impure deeds
one becomes impure."

—*The Brihadaranyaka*

Hindu saint like Ramakrishna, or one like Jesus or Muhammad or the Buddha. For Hindus, the idea of reincarnation provides both hope and a sense of justification. A well-lived life will make your next life freer and more blissful. Although you may be suffering now because of previous bad deeds, it is possible to improve your lot in the next life by living well in this one.

It is even possible to achieve liberation *(moksha)* permanently and remove oneself from the endless rounds of rebirth and re-death. Liberation can be obtained in *this* world, in the here and now. This is in contradistinction to the conventional Western concept that release can be obtained only after death in an otherworldly paradise. The Hindu *moksha* is not a place, nor does it occur in "time." It is beyond space and time, a state that the Hindus refer to as "unconditioned."

*Moksha* is the ultimate goal of all Hindu people. It means not only to be liberated as a person, but finally to be liberated *from* personhood, that is, to escape the bounds and limits of our own egos, our own personalities, to achieve a unity with the ultimate source of being. This is one of the most difficult Hindu concepts for Westerners to accept. Our tradition teaches us to fulfill our personalities, not lose them. For Hindus, however, escaping from ourselves means escaping from all the physical and mental and spiritual limitations that have defined us. Only then can we be truly free.

The way to this liberated state is to remove the veil of ignorance *(maya)* that produces the conditions that make for karma and the endless round of rebirth.

## MAYA

*Maya* is the world of appearances: the everyday universe of sights and sounds. The word comes from the Sanskrit root *ma,* which means to "measure out" or "construct."

Although *maya* is not exactly an illusory world, as is often stated, neither is it truly real. In fact, it's deceptive, and covers the truly real like a veil. It is deceptive because to our eyes, the one reality appears to be a multiplicity, and the changeless appears as a series of changing events. It's the appearance, and not the real that is termed *maya*. Interestingly, *maya* is conceived as a feminine principle. Naturally.

Originally, the word *maya* referred to the miraculous ability of the immaterial gods to create a material universe. (That is a good trick.) Here's another way of looking at *maya: Maya* is formed of matter, and matter is what hides the truly real. The true self is nonmaterial and the more closely we connect with our true self, the easier it will be to pierce the world of matter into the truth beyond it. To end the perception of *maya,* one must enter into the spiritual disciplines that will reveal reality as it truly is.

## THE CYCLES OF THE UNIVERSE

Strongly connected to the moral theory of reincarnation and karma is the Hindu metaphysical view of the universe. The universe itself moves through cycles called *kalpas*. Each *kalpa* equals 4,320,000,000 human years, which is 12,000 divine years. A thousand *kalpas* is one day in the life of Brahma, a so-called Brahma day. (There's a Brahma night too, a period just as long, during which the universe rests. This is a period of "pure potentiality.")

Since this is a little too much to manage for ordinary folks, Hinduism conveniently splits the *kalpas* up into slightly (only slightly) more manageable "days" or "ages" or *yugas*. The great age is the Satyayuga—the Age of Wisdom, a time when people dwelt in knowledge of the Brahman and in harmony with each other. Everyone lived for about 100,000 years. Progressively, however, things went downhill, through the Tretayuga and Dvaparayuga, wherein human life spans were only 10,000 and 1,000 years, respectively.

Now we live in the worst age of all, the Kaliyuga. This is the Age of Darkness, a time of discord and unhappiness. The average life span is only 100 years. (This may sound high, but the ancient Hindus liked to look on the bright side.) Only liars, murderers, and cheaters prosper in this "Age of Iron." It began on the night of February 17/18 in 3102 B.C.E., when the god Krishna died. And it will last 432,000 years, so we still have a way to go. At the very beginning of the Kaliyuga, it is said that the god Vishnu was incarnated as Vyasa to put the Vedas in writing. (People were too stupid and evil to learn them by heart anymore.)

Only a small bit of truth remains to us in this age. Still, even while we speak, the conditions are developing for a new Satyayuga. At the end of this age, Brahma or Vishnu will appear among us as Kalki, agent of destruction. He will be mounted on a white horse and wield a sword. (See Revelation in the Christian Bible for a comparison.) The good will survive, however, and the world will be re-created.

This process will be repeated over a period of 311 trillion and forty earth years, until Brahma the god finally dies and the physical universe comes to an end. At least that's one theory.

## THE FOUR GOALS OF LIFE

Hinduism acknowledges four legitimate goals *(purusarthas)* of life: pleasure, usually sexual *(kama);* material wealth *(artha);* social and religious duty *(dharma);* and finally spiritual liberation or release *(moksha).* The fourth goal, originally part of *dharma,* was later considered a separate category. Each *purusartha* is worthwhile on its own, but *moksha* is without doubt the highest goal.

The word *dharma* is an honored one in both Hinduism and Buddhism (where it refers to the Buddha's teachings). It appears one hundred and thirty times in the Rig Veda and has expanded its meaning over time. In its earliest formulation, it probably meant "ritual." Later *dharma* came to mean "cosmic order," somewhat akin to the idea of Rita, the old Vedic god. Still later it referred to the human/divine connection. In this light, human conduct was regarded as both a cause and result of the great *dharma* of the universe. One source I consulted describes *dharma* as "an abstract Sanskrit term that is not easy to grasp," which was less than helpful. Simply put, however, *dharma* is the law of being. In addition, every individual has his own personal *dharma.*

## THE FOUR PATHS

It should come as no surprise that Hindus accept more than one path *(marga)* to liberation. (Note that the words *marga* and *yoga* are

---

### HINDU SEX

*The famous Kama Sutra by Vatsyayana is a sex manual listing sixteen kinds of kisses. It also discusses various aphrodisiacs as well as the importance of biting and scratching during sex. This particular Kama Sutra is only one of a number of such works and is considerably more respectable than most of the others.*

often used interchangeably. As this causes great confusion for many Westerners, I'll use *marga* when referring to a spiritual path in the traditional Hindu sense.)

The different paths have been developed to help people attain a union with the divine, and Hindus are encouraged to find the *marga* suited to their own natures. One could argue that this ideal is undermined in practice, because there is a significant correlation between an individual's caste and the *marga* that is appropriate for him or her. Each of the following four chapters is devoted to a particular *marga*, so you'll get a lot more detail on how a Hindu attains *moksha*.

## THE ROLE OF THE GURU

*Guru* is a Sanskrit term, meaning teacher, but it's a lot more than that. In Indian tradition, the guru is an almost godlike being, whom the student reveres above every other human person, including his own parents. Most gurus, but not all, belong to the Brahmin caste.

The guru is usually charged with teaching his disciple both regular studies and secret knowledge, including a personal mantra. For all yoga disciplines, a guru is absolutely essential. Most gurus have traditionally been male, but nowadays, female gurus are becoming increasingly common.

The role of the guru is to help his student reach liberation. It is not enough to study the Vedas; they must be explained by a guru, and then reasoned about together. The guru doesn't just teach scripture. He teaches life, using his own as an example. There is no room for separation of theoretical and living knowledge in Hinduism. (The great Hindu mystic Ramakrishna did say that a very few people could achieve liberation without guidance from a guru. But not many.)

Disciples may kiss the toes of their guru, a courtesy that repels many Western observers. However, this is a common Indian custom. Children may kiss the feet of their parents and grandparents. No one thinks anything about it.

Not every guru is right for every disciple, and many gurus, after a cursory examination of the aspirant, will send him to a different master, one he feels is more in tune with that person's specific needs. It's not rejection so much as guidance to a different path.

**DOING** *DARSHAN*
*Sometimes disciples merely stand in the presence of their guru, absorbing spirituality like osmosis. This practice is called* darshan, *meaning "presence."*

## CHAPTER RECAP

- The four Vedas are the sacred scriptures of Hinduism.

- Important Vedic gods include Agni, the fire god; Indra, the thunder god; and Soma, the god of delight and immortality.

- Behind all the gods is the ultimate divinity known as Brahman, the God beyond God.

- The cause and effect laws of karma guide one's destiny, and *samsara* is the eternal round of birth, death, and rebirth.

- This world is *maya,* that is, not ultimately real.

- To reach salvation, Hindus often employ the services of a guru, or teacher.

*Recommended Reading*

Edgerton, Franklin. *The Beginnings of Hindu Philosophy.* Cambridge, MA: Harvard University Press, 1965.

# Raja Marga—

## *The Path of Mental and Physical Discipline*

The word *marga* is Sanskrit for "path" or "way." As a way to truth and liberation, the yogic *marga* relies on spiritual and physical discipline in the form of meditation and, sometimes, ascetic practices.

### RAJA YOGA—THE ROYAL ROAD

Traditionally, *raja* yoga was followed by the *Kshatriya* or warrior caste, although there is no specific rule about it. (Chapter 6 of the Bhagavad Gita gives basic instructions for meditation, thus emphasizing the ultimate unity of meditating and doing battle.)

An important first step in *raja* yoga is *hatha* yoga. As a separate discipline, *hatha* yoga developed in the ninth through twelfth centuries, after the *raja* yoga system, discussed in this chapter, was established. Today *hatha* yoga adherents believe their practice is a grounding discipline for more advanced yoga.

Literally translated "force" or "power" yoga, *hatha* yoga is a physical yoga taught in YMCAs and health clubs all over the world. It emphasizes physical discipline and relaxation techniques, and, in its more severe forms, is a training exercise for more advanced yoga endeavors. Some of the postures taught in *hatha* yoga are positively painful; some believe that the very difficulty of these positions is conducive to mental health. At any rate, you don't need to be a Hindu to practice *hatha* yoga, and most practitioners, at least in the West, draw no connection between their spiritual development and yoga postures.

The central techniques of *hatha* yoga involve regulated breathing *(prana)* and sustained body postures *(asana)*. The main object of the breathing exercises is to unite the sun-breath *(ha)* that controls vital energy, with the moon-breath *(tha)*, which takes away body waste.

### The Yoga System of Patanjali

The founder of the *raja* (royal) yoga system of meditation was Patanjali, who lived sometime between the first century B.C.E. and the third century C.E. His great work is the Yogasutra. For Patanjali, *raja* yoga is the path of mental and physical discipline, with the object of stilling the mind. The final goal, however, is not to become more organized, lose weight, or achieve better job performance, but to experience a oneness with the ultimate Ground of Being, the divinely Real. It is considered as much a science and a practice as it is a theory or religion. "Yoga," says Patanjali, "involves ascetic practices, study of sacred works, and a dedication to the Lord of Yoga. Its purpose is to attain purest meditation, and to weaken the forces of corruption." In case you're wondering what these corruptive forces are, Patanjali lists them: passion, hate, ignorance, self-centeredness, and the will to live!

The idea that heroic meditation will reduce one's desire to survive does not recommend it from the Western viewpoint, but one must remember that the yogin seeks something far more important than the temporary life on this earth. He seeks eternal liberation. It is true that this path is so difficult and time-consuming that only ascetics traditionally undertake it.

All meditation, whether Hindu, Buddhist, or Taoist, has the same goal: to replace ordinary perception and logical thought-patterns with direct experience. Direct experience is not the same as ordinary perception, even if it sounds the same. Ordinary perception is relative or deceptive. Far objects appear small. Ropes look like snakes, or vice versa. Enemies may appear to be friends. Not only do our senses frequently deceive us, but in fact they *must* deceive us, even if only by giving us partial, rather than full, knowledge.

**HOT YOGA**

*The aptly named "hot yoga" is practiced in room temperatures exceeding 100 degrees. Hot yoga is offered for curing various physical complaints from obesity to diabetes. Although it may sound odd to practice yoga in such extreme heat, when you stop to think of it, that is what India is like most of the year.*

For example, we must look at a particular object, say a brick wall, from a particular position, at a particular time. We can't help it. The laws of physics assure us that only one body can occupy any one space at any one time. Someone else may be looking at the same object at the same time, but then he must be standing somewhere else. Or he might stand in the same spot, but then he has to stand there at a different time. Both time and viewpoint change what is seen—even if both parties have 20-20 vision.

Besides, human beings can see only part of the wall; we can't see what's on the other side of it. And our human vision is limited to only a portion of the light spectrum; the bricks might look entirely different to a honeybee, which has more resources in this regard than we do. So the senses aren't very good reporters even of the reality we think we know, much less of any ultimate reality beyond our senses. That's where meditation comes in. By concentrating the mind, meditation opens the spirit to direct experience, driving through the sensuous world into the ultimate reality that only those who are trained to "see" it can know.

"A fool sees not the same tree that a wise man sees."

—*William Blake*

---

### THEM AND US

*In Hinduism, meditation goes back to the Rig Veda. The closest Western equivalent is "contemplation," which refers to a variety of ways of thinking about something. Unlike meditation, contemplation is not meant to still the mind or to improve concentration. It is a mental activity rather than a discipline or spiritual practice. Put another way, contemplation is the development of thought. Meditation is the focusing of the mind, combined with the absence of specific "thought." Thomas Merton (1915–1968), the Trappist monk and Zen Buddhist scholar, joined Christian contemplation with Eastern meditation in his concept of "contemplative meditation."*

---

According to Patanjali, the eight steps of yoga (to be performed sequentially, or simultaneously, as the practitioner sees fit), are as follows:

1. Abstention from the five evils *(yama):* violence, deceit, theft, sexual impurity, and greed.

2. Various means of self-discipline *(niyana):* cleanliness, contentment, scripture study, bodily discipline, prayer, and devotion.

3. Posture exercises *(asana):* The most famous *asana* is the Lotus position, but there are others: Greeting the Sun, the Locust, the Bow, the Peacock, the Triangle, and the Wheel.

4. Breathing exercises *(pranayama):* controlling the inhalation, exhalation, and rhythm of breathing.

5. Withdrawing the mind from sense objects *(pratahara):* closing the mind to outside distractions is absolutely essential to success.

6. Concentration, or steadying the mind *(dharana):* focusing on one object only, the so-called one-pointed concentration.

7. Deep meditation *(dhyana):* deeply engaging in the intentional act of meditation itself. If one is in deep concentration, even the arrival of a fierce tiger would not interfere with one's concentration. At least that's what they say.

8. Super-conscious absorption in the ultimate *(samadhi):* knowledge of being one with the universe. At this point, the meditator is calm and free from all desire. He has achieved *citta,* pure awareness. The spirit becomes absolutely separate from the body.

To outsiders, *samadhi* looks like a trance, but it isn't. It is a transcendental state that brings with it ultimate knowledge. This is knowledge that cannot be won in any ordinary way, not something one can find in books. Neither is it knowledge that contradicts reason and common sense; it goes beyond them, but it never defies or rejects them.

Yoga is extremely difficult, of course. Even the god Krishna admits as much in the Bhagavad Gita. "Beyond denial," he says, "it is hard for man to restrain his wavering heart. Still, it may grow restrained by habit and by self-command. Yoga does not come easily; only he who is master of himself shall win it."

The Bhagavad Gita also describes the perfect yogin:

---

**THE PURE LIFE-FORCE**

*In yoga there are five breath forces. The fifth, prana, is the pure life-force, or energy. It is depicted as a horse whose energy pulls the chariots of the gods.*

---

**THE PERFECT POSTURE**

*To attain the Lotus position (padmasana), seat yourself in a quiet place. Cross your legs, with each foot touching the opposite thigh. Rest your hands on the knees, thumbs up. Focus on the tip of your nose. This is sometimes called the "perfect posture" and is supposed to be very comfortable, at least for Indians. Most Westerners find it excruciating.*

The sovereign soul
Of him who lives self-governed and at peace
Is centered in itself, taking alike
Pleasure and pain; heat, cold; glory and shame.
He is the Yogin...
With joy of light and truth; dwelling apart
Upon a peak
Whereto the clod, the rock, the glistening gold
Show all as one...
Being of equal grace to comrades, friends...enemies,
Aliens and kinsmen; loving all alike... Sequestered should
    he sit,
Steadfastly meditating, solitary,
His thoughts controlled, his passions laid away,
Quit of belongings...
There, setting hard his mind upon The One,
Restraining heart and senses, silent, calm,
Let him accomplish Yoga, and achieve
Pureness of soul..."

*(Trans. Sir Edwin Arnold. Boston: Roberts Brothers, 1891, p. 62.)*

## SIDDHI—*PARANORMAL YOGIC POWERS*

The Sanskrit word *siddhi* means "complete attainment" or "perfect." *Siddhi* yoga, for masters only, explores the possibility of achieving supra-human feats while still in human form. These strange abilities are not sought after for themselves, however; they are a manifestation of the powers of concentration of a great yogin. For the spiritual master, they are by-products of something more important: total awareness. Traditionally, there are eight manifestations of psychic power, although texts differ as to which eight comprise them. Some examples include clairvoyance or clairaudience, becoming extremely small or large, vanishing from sight, touching the moon, moving with extreme speed from one place to another, and control over all physical things. More specifically, and less pleasantly, the Yogatattva Upanishad claims the yogin can turn iron into gold by smearing his urine and excrement on it. (It's not clear whether the resultant gold would be likewise coated.)

**HOW THE PREGNANT PAUSE**

*In large numbers, pregnant women are opting for yoga rather than Lamaze when preparing for childbirth. Yoga practice keeps blood pressure down, helps one relax, and provides important breathing techniques useful at the big moment. Special classes in Iyengar yoga, which focuses on the back, spine, and breathing, are offered just for pregnant women.*

Orthodox masters tend to downplay these excursions into the realm of psychic phenomena. The classic practitioner Sankya Karika, prosaically lists eight increasingly strenuous attitudes of mind as worthy of pursuit: reasoning, close study, learning from a master, discussion with learned people, generosity, detachment from psychological suffering, detachment from interpersonal suffering, and detachment from the suffering inflicted by one's fate.

## CHAPTER RECAP

- *Raja* yoga, or royal yoga, combines meditation with physical discipline.

- Patajali wrote the first treatise on *raja* yoga.

- *Hatha* yoga (force yoga), which is part of *raja* yoga, uses breathing techniques *(prana)* with body postures *(asana)*.

- One goal of meditation is to quiet the mind.

- *Siddhi* yogins are reputed to have attained supra-human powers.

*Recommended Reading*

Bashan, A. L. *The Origins and Development of Classical Hinduism.* Boston: Beacon Press, 1989.

Davich, Victor N., *The Best Guide to Meditation.* Los Angeles: Renaissance Books, 1998.

Eliade, Mircea. *Yoga: Immortality and Freedom.* Princeton, NJ: Princeton University Press, 1973.

Knipe, David M. *Hinduism.* New York: HarperCollins, 1991.

Swami Vishnudevananda. *The Complete Illustrated Book of Yoga.* New York: Simon & Schuster, Inc., 1972.

# Karma Marga—The Path of Work and Action

The karma *marga* has been traditionally the path of the Kshatriyas, or warrior caste. (Today this group also includes lawyers.) Much of the Bhagavad Gita concerns a discussion of *dharma* in relation to war. (The word *karma* means "deed" in Sanskrit, and so this path is the path of deeds or actions.) The kind of actions available to the karma yogin varies, but the term is most commonly used to mean responsible action in the world, action that can include service to one's nation, community, and caste. In fact, the caste system, notorious around the world, has its roots in the concept of karma *marga*.

## THE LAWS OF MANU AND THE CASTE SYSTEM

The caste system has probably aroused more negative comment than any other single element of Hindu culture. No one is really sure how or even when it started, but it was going strong by about 500 B.C.E. (There is reference to the caste system in the Rig Veda, but the system may not have been consolidated until later.) The great Indian epic, Bhagavad Gita, notes it approvingly, but some other authoritative texts do not mention it or pass it off as apparently insignificant.

Whenever the origins of the caste system, it's pretty certain that one reason for its development was India's multiracial society.

"A husband, though devoid of virtue, or seeking pleasure elsewhere, must be constantly worshipped as a god by a faithful wife."

—*Manu*

A common term for the system, *varna*, literally means "color." There's no Indian language word that correlates precisely with the English word *caste*, which comes from Portuguese. The Indians use one of two words: *varna* or *jati* (the word most often used today), which means birth group. And although caste is now inherited, some early literature argued that it ought to be assigned by conduct rather than birth. That idea never caught on.

One ancient text, the *Bhavishya Purana*, deplored the whole idea of the caste system. "Since all people of whatever caste are the children of God, they all belong to the same caste," it argued. That idea never caught on either.

We can blame part of the caste system on Manu and his Laws. Manu was a legendary king or demigod. Even though he wasn't real, medieval rulers of India all claimed to be descended from him. (This puts a question mark on their own reality, it would seem to me, but perhaps they didn't see it that way.)

The mythical Manu's laws attempt to account for the development of the caste system. According to him, castes have their origin in Purusha, the Divine Primeval Person. Purusha's head turns into the Brahmins, his arms are the Ksashitriya, his abdomen the Vaishya, and his feet the Shudra.

Manu's famous Laws (written between 300 B.C.E. and 300 C.E.) consist of twelve chapters and 2,694 couplets. They contain several remarks (aside from those concerning the caste system) that irritate modern sensibilities.

Men should control their wives by keeping them busy "making and spending money, doing purification rituals, cooking, and looking after the furniture." He also lists the six things that corrupt women: drinking, associating with ne'er-do-wells, being apart from their husbands, wandering around, living in other people's homes, and sleeping!

More severe than Manu are the remarks in the *Padmapurana*: "Even if her husband is abusive, immoral, a drunkard, a gambler, a whoremonger, without love for his home, a raving lunatic . . . a wife must always look upon him as god."

Out of this mindset came the practice of suttee *(sati),* whereby a high-caste widow was expected to fling herself upon the burning funeral pyre of her deceased husband. (Low-caste women didn't bother.) Most Hindus considered it the woman's fault if the husband died first; her bad karma was sticking to him. If she declined to throw herself into the funeral fire, she might be helped along by her dead hubby's relatives, who didn't want the responsibility of feeding another mouth. In some cases, such as before a war, women were urged to kill themselves in advance, just in case.

Even women who didn't kill themselves had a bad time. They were expected to dress in horrible clothes, sleep on the floor, and keep out of everybody's way. No wonder some women preferred death. The British and Indian reformers worked together to out-law suttee, and the practice is almost nonexistent in India today.

### The Duties of the Social Classes

The Laws of Manu claim that the rigid social classes were devised to protect the universe, by making sure that all essential tasks are properly performed. (It does seem to be true that unless you specifically assign someone to take out the trash or clean the cat litter box, it won't get done.) Each caste had its own duties, and its own rituals and taboos.

Manu discusses only four castes, although hundreds of sub-castes developed through the ensuing years. Here they are, in descending rank. Because the members of the first three go through a rite of initiation, they are "twice-born."

1. Priestly, scholarly class (Brahmins): The Brahmins make up the "spiritual" caste. Their job is to teach, study the Vedas, perform sacrifices, and give and accept alms. Originally they did no manual labor.

2. Warrior and ruler class (Kshatriya): This is the "dynamic" or aristocratic caste. The role of the Kshatriyas is to protect society and to give gifts. They offer sacrifices, study the Vedas, and refrain from sensual indulgence. The Kshatriyas held all the political power, as the Brahmins held the religious power. Unlike the other twice-born castes, the Kshatriyas are permitted to eat meat and drink alcohol.

3. Merchant and crafts class (Vaishyas): This is the "economic" or business caste. The Vaishyas tend cattle, give

**A GOOD WIFE**

*The word* sati *actually translates as "good wife."*

gifts, offer sacrifices, lend money, and cultivate the land. Today many are involved in banking. Most are vegetarians.

4. Laboring and peasant class (Shudras): This is the "material" caste. Their job is to serve the other three castes, especially the Brahmins, and perform manual labor. Manu suggests that if they don't serve willingly, they can be compelled to do so as slaves. Unlike the upper three castes, they are referred to as "once-born."

In keeping with the color-code idea, one character in the great Indian epic, the Mahabharata, claims that Brahmins are fair, warriors are "reddish," merchants are yellowish, and Shudras are black. Another character responds that if that's the case, there was a lot of caste-mixing going on.

Today the caste system is more complex than ever. Many castes are "functional," that is, based upon their activities and career opportunities. There are also "race" castes that are organized along color or ethnic lines and "sect" castes that are organized on religious grounds.

Castes generally form a cohesive social unit, and members are discouraged from marrying or even eating with those outside their caste. (It sometimes happens that a woman is of lower caste than her husband. Somewhat more rarely, the wife is of higher caste.) Each caste has its own rites and dietary practices. Members of higher castes (the "twice-born") consider it a "pollution" to eat with a member of a lower caste. Even unknowing contact can result in serious caste contamination.

---

### THE TWICE-BORN

*The term* twice-born *refers to the initiation, or sacred thread, ceremony performed in the top three classes. (Actually, it's a cord made of three threads, worn over the left shoulder.) Only old, previously incarnated souls get born into a twice-born caste. When the candidate has gone through the ceremony, he is said to have been born again. Only these castes may study the Vedas.*

---

It seems pretty obvious that the easiest job is being a Brahmin. Manu tells us that the very birth of a Brahmin is the eternal incarnation of sacred law. He further informs us that the Brahmin is the highest of all created things. Most Brahmins tend to agree. (Actually, Manu was supposedly some sort of king, and he therefore would have been a member of the Kshatirya caste. Because there was probably no Manu ever, however, his Laws were undoubtedly written by members of the you-know-what caste.) Today the caste system is weakening in urban areas, but remains very strong in the country, especially in the south of India.

### The Outcastes

There exists yet another caste—the Outcastes, or Untouchables (Mlechcha or Dalits). In Hindu thought, the Outcastes are polluting the Hindus; yet they comprise about 15 percent of the population.

Originally the Untouchables belonged to the Shudra caste, but because of the "polluting" nature of the work they were assigned, some gradually became "Outcastes," that is, outside every caste.

The Untouchables lack the most basic connections with other castes. In most places they cannot even use the same wells as caste Hindus. The higher caste Hindus call them "walking carrion." These unfortunate people perform the most forbidden and "lowest" jobs: tanning leather, handling corpses, and cleaning toilets. Gandhi called them the *"Harijan,"* the children of God, to indicate to other castes their worth, but they still suffer enormous, if unofficial, discrimination. Although Untouchables may now legally enter any temple in India, in practice, old taboos hold strong, and most Untouchables use their own temples. Technically, "untouchability" has been illegal since 1948, but no one pays much attention to that.

**HINDU HIGHLIGHT**

*Traditionally, Outcastes were so unclean that even the shadow of one could defile a Brahmin.*

## MANU ON THE FOUR STAGES OF LIFE

The four stages of life *(the ashramas),* apply only to the top three castes: the "twice-born." (*Shudras* apparently had no life-stages.) Almost no one today follows this path precisely as set out by Manu, especially the final two stages. (In fact, it's likely that it always was an ideal honored more in the breach than in the observance.) However, they are still admired as a basic principle. It should be noted that these life-stages were traditionally devised for males only, although today a few women follow them also. Each life-stage lasts approximately twenty-five years.

### The Student Stage

In India, the student stage is known as the *brahmacarin.* Literally, the word *brahmacarin* means "wandering about in the Brahman," a colorful (if singularly uninstructive) phrase. At this stage, which begins traditionally at twelve years of age, (but may start as early as eight), a young man goes to live in the house of his teacher and begins study of the Vedas, a study which may last for more than eight years. During this time, he lives as a member of the family. He is expected to remain celibate. He learns to control his sensual desires into order to open himself up to the knowledge and understanding of the Brahman. He also undertakes necessary training in the sciences and arts. Nowadays women also receive the benefits of education, although not often with a guru.

> "He who understands his duty to society truly lives. All others shall be counted among the dead."
>
> —*Tirukural*

### The Householder Stage

During this active stage of life *(grhastha)*, men were expected to marry and raise a family, especially sons. (Most Hindu males marry between the ages of twenty and twenty-four.) The male is expected to tend the sacred fire. The householder stage is often associated with the life-goal of *artha,* or wealth. The householder also discharges his duties to the community, in accordance with his caste responsibilities. "Perform your required responsibilities," says the Bhagavad Gita. "Action is better than non-action." This, of course, is following one's earthly *dharma.* Today women are often included as a matter of course; they are expected to work and serve their community in much the same way as a man.

### The Forest Dweller

The forest dwelling *vanaprastha* stage, is the time of retirement from the world, although the wife may accompany her husband. The time of "retirement" varies, but usually occurs when the first grandchildren arrive. Here the seeker learns to be free of most attachments. Today, most people who enter this stage stay at home, but eat, meditate, and study apart from the rest of the family.

### The World Renouncer and Wandering Ascetic

In this stage *(sannyasin),* all attachments are renounced. "No one belongs to me and I belong to no one," the renunciate vows.

Very, very few people pass on to this optional stage. A man must leave his spouse behind, but he must make sure that she will be provided for. By ancient tradition, only males can attain the state of *sannyasin,* but now women sometimes also embark on this lonely journey. Some *sannyasins* wear handsome saffron robes, while others dress in dirty rags (or go naked). Most have long, matted hair, a sign of austerity, but more hygienic-minded *sannyasin* shave their heads. Generally, a *sannyasin's* only possessions are his begging bowl and a staff, although some spring for a parasol as well.

The *sannyasin* even renounces his name and his caste. This is a legal commitment—the *sannyasin* is dead to the world and may not lawfully resume his former life. He even gives up his Vedic rituals. Because he does not expend his sexual energy, common belief ascribes to him great powers.

Despite his physical hardships, the *sannyasin* lives in a state of joy, not agony. He renounces the world because he is ready to renounce it, because he has seen through its snares and deceptions. He is leaving behind him nothing of value. If anything, the *sannyasin* feels pity for those who cannot relinquish their hold on illusion. His many austerities have purified his body and soul from attachment to things of this world.

The *sannyasin* seeks to connect with the ultimate goal: *moksha (mukti)* or liberation. Once he has attained it, he is free from bondage to *maya, samsara,* and *karma. Moksha* is a positive, joyful state of complete perfection. Unfortunately for half the human race, traditional scholars held that only men could attain *moksha.* If you are a woman, you must be reborn as a man. There's always something.

**RENUNCIATE OPTIONS**

*Some* sannyasin *choose to enter an ashram, a place of retreat and study rather than become nomads. This is permitted.*

## THE BHAGAVAD GITA—THE CELESTIAL SONG

The Gita, as it is familiarly known, is actually Book 6 of the huge epic, the Mahabharata. The Mahabharata is 100,000 verses long, all in Sanskrit. This makes it the world's longest poem. It was also turned into a very long Broadway play. Although now included as part of the Mahabharata, the Gita is often printed separately from its parent epic. Most scholars think the Gita was "added in" to the Mahabharata by later editors.

Despite its great length, the Mahabharata is a fabulous read, containing stories, commentary, moral instruction, dialogue, and celebration. More than perhaps any other work, it captures the spirit of all India. I'd like to give a summary of the Mahabharata, but it's impossible. All the characters go by several different names, they are all related to one another in various ways, and the plot is too convoluted to follow, let alone recall or retell.

The Gita contains eighteen sections, about 700 two-line stanzas. It dates from about 100 B.C.E., although the original source was probably written several hundred years earlier. The setting is a battle between the Pandavas (the good guys) and their cousins the Kauravas (the bad guys). (The actual location isn't far from modern New Delhi.) The book is a dialogue between the epic's hero, Arjuna, and the god Krishna, who has been playing the role of his charioteer.

---

**THE GITA IN ENGLISH**

*The first English translation of the Bhagavad Gita appeared back in 1785. It was the first full-length translation of a Sanskrit work into any Western language. Oddly enough, its great appeal to many Western writers and philosophers helped boost its prestige in its own homeland.*

---

### Krishna—Avatar of Vishnu

Krishna is the seventh avatar of Vishnu, and as a historical character is said to have died in 3102 B.C.E. (Arjuna went to his funeral.) He was "born" to a human couple, although they suspected something was up when the baby emerged blue-black, with four arms and hands. One hand bore a mace, another a conch, a third a discus, and a fourth a lotus. They trembled with fright until Krishna graciously agreed to reappear as a normal baby.

**A GOD IN DISGUISE**

*An avatar is a human or animal "disguise" a god may wear when embarking on an earthly mission.*

Although he's blue, Krishna is not only devilishly good-looking but is also a great charioteer and an excellent flautist. He is quite well-known as a lover. He often appears as a cowherd, who gathers about him adoring married women who leave their husbands to romp in the woods with the god. This is all metaphorical, of course. The women represent the absolute love and devotion of the Krishna worshipper.

Although the Gita is part of a human-created epic and is hence classed as *smriti,* or not-divinely inspired, the actual words of Krishna recorded in the epic are considered as *shruti,* or divinely inspired and infallible. And Krishna's infallible words are that a person is bound by his *dharma* to engage in the world, while at the same time remaining aloof from it. In fact, if one were to summarize the message of the Gita, one would have to say that although it teaches salvation through works, it also gives a nod to loving grace, suggesting that the almighty Lord of the Universe is willing to come down to earth, counsel people, and aid them in attaining their goals. This is a new idea for Hinduism and very different from the pull-yourself-up-by-the-bootstraps approach of the Upanishads. This approach makes the work greatly beloved.

### Arjuna—The Warrior

The warrior Arjuna is something of a deity himself, a son of the ancient Vedic god Indra. As a human, however, he belongs to the warrior class, the Kshatriya, and knows that it is his caste duty to fight for the right. He is an excellent bowman (a southpaw), and as an added bonus he has two inexhaustible quivers. (His keen archery skills won him a wife, Draupadi, whom he politely shared with his five brothers. Arjuna was always her favorite, however.)

Despite being such a great warrior, Arjuna has an aversion to killing, especially to killing his own relatives. He sees the futility of all war and does not wish to stain his soul with blood. This places Arjuna in a difficult position, so difficult, in fact, that he sits himself down and begins blubbering like a child. Obviously, it's time for the god to take action.

Krishna explains to Arjuna that provided his cause is just, and that he is not undertaking the action for glory or gain, Arjuna must follow his prescribed duty. The real battlefield, Krishna tells him, is not the physical one they're on, but the field of *dharma*. Arjuna is bound to follow the path of karma yoga—the path of dedicated action, which itself is a form of worship. In fact, Arjuna is duty-bound to fight by his karma, his *dharma,* and his inmost nature. In more brutal terms, the killer must kill, and the victim must die. What makes the difference is the attitude with which he will fight, and that remains in his control. And

> "Believe me, whatever you see in this world that is beautiful and glorious, whatever is forceful and mighty, know that he is the very splendor, light, and energy of Me."
>
> —*Krishna, in the Gita*

---

**TALES OF KRISHNA**

*Some of the best-loved stories of Krishna concern his childhood. As a kid, someone noticed that he was eating dirt and pointed it out to his mother, Yashoda. When Yashoda looked into the godlet's mouth, however, she saw there the entire universe, born and unborn, visible and invisible. She then understood that the whole cosmos is part of Krishna's play. At the same time, she got a hint of exactly whom she was dealing with. Krishna's wife is the cowgirl Radha, who, like her husband, is a greatly beloved figure in Hindu mythology. Radha has another, divine form—that of Lakshmi, in which she is married to Vishnu himself.*

in the long view, Krishna tells him, victory and defeat are pretty much alike anyway.

## Who Is the Yogin?

"The perfect yogin," counsels Krishna, "acts, but acts unmoved by passion and unbound by deeds, setting results aside." This means that if Arjuna were to fight in order to gain glory, or to achieve any selfish goal, his work would stain his soul, but if he fights with "detachment," pure of soul, he is fulfilling his *dharmic* obligation. If he fights "with malice" he would be breaking a powerful Hindu sanction—that of *ahimsa,* or nonviolence.

The actions of the karma yogin are selfless. Such a yogin does not consider the consequences of his actions, only their rightness. He renounces bondage to material things and abandons the fruits or material rewards of his actions. Thus he rises above the world of *maya* or illusion. He understands that victory and defeat, gain and loss, and love and hate are truly one. The yogin is skill-in-action.

Although Arjuna did win the war, it's only fair to report that many years later he was killed, as result of being too proud of his heroism. It was all karma, the result of his previous deeds.

The Gita, however, is more than an adventure tale. It also contains immortal words about the nature of the Brahman, the Ground of Being of the universe: "It is not born, nor does it ever die. Nor having come into being, will it ever cease to be. This ancient one is unborn, eternal, everlasting, and is not killed when the body dies." In its earliest form, found in the Vedas, the Brahman was understood to be a powerful, if amorphous, force underlying the universe. As Hinduism developed, the concept of the Brahman became more philosophical. God is not to be found, counsels Krishna, in the world of appearances. One must seek beyond, through, and above this world to attain a true realization of the ultimate.

**KRISHNA'S HONORIFICS**

*In the Bhagavad Gita, Krishna has forty-nine titles. Some of them are: Lord of the Senses, Protector of Cows, the Beyond, the Friend, the All, the Immeasurable One, the Lord of Yoga.*

---

**THE TIMELESS BHAGAVAD GITA**

*J. Robert Oppenheimer was a physicist who contributed to the development of atomic energy for military use. As Oppenheimer watched the testing of the first atomic bomb, he is said to have recited from the Bhagavad Gita:*

*I am become death, the shatterer of worlds:*
*Waiting that hour that ripens to their doom.*

---

The Gita also has features of theism—the belief in a personal god, in this case Krishna. One thing that makes the Gita so revered among all Hindus is its broad sweep, for it contains elements of devotional Hinduism, and philosophical Hinduism, as well as instruction in karma yoga. It doesn't stake out just one road to the divine. All paths are accepted as equally valid. And that is the soul of Hinduism itself.

## CHAPTER RECAP

- Karma yoga is the yoga of action and is fulfilled through one's life and deeds.

- One's station in life is ordained by one's hereditary place in the caste system.

- There are four main castes: Brahmins, leaders, merchant class, and laborers.

- The Untouchables comprise a fifth group of people—the lowest of all.

- Traditionally, high-caste Hindu males follow four stages in life: student, householder, hermit, and wandering ascetic.

- The great Indian epic the Bhagavad Gita teaches the yoga of action, the yoga of meditation, and the yoga of love.

### GANDHI'S GITA

*The Bhagavad Gita was a particularly holy text to Mahatma Gandhi, who, interestingly enough, never read it until he lived in England. He interpreted its call to fight in a spiritual rather than a physical battle, and this idea has become very influential among modern Hindus.*

*Recommended Reading*

Eck, Diane. *Darsan: Seeing the Divine Image in India, second ed.* Chambersburg, PA: Anima Books, 1985.

O'Flaherty, Wendy, ed. *Karma and Rebirth in Classical Indian Traditions.* Berkeley, CA: University of California Press, 1980.

Sharpe, Eric J. *The Universal Gita: Western Images of the Bhagavad Gita.* Chicago: Open Court Publishing Company, 1985.

The Song of God: Bhagavad Gita. Trans. Swami Prabhavananda and Christopher Isherwood. New York: Mentor, 1972. Other excellent translations are also available.

Zaehner, R. C. *Hinduism.* New York: Oxford University Press, Inc., 1962.

# Jnana Marga—

## *The Path of Knowledge*

*Jnana marga* is the path of spiritual wisdom and is considered the most difficult of all the *margas*. It relies more on reason, and less on meditation, than some of the other paths. *Jnana marga,* however, is not *just* reason and intellectualism. It also cultivates the great spiritual values, without which one cannot reach *moksha*.

Traditionally, *jnana marga* was the preferred path for the Brahmin class, or for intellectuals in general. One who achieves liberation through *jnana marga* must achieve first the Six Excellences:

1. Tranquility

2. Control over the senses

3. Renunciation

4. Endurance

5. Concentration or faith in the things of spirit

6. Longing for liberation

There are six orthodox *(astika),* or fully accepted, schools of Indian *jnana* philosophy—the *Nyaya,* the *Vaisheshika,* the *Purva Mimansa,* the Yoga, the *Sankhya,* and the *Vedanta.* They are orthodox

**NAME THOSE UPANISHADS**

*There are ten major Upanishads: Isa, Kena, Katha, Prasna, Mundaka, Mandukya, Chandogya, Taittiriya, Aitarea, and Brihadaranyaka, with three others also widely regarded as authoritative. Although they have broad areas of agreement, they differ on many important points of philosophy.*

because they all consider the Vedas to be divine and authoritative. Because the *Vedanta* system is so popular, I'll focus on it for most of this discussion. A seventh school, *Carvaka,* is considered unorthodox because of its deep skepticism. (Although *Carvaka* is sometimes considered atheistic, this is difficult to prove. Sanskrit doesn't even have a word for atheism in its vocabulary.)

The *Nyaya* system and the *Vaisheshika* system are closely related schools; the first focuses on the logic, and the second on metaphysics. The *Purva Mimansa* school deals with critical analysis of the Vedas as an eternal, author-less scripture. All these schools deal with highly technical matters beyond the reach of most beginners.

Patanjali's Yoga system (discussed in chapter 3), is closely allied to the *Sankhya* system, but because of its emphasis on physical training, and the importance it has acquired in the West, it is often considered separately.

The *Sankhya* school's dualistic philosophy is similar to traditional Western views of the universe. It may be the oldest of Hindu philosophical schools as well, whose legendary founder was Kapila, who lived in the seventh century B.C.E. According to this school, there exist two eternal realities: pure spirit *(purusha)* and matter *(prakriti)*. These two are real entities—not *maya* or a product of illusion. The natural world is made up of twenty-four elements, including things such as "intellect," which most of us don't think of as elements. The spiritual world is composed of an infinite number of independent, eternal souls. Somehow, these souls got attached to bodies. Their main goal is to get free of them. This school rejects the concept of a personal god.

## THE VEDANTA SYSTEM AND THE UPANISHADS

The *Vedanta* school focuses on the Upanishads for its inspiration. The word *Upanishad* means "sitting near" and refers to the custom of students sitting close by their gurus to hear the truth. The truth of the Upanishads is that of ultimate things: the self, the cosmos, and God. The Upanishads are also called the Vedanta, "the end (or concluding part) of the Vedas," and the two terms may be used interchangeably.

There are 108 Upanishads altogether, most of them composed as a dialogue between a student and teacher. Some are prose, others poetry, and some a combination of both. The Upanishads were written between 900 and 400 B.C.E, with the prose works possibly older than the poetry. They vary greatly in length, style, and tone.

One of my favorites, the Brihadaranyaka, features a dialogue between a sage and a woman named Gargi. Having women featured in intellectual roles is rare in Hindu literature, and Gargi asks some of the most thoughtful questions of all. She wants to know what "It" is, that entity which reaches across, binds together, and separates all other things. The answering wise man, Yajnavalkya, tells her that "It" is "not coarse, not fine, not short, not long, not glowing, not adhesive, without shadow and without darkness, without air and without space, without stickiness...." He continues in this vein for some time.

Many of the Upanishads express the views of the *Vedanta* school of philosophy, whose founder was the south Indian philosopher Shankara *(Samkara)* the so-called "mystic of the soul" (c. 788 to 820 or 700 to 750 C.E.).

As a child, Shankara tricked his mother into letting him join a religious order by pretending that a crocodile was about to eat him, and wouldn't let go unless he promised to take ascetic vows. The mother fell for this unlikely tale, and Shankara was on his way to founding a philosophical school. Perhaps to make up for the crocodile story, he supposedly caused a river to flow miraculously nearer to his mother's house, so that she would have an easier time getting water. According to the story, Shankara died in the Himalayas, after having established monasteries in each of the four corners of India. One tradition says he wrote more than 300 Sanskrit works. Because he died when only thirty-two years old, one hopes, for his sake, that the books were short ones.

*Vedanta* is probably the most important philosophical school in Hinduism, both for its intrinsic interest and its powerful influence on other, including Western, philosophies. Its main thrust is metaphysical, meaning that it concerns the ultimate nature of reality. Another word for the *Vedanta* system is *Advaita*, meaning nondualist. According to *Vedanta* thought, the way we commonly perceive the universe, as an entity divided into spirit and matter, a

**THE MYSTIC OF THE SOUL**

*Some Hindus believe that Shankara was the reincarnation of the god Shiva. This would not have pleased Shankara, who denied the existence of or devotion to any god or goddess.*

dualist view, is incorrect. The world is not separate from God. *Vedantans* refuse to commit themselves formally to the apparently logical corollary that if there are not multiple entities in the universe, there must be only one entity, or none at all. Such a view would make them monists, a label they refuse to accept. The foundation of the universe, the Brahman, is beyond all qualifiers. *Vedantans* regard the label "monist" as too restrictive, both linguistically and metaphysically. They say that if one says "one," one is opening the door to "two," and then even "three" or "four." Saying "not one" slams this door shut, at least in their mind. The rejection of the term *monist* is thus a matter of principle. For practical purposes, however, they are monists—they accept only one truly real entity in the universe. And that reality is a spiritual essence, the all-pervading Brahman. The concept that a spirituality infuses everything is familiar to Westerners. For example:

> And I have felt
> A presence that disturbs me with the joy
> Of elevated thoughts, a sense sublime
> Of something far more deeply interfused,
> Whose dwelling is the light of setting suns,
> And the round ocean and the living air,
> And the blue sky, and in the mind of man:
> A motion and a spirit, that impels
> All thinking things, all objects of all thought,
> And rolls through all things.
>
> —*William Wordsworth*

For *Vedantans,* the main problem we humans face is ignorance *(avidya).* They use this word in a radical way. For them, it doesn't just mean "non-knowing." It means "not knowing" in such a deep and powerful way that keeps us from knowing, that it makes us cling to our ignorance and mistake it for knowledge, the way a desert wanderer clings to a mirage. This teaching is in harmony with that of the ancient Rig Veda, which cries, "O self-luminous Brahman, remove the veil of ignorance from before me, that I may behold thy light."

Shankara claimed that once a person attained true knowledge, he would be released from the cycle of rebirth and redeath.

He emphasized that this knowledge and the bliss that comes from it could be obtained in the present life. He also gave some indications as to what that knowledge consists of. It means knowing the soul.

## KNOWING THE SOUL

When Hindus use the word *soul,* they don't mean it the way Western religions do—as some immortal piece of personal ego. Immortal it is, personal it is not. In fact, thinking of the soul as some indestructible collection of one's thoughts, feelings, and experiences is exactly the wrong way to look at this important Hindu concept.

The most common Hindu philosophical term for "soul" is *atman,* but atman is a much larger concept than its Western counterpart. It refers to the timeless divinity within each person, a divinity that everyone shares. (The Yajur Veda says that the soul pervades reality like the butter in milk.) It is sometimes called the "subtle self."

*Atman* is cognate to the English word *atmosphere* and in fact, the word originally meant "breath." The person breathes in his soul the way he breathes in the air: it doesn't belong to him, although he depends upon it. The soul has no shape of its own but accommodates the capacities of the breather. In and of itself, the soul is indistinguishable from the vastness of the atmosphere; it is one with it. Yet at the same time, it's the inmost self of him who breathes it in.

**SOUL IN THE SINGULAR**

*Once in a while, especially in ordinary language, another word for soul is used, jiva. This refers to the single individual spirit of each person.*

---

**TO BE GREAT**

The word Brahman comes from a Sanskrit stem meaning "to be great." In one of its more esoteric comments, the Upanishads portray the Brahman as anna-prana-manas-vijnana-ananda-chit-sat. In case you're wondering, this means: physical, vital, mental, awareness, blissful, conscious, full totality of being.

---

Ultimately, the Atman is one with the Brahman, the Eternal, Uncreated, Ground of Being of the universe. The important thing is to *experience* this truth, not just read about it.

Shankara goes to a great deal of trouble to explain that the usual things we think of as "ourselves" (body, energy, mind, intellect, or ego) are just "coverings." Look beneath them to find who you really are. To clarify this idea, I have included here a passage from his *Crest-Jewel of Discrimination,* one of his more popular and non-scholarly works. Its charm is largely due to its poetic evocation of the nature of the Brahman/Atman.

> I, the Atman, am Brahma. I am Vishnu. I am Shiva.
>
> I am the universe. Nothing is, but I am. I dwell within: I am without. I am before and behind. I am in the south and I am in the north. I am above and I am below...
>
> This entire universe of which we speak and think is nothing but Brahman... There is nothing else...
>
> The scripture says, "The Infinite is where man sees nothing else, hears nothing else, knows nothing else." In the Infinite, the scripture tells us, there is no duality—thereby correcting our false idea that existence is manifold.
>
> I am Brahman, the supreme, all pervading like the ether, stainless, indivisible, unbounded, unmoved, unchanging. I have neither inside nor outside. I alone am. I am one without a second. What else is there to be known?

Shankara also did his best to rebut Buddhist philosophy, which was gaining ground in India at the time. Since Buddhism there was eventually re-absorbed into Hinduism, we could say that Shankara succeeded in his task.

## KNOWING THE BRAHMAN

As if the idea of Brahman isn't hard enough, it so happens that Brahman can be understood in two different ways. One way is the *Saguna* Brahman, which means the Brahman "with attributes." The *Saguna* Brahman has all the qualities we normally ascribe to God, like wisdom, power, and goodness, but the real Brahman is the *Nirguna* Brahman, the Brahman without attributes. After all, all attributes are limiting. For example, if we say a person is female, then she is not male. If a person is 5'4", he cannot be 6'5". If we ascribe attributes to the Brahman, we limit the Brahman. And the Brahman cannot be limited. For some Hindu thinkers, even to say "Brahman exists" is too limiting. This is why he is often spoken of only in negatives, "not this, not this" *(neti, neti),* and why nondualists use a negative term to describe their philosophy.

In the Chandogya Upanishad, the priestly Aruni tells his son Svetaketu a series of parables to explain this point:

> Just as the bees make honey by collecting the nectar from all kinds of flowers, and the nectar no longer knows from what tree it originally came, so when all creatures have merged with the Ultimate Reality, they are no longer aware of their individual identity.
>
> Just as all the rivers run to the sea, where their waters intermingle without knowledge of their source, so do all creatures, tigers, bears, gnats, and mosquitoes, come to the Ultimate Reality without knowing their origins.

It is also true that each person may experience the Brahman differently. This is an important point. The Brahman can be truly known and truly experienced. Blind faith and sacrifice are not relevant here.

Then comes the master phrase of nondualist philosophy: *Tat tvam asi:* "That art thou," the philosophy of self-identification. In other words, the Atman and the Brahman are one. As the Ground of Being, the Brahman is present in all things.

In another series of parables, Aruni points out that although clay can be transformed into many things, it remains clay. And every thing into which it is transformed, whether it's a pot or a statue, remains clay too. He then goes on to give several other examples of like nature, just to make sure that his son gets the idea.

In any case, when the Brahman *must* be described in words, it is called *Satchitananda,* which means "perfect being, perfect knowledge, perfect bliss." The Being referred to is not mere existence, nor is it only potential being. It is being in its fullness, in its plentitude, and in its absolute reality. (The word for Being, *sat,* also carries the connotation of righteousness.) Knowledge *(chit)* has nothing to do with what's found in books, or learned in school, or perceived by the casual observer. Knowledge is experienced realization. (It's the difference between reading about pregnancy and being pregnant.) And bliss *(ananda)* is not the kind of bliss that comes from a happy marriage or even a really good bar of chocolate. It's much, much more. Apparently, it is even more than any heaven can provide.

"It is this very fineness which ensouls all this world, it is the true one, it is the soul."
—*Chandogya Upanishad*

## Ramanuja and Qualified Nondualism

Brme said that Atman and Brahman are not the same—they are just "related." For instance, the Brahman is the knowledge, and the Atman is the knower. Or the Brahman is love, and the Atman is the lover.

The eleventh century Vaishnavite philosopher Ramanuja (c. 1040–1137) pointed out that if the Atman and the Brahman were one thing, there would be no point in worship, because you'd be worshipping yourself. That seems true; however, those who believe the Brahman and Atman are the same don't practice worship anyway. In Ramanuja's philosophy, the soul always has a self-knowledge apart from God. Ramanuja called his theory "qualified nondualism," and said that although the Brahman is really one, he has two aspects—mind and matter. Avatars and yogic visions give us a partial idea of the true divinity. Furthermore, he conceived of ultimate reality as a person (sort of) with the qualities of omniscience, omnipotence, loving kindness, and mercy. Whether this helps or not is up to you.

## Madhva and Dualism

Still further to the right (almost Western in fact) is the position of Madhva, a thirteenth century Vaishnavite theologian. Madhva was a dualist, claiming that each soul was distinct from God and separate from every other soul. Madhva also taught that some souls are predestined to eternal damnation. This Calvinistic outlook is found nowhere else in the Hindu tradition. Because of certain suspicious elements in Madhva's biography—he walked on water, fed casts of thousands, and so forth—some scholars suspect his philosophy was contaminated by Christianity. Certainly he was exposed to Christian missionary influence in the area around Madras where he lived.

## KNOWING THE COSMOS

In Hindu philosophy, the universe is organized into seven planes. Each of these has two aspects—the positive *Loka* and the negative *Tala*. In Western terminology, the *Lokas* are like heaven, and the *Talas* like hell, although neither is a permanent lodging for the soul. (Only the Brahman is forever.) From highest to lowest, the *Lokas* are:

1. *Satya-Loka:* the plane of ultimate existence or truth, where Brahma resides.

2. *Tapar-Loka:* plane of self-aware energy, where the demigods who do not have to return to earth dwell.

3. *Janar-Loka:* plane of creative delight, where Brahma's children live.

4. *Mahar-Loka:* plane of great consciousness, where the saints live.

5. *Svar-Loka:* plane of luminous mind, between the sun and north star where Indra lives.

6. *Bhuvar-Loka:* plane of vital becoming between the earth and sun. Here live the sages.

7. *Bhur-Loka:* plane of material becoming.

The corresponding *Talas* are:

1. *Atala:* plane of no place, extinction.

2. *Vitala:* plane of spiritual darkness.

3. *Sutala:* plane of desire and passion.

4. *Rasatala:* plane of sensual pleasure.

5. *Talatala:* plane of self-indulgence.

6. *Mahatala:* plane of darkness ruled by the ego.

7. *Patala:* plane of ignorance and darkness.

Most human beings reside in the *Bhuvar-Loka* most of the time. Hinduism has no concept of a permanent hell, still less of a Satan. Hell is merely a state of being that we ourselves have produced from our own selfishness, ignorance, and desire. It is a result of our own karma, not a place designed by a god for our punishment.

"The fourth state of consciousness is not that which is conscious of the subjective, nor that which is conscious of the objective, nor that which is conscious of both, nor that which is simple consciousness, nor that which is all-sentient mass, nor that which is all darkness. It is unseen, transcendent, the sole essence of the consciousness of the self, the completion of the world."

—*Mandukya Upandishad*

## DEALING WITH DEATH

One of the most beloved and important scriptures in Hinduism is the Katha Upanishad. Here a boy, Nachiketas, is offered up to Yama, the Lord of Death. Curiously, the boy's name means "not-conscious." (That has to be symbolic of something.) This Upanishad is mostly a dialogue between the boy and Death, in which the boy tries to find out what the afterlife is like. When the question is finally answered, however, the reader is still not real sure.

## THE SACRED AUM

In the Upanishads we also find mention of the supreme sacred syllable: AUM, the mother of all sounds. It is sometimes spelled "om," but this is less exact, because there are supposed to be three distinct sounds. The Mandukya Upanishad says that there are really four sounds (not three) involved: the three audible sounds, and the following silence, which represents the Atman in the state of self-realization. This fourth "sound" corresponds to *Turiya*, the fourth state of consciousness *(samadhi)*. "The fourth is without an element, with which there can be no dealing, the cessation of development, benign, without a second. Thus AUM is the Atman indeed."

The two marks on top are the sun and moon. When "AUM" is correctly chanted, the chanter vibrates to the sound of the cosmos and ultimately he becomes the mantra itself.

All words are said to be derived from this one sound. It is chanted at the beginning of all holy ceremonies, for its three separate sounds ("A," "U," and "M") represent the three aspects of the divine: the outer divine, the inner divine, and the super-conscious divine. According to other sources, each element of the word speaks to a different part of the creative process. The A stands for the creating God Brahma, the U stands for the preserving god Vishnu, and the final M stands for Shiva and the end of existence. This is because you have to close your mouth to make the M sound.

In other schemes, the letters correspond with the three worlds, or with the three states of consciousness: ordinary waking, dreaming, and dreamless sleep.

The last words of the Gita are "AUM, that Boundless Reality." That says it all.

> "AUM! This syllable is this whole world. Its further explanation is: the past, the present, the future—everything is just the word AUM."
>
> —*Mandukya Upanishad*

**THE AUM IN SANSKRIT**

## CHAPTER RECAP

- *Jnana marga* is the *marga* of knowledge.

- There are six orthodox schools of *jnana marga,* but the most important is the *Vedanta,* or nondualist school.

- *Vedanta* teaches that the human soul and the ultimate divinity are the same.

- The sacred syllable "AUM" expresses the boundless reality of the Brahman and the Atman.

*Recommended Reading*

The Upanishads. Trans. Swami Prabhavananda and Frederick Manchester. New York: Mentor, 1970.

Younger, Paul. *Introduction to Indian Religious Thought.* Philadelphia: The Westminster Press, 1962.

# Bhakti Marga—

## *The Path of Devotion*

*T*he vast majority of Hindu worshippers, most of whom belong to the Shudra or laboring castes, classify themselves as followers of the *bhakti marga*. This is the path of devotion. It doesn't center on sacrifice as did the ancient Vedic religion, or on *dharmic* responsibility like karma *marga*, or on weird physical postures like *hatha* yoga, or on abstruse philosophical knowledge like *jnana marga*.

In this popular tradition, devotees often refer to the ultimate as God, by whom they mean a divine person, much like the Christian, Jewish, and Islamic notion. For these worshipers, *bhakti* is like a rope that helps them climb to God—or pulls God down to them. Although *bhakti* Hindus may in theory worship as many gods as they like, most confine their devotions to one god only. That god represents the ultimate Brahman, but it is certainly easier to worship the ultimate in a "human" form. The ultimate goal of *bhakti* devotees is a meeting with the divinity, whether that divinity is Shiva, Vishnu, or the Goddess. It is less concerned with transcending the ego than are the other paths. *Surrender* is a more apt word, and the surrender is to the deity in love.

One of the founders of the modern *bhakti* movement, a philosopher named Narada, listed eleven forms of devotion. These include first being in awe of God, and then learning to regard him as the supreme person and entering into a personal relationship with him,

A YOGIN'S LIFE

*For a fascinating account of the life of a modern yogin, there's no more interesting work than the classic* Autobiography of a Yogi, *by Paramahansa Yogananda. It has been a major influence in attracting people to the religion and philosophy of India.*

which might take the form of friend, lover, child, or servant. Narada appeared to emphasize servantship *(dasya)* to God as the best way to liberation. He believed that the chief obstacles to liberation were wealth, sex, and atheists. He further suggested that too much discussion about God might be dangerous, because it can never lead to certainty. He thought instead that people should pray incessantly to God and seek his love alone. When the goal is attained, we will become fulfilled, immortal, and happy.

In *bhakti marga*, the devotee worships, perhaps exclusively, one manifestation of the Brahman. This manifestation is usually one of the so-called Hindu trinity, or else a female goddess who represents the real power of that deity. Some *bhakti* yogins worship their guru, who they believe has the spirit of God.

The point of *bhakti* yoga is to surrender completely to God, and thus attempt to gain either unity with him or else to enjoy his love and company forever, depending on one's bent (dualist or nondualist). Many forms of devotion are practiced, including singing hymns, worshipping symbols, and offerings. The last can include flowers, candles, clothing, jewels, incense, and prayers.

Another practice of *bhakti marga* is "making *japa*" or reciting a mantra. (The word *mantra* comes from the Sanskrit and means "crossing the mind.") In a similar vein, some *bhaktis* repeat the name of God, or a series of holy words. The object is to lead the devotee to a higher consciousness. According to tradition, this is the easiest way to achieve union with God.

## THE TRIMURTI: *THE HOLY THREE*

The Hindu *trimurti* or trinity are Brahma, Vishnu, and Shiva—the creator, the preserver, and the destroyer of the universe. All, however, are but manifestations of the Brahman.

### Brahma—The Lonely Creator

Brahma is the king-creator god, born from a lotus blossom that grows from the navel of Vishnu, another member of the trinity. Another, more philosophical, notion is that Brahma was born from a golden nucleus or egg *(hiranyagarbha)* that was sparked by the first cause like kindling from a match. Some Hindus say that Brahma was born when fire and priesthood joined together. Regardless of how he got here, Brahma now lives on the mythical Mount Meru in the Himalayas. (Brahma is usually worshipped along with Shiva or Vishnu rather than separately. Only two temples in all India are dedicated to him alone.)

Brahma carries a rosary of beads, seeds, or flowers, all of which represent the continuous passing of time. He is most familiar as a source of knowledge and a teacher

> **LOTUS LORE**
>
> *Some traditions say that before creation, the entire world was a golden lotus. The lotus is a traditional symbol of nonattachment in Hinduism. This is because it remains dry as it floats serenely above the water and mud that gave it birth. It is also a symbol of spirituality and fertility. The goddess of the lotus is Padma, and she is very ancient, dating back to pre-Vedic days. For Buddhists, too, the lotus is an important symbol. The Buddha is said to have "lotus eyes and lotus feet."*

of human beings. He is depicted with four faces and four arms, and is often shown with a goose. His four faces look in four directions, so Brahma sees and knows all.

## Vishnu—The Benevolent Preserver

Of all the Hindu gods, Vishnu most strongly resembles the idea Westerners have of "God." His worshippers are known as Vaishnavites, most of whom belong to either the Krishna or the Rama sect, depending on which of Vishnu's many forms they wish to honor.

One set of the *bhakti* sacred scriptures, the Puranas, are devoted to Vishnu. The other two are devoted to Brahma and Shiva. The Puranas were compiled between 300 and 1600 C.E. and remain a popular mythology of India. (Another set of scriptures, the Agamas, is used for rituals.) They say that if you really want to know Hinduism, read the Puranas.

Vishnu is often shown as sleeping on a vast serpent, Ananta (meaning "without end"). Both float on an endless, milky ocean. Hindus say that he is dreaming the universe, and this image is a staple of Indian art. (From his navel grows the lotus that bears Brahma.) His fabled home is Vaikuntha, a paradise of pools, jewels, and of course, lotuses.

Vishnu's mount is Garuda, a strange, eagle-like being. Garuda has quite a few adventures of his own, the most notable of which is killing the serpents that guard *soma*, the elixir of immortality.

**EARLY GODS**

*Originally, Vishnu may have been a sun god, as Shiva was originally a moon god.*

(The snakes were guarding it on behalf of some gods, who had stolen it themselves from some demons.) Garuda is a mediator between gods and demons; he is also the sworn enemy of snakes. If you look carefully, also, you might notice that Garuda is today the symbol of Indonesian Airlines.

According to Indian legend, when a sage was wandering around trying to find the best god, he awakened Vishnu by kicking him. Instead of having a temper tantrum, Vishnu rubbed the sage's foot, concerned that he had hurt himself. The sage then declared Vishnu the wisest of the gods. Or at any rate, the nicest.

Vishnu also takes in the entire cosmos in three great strides: earth in one stride, heaven in another, and the supreme state of being/knowledge/bliss in the third.

### The Avatars of Vishnu

Strong and protective, the crown-bearing Vishnu takes on earthly form from time to time, in order to help the world. Such a being is known as an avatar, a word that literally means "descent." An avatar acts as an intermediary between the god and human beings.

Vishnu traditionally has ten avatars, although some devotees count thirty-nine altogether. A common list of Vishnu's avatars includes: a fish who saved Manu from a great flood, a tortoise who helped the gods obtain the nectar of immortality, a boar who saved the earth from sinking into the ocean, a man/lion who saved a devotee from persecution, a dwarf who saved the world from a great demon, Rama-with-an-Ax who restored authority to the Brahmins, Krishna, and even the Buddha. (This last doesn't make Buddhists very happy.) The last avatar, Kalki, is yet to come. He will destroy the barbarians and bring about a new order on earth.

Krishna and Rama are Vishnu's most famous avatars. Krishna is usually shown as a young man, or even as a boy. Sometimes, though, he is shown with many arms and legs, which demonstrate his power. He's usually depicted as blue. He appears in the Bhagavad Gita in yet another guise, the Charioteer.

Rama is the hero of another epic, the *Ramayana* ("The Adventures of Rama"). It was supposedly written by Valkimi around 100 or 200 B.C.E., and contains 48,000 lines of eight syllables each. *The Ramayana* is a story of good and evil. Rama (who may have been a historical character) loses his bride Sita to the demon Ravana, who kidnaps her and takes her away to Lanka, his island kingdom. Ravana is easy to spot, because he has ten heads and twenty arms, although he can change shape at will. Eventually, Sita is located by the king of the monkeys, Hanuman. Hanuman's father was Vayu, the Vedic god of wind. His mother was a mortal woman known for her extraordinary beauty. Together, they created a monkey.

During the battle for Sita, Rama was badly hurt. Hanuman to the rescue! He knew that a healing herb grew on a far mountain, and he raced to get it. Unfortunately, he didn't know exactly what herb to pick, so he just grabbed the whole mountain and brought it back. That worked. Rama gave the monkey a lovely bracelet of gold and pearls as a reward, but Hanuman just chewed it up and threw it away. It was worthless to him, he said, because it didn't have Rama's name on it. "Well, if you feel like that," sneered one of his friends (a bear), "you might as well throw your whole body away." At that point, Hanuman ripped open his chest so that his innards were exposed. Every bone, every sinew, every muscle, had the word *Rama* written on it. Today he is revered throughout India, as the model of devotion to God. He is also the object of devotion for those who need great strength.

> ### GANDHI'S LAST WORDS
>
> *As he lay dying from an assassin's bullet, Mahatma Gandhi (1869–1948), muttered his last words "Ram. Ram. Ram." to Rama. Gandhi was the ultimate exemplar of the Hindu principle of nonviolence. He gained great fame for almost single-handedly delivering India from its British occupiers—without the use of violence, although he did every other thing he could think of, including having himself jailed on several occasions. He also made use of strikes, marches, and media spin. He was so beloved by the Indian people that they called him* bapuji, *"dear father."*

Finally there is a battle between Rama and Ravana, *mano a mano*. Rama wins, of course, shooting an arrow blessed with Vedic mantras right into Ravana's heart. But the epic isn't over yet. Rama decides to test Sita's loyalty by accusing her of adultery. He puts her to the test of fire, but Sita is protected by Agni. He still doesn't give up, however, and subjects her to test after test. Finally poor Sita turns into pure blazing light, confesses her undying love for Rama, and melts into the earth. This is supposed to be something of a happy ending, and according to some authorities, is intended to show how highly women are venerated in Hindu society. *The Ramayana* is acted out every year in India.

### Shiva—The Terrifying Destroyer

Shiva represents an utterly different aspect of the divine from the friendly Vishnu. Shiva is the Destroyer God, a wild being. In some ways Shiva is a new god, but he has powerful connections with the ancient Vedic god Rudra and can be said to have merged with him. Like Rudra, he has both his positive and negative aspects, but Shiva has a more complete set of personal characteristics. His signature qualities are truth, energy, and darkness—a powerful, but frightening combination. The breathing of Shiva both creates and destroys the world.

**IN OTHER WORDS**

*The word Shiva actually means "kindly" or "lucky." His more gentle aspect is celebrated in the southern part of India, while people in the north pay more attention to his destructive aspects, or Rudha-nature. In that guise he presides over cremation grounds.*

Those who worship Shiva are called Shaivites. Modern Shaivites believe that Shiva is the ultimate god made manifest in a "visible" form. Shaivism is most popular today in south India, especially around Madras. Shaivites themselves come in several varieties. Some sprinkle their bodies with ashes and practice a special yoga, while others, such as practitioners in Kashmir, worship Shiva in his most terrible aspect.

The god is often thought of as being enthroned among the ice-clad Himalayas, on Mount Kailasa. Another way of picturing him is as the divine dancer, or Lord of the Dance, the Nataraja. In this form (first depicted more than a thousand years ago) he bears the fire of destruction and the drum of creation. His dancing platform is a demonic dwarf, who represents ignorance. His long hair (an emblem of a yogin) flies in the wind. He is surrounded by the flames of destruction. Shaivites insist that this destruction is not a totally negative thing, pointing out that destruction is necessary for the creation of new life. Besides, Shiva never destroys the world until everything has gone to hell anyway.

### Ganesha

Shiva has a very popular stepson, Ganesha, the elephant-headed god of wisdom, time, and good fortune. He is known as lord over the dwarf-demons (who are always causing trouble of one kind or another). He is the patron of all the arts and sciences, and Shiva has directed that people should worship Ganesha even before himself.

Ganesha has another role, however: the Lord of Obstacles. Not only does he place obstacles in your path, he also removes them. Devotees of Shiva believe that Ganesha is the embodiment of karmic laws. Ganesha lost his real head (stories vary about how), and the elephant head is a replacement. His mother, Parvati, threatened to destroy the universe unless a substitute head was found—and fast. At any rate, the elephant head quickly distinguishes Ganesha from all the other 330,000,000 Hindu gods. (This is an approximate number. Figures vary, and I don't think there's a list anywhere.) Ganesha has only one tusk—the other one got knocked out by a guy named Parashurama. He has a big sweet tooth and is always depicted with some candy in one hand. (He also carries a noose and goad.)

Ganesha is sometimes thought of as a teacher, who lays down tests for his students—only to help them become stronger for it. For this reason, perhaps, Ganesha is the god of education. He helps us make decisions, but also expects us to use our intelligence. No aim can be accomplished without his assistance.

### The Lingam and Yoni Emblems

Everywhere you go in India, you see lingams, stone or marble pillars, often very large, in honor of Shiva. Many lingams are engraved with the face (or multiple faces) of the god. Others are plain, but no matter how simple or elaborate they are, many look remarkably like erect penises. Some Hindus will assure you this is merely a coincidence, and point out other lingams that are abstract, oblong shapes, with no overt phallic features.

Whatever the truth of it, Shiva is most often depicted in the lingam emblem; in fact, one of his nicknames is Sthanu, "the pillar." Abstract or not, it's hard to get away from the idea of Shiva as a sex symbol. (The lingam is considered "hot," and cooling water or milk is often poured over it as a form of devotion.) The lingam represents Shiva in his creative aspect, the flip side of destruction. To make his paradoxical nature clear, Shiva, although he is an ascetic yogin, is often shown with an erection. (Actually, Shiva has four aspects: fearsome, benign, sensual, and ascetic.)

The lingam is often shown embedded in a yoni (vaginal) emblem, which represents Shakti, Shiva's female aspect or consort.

**THE STORY OF SHIVA**

*Worship of Shiva may be very old, probably dating back to the original inhabitants of the region, the Dravidians. In his earliest representations, in the Indus Valley Civilization, seals were found with a meditating Shivalike figure.*

These images go all the way back to the Indus Valley Civilization. Modern Shaivites sometimes say that the lingam represents Shiva in his ultimate, invisible aspect, while the yoni represents Shiva made manifest.

Young girls in particular pay devotion to the lingam; it's one way to get a good husband. There's even a sect of Hindus called the Lingayat who wear little stone lingams around their necks or on their left arms from the very day of their birth. (This interesting group also permits widows to remarry and has no problem with female *sannyasins*.)

---

**HINDU HIGHLIGHT**

*On September 21, 1995, many statues of Shiva all over India suddenly began drinking milk offered by their devotees. Some drank a bucketful of the stuff. Even more amazing, to many Indians, was the fact that the Shiva statues accepted milk from anybody, from every caste. This miracle lasted only one day, but was pretty convincing to everyone who experienced it.*

---

## WORSHIP OF THE FEMININE

From very ancient times, goddesses were popular in India. The Indus Valley Civilization had a well-established goddess cult, and even the patriarchal Aryans had female deities. In classical Hindu culture, however, female goddesses were usually reduced to the status of consorts of the males. All this began to change around 500 C.E., when goddesses came into their own. There is even a Great Goddess, Mahadevi, who contains all lesser manifestations of feminine divinity within her. According to many Hindus, she ranks above *all* other gods, both male and female, and is identified with the Brahman.

In *bhakti* Hinduism, the female divinities are called Devas. Some are nurturing and loving mother goddesses, others are destructive and fearsome beings. Often the same deities combine both qualities but assume a different alias for each activity. Among the more benevolent goddesses is Lakshmi, the goddess of beauty, riches, and good luck. She is a consort of Vishnu, and in Indian art, is often shown rubbing his leg.

Another beloved goddess is Parvati, a consort of Shiva. She is more than a mere wife, however. She is a *shakti*—one who expresses the power and energy of creation. As such, she can be worshipped along with her male consort, or separately. (About 15 million Hindus are worshippers of *shakti*.) In this guise, the *shakti* is regarded as having created the world out of a sense of *lila* or playfulness. The whole concept of divine *lila* is an important part of the Vaishnava tradition. This doesn't mean that God is frivolous, however. It means that he (or she) acts in a spontaneous way; God didn't *need* to create the universe, but did so freely and joyfully.

The main destructive goddesses are Kali and awe-inspiring Durga, both extremely popular in India today. Sacrifices of goats are regularly made to them, in contradistinction to the typical Hindu emphasis on nonviolence. This seems odd to Westerners, but Hindus believe it's smart to pay homage to those who wield power.

Ten-armed Durga, a pre-Vedic deity, is a warrior goddess. She wears a halo and always looks calm, no matter what's happening around her. (She looks nice enough, but be careful of the weapons she carries. She also rides a tiger. In fact, Durga is exactly the same color as a tiger.) Durga's most famous exploits involve killing buffalo demons. The buffalo demons were way beyond the powers of the male gods, and they had to ask Durga for help. (The text adds that the demons went to perdition. One wonders where they came from.) During the battle, Durga gives birth to Kali. (At least that's one story, but there are others. In many accounts Durga and Kali are actually interchangeable.)

Dark Kali (the Black One) is Shiva's consort, and when she is in the picture she's more powerful than Shiva and completely dominates him. In this aspect, she too is a *shakti*. Bengalis called her the supreme mother, although her motherly aspects seem to be slightly obscured, because her main ornament is a necklace of human skulls. Sometimes, each skull is inscribed with a letter of the Sanskrit alphabet. Odd as this seems, it represents that Kali brought beings into creation by naming them. For more about the odd relationship between Shiva and Kali, see chapter 18 on Tantra.

A fairly recent goddess is Manasa, queen of the snakes. Although she is not the most attractive of deities, having broken hips and blind in one eye, her blessing will cure snakebite, still a serious problem in India. A similar healing goddess is Sitala, who can cure smallpox.

OH! CALCUTTA!

*The city of Calcutta is named after a great temple in Kali's honor.*

UH OH! CALCUTTA!

*American Beat poet Allen Ginsberg went to Calcutta himself. He said it was the world's most liberated city. I am not sure what his ultimate plans were, but he didn't stay long. It was too hot.*

## TEMPLES AND WORSHIP

Temples are a fairly recent development in the history of Hinduism. Most arose during the medieval period (600–1800 C.E.). (As seems to be true about everything in Hinduism, the medieval period lasted a lot longer for them than it did for Westerners.) The rise of the temple was a result of the development of *bhakti* Hinduism, because Hindu temples are devoted to the worship of a god or gods. Hindus, however, are never required to enter a temple. Only religious practices done at home are obligatory.

When Westerners think of a temple, they think of a building. In Hinduism, however, the ideal is not one single building, but an entire complex of richly decorated structures. The original temples were made of wood and decorated with elaborate carvings. Later, stone temples were built to duplicate the look of the earlier wood. Most temples contain a gateway, a courtyard and bell, a terrace, and a purification tank (especially if no river is close by). There is a spire that symbolizes the aspiring spirit of the devotee. The actual deity is kept within a small, poorly lit, inner room, a sort of Holy of Holies.

The temple is considered to be the home of the god; many temples are constructed to honor gods often worshipped together like Shiva and Parvati.

To facilitate religious practice at home, many Indian households contain a special room devoted to *puja* worship. In *puja*, the devotee offers flowers or food to his favored deity. The image of the deity is merely an image, and every devout Hindu knows this. *Puja* is not idol worship; it is merely a way of honoring the divine that exists in all things.

**TEMPLES OF YORE**

*Ancient temples may have had sacred prostitutes associated with them, but this practice has gone out of fashion.*

## CEREMONIES

Ceremonies mark the most important life passages in Hindu life. The ancient scriptures list sixteen such ceremonies, including ceremonies at conception and a hair-braiding ceremony for the mom during pregnancy. Also important are the baby-naming ceremony *(namakarana)*, weaning *(annaprasana)*, initiation for the twice-born, *(upanayana)*, marriage *(vavaha)*, and the funeral *(sraddha)*. The ancient Vedic custom of *sraddha*, a word meaning "respect," is an offering system that has survived into the present. Without the correct ceremonies, an ancestor may become a problem—an annoying or dangerous ghost. Special rites are performed at the time of death to keep this from happening. Curiously, this practice, which smacks of ancestor worship, is not Vedic in origin. It may have been an innovation, or part of the original Dravidian culture. In *sraddha*, rice balls, which may represent a kind of new body for the dead, are offered by a male descendant. Interestingly, rites are offered only for adults—young people who die receive no special rites.

Daily ceremonies are generally performed at home. They include meditations and prayers. There are a few weekly or monthly rituals also, but certainly most Hindus do not observe every possible ritual. One would have time for nothing else.

Given the number and variety of Hindu ceremonies, I'll focus on a few of my favorites. One of these is the daily care of the deity. The deity, or in the case of Shiva, the lingam that represents him, is bathed each day and anointed with sandalwood paste. Refreshment is offered to him each afternoon or at sundown. (During the hottest portion of each day, the deity should be taking his siesta.) At night, the god is ceremoniously dressed for the evening and put to bed.

It is common for sacrifices of fruits and flowers to be offered to the deity, and at Kalighat in Calcutta, animal sacrifices are made to the fearsome goddess Kali. This is an extremely unusual practice, not done elsewhere in India. Many devotions in Hinduism involve *ghee*, which is simply the Hindi word for clarified butter. *Ghee* is most often used in sprinkling on the sacred fire, in remembrance of ancient devotions to Agni, the Vedic fire god.

**ONE TYPE OF OFFERING**

*To gain protection from the gods, Hindu women often make rice paste patterns on the ground in front of their homes.*

## COW VENERATION

From very ancient times, cows have been a powerful symbol of good. For the Hindus they represent fertility *(prithivi)* and abundance *(aditi)*. The cow's products: milk, butter, dung, and so forth are considered to be "gifts" to be used for spiritual cleansing. Cow dung is actually used as a disinfectant in floor washing. Dying persons are encouraged to grasp the tail of a cow backed up to their bedsides; it helps in the next life.

The Vedas include some special hymns to the cow, who is often referred to as "our mother." Cows also represent the entire nonhuman world and remind us that all life, not just human life, is sacred. Vishnu's paradise is sometimes called "the heaven of cows."

In the modern world, Gandhi claimed that cow protection was Hinduism's gift to the world, as it emphasized the bond between all living things.

In mythology, the cow is the consort of Shiva's great white bull-with-the-black-tail Nandi, and as such, she grants wishes. (*Nandi*, whose name means "joyful," is also the ideal worshipper of Shiva.)

---

### THE BRAHMIN'S BOVINE

*Although the ancient Aryans thought highly of cows, they nonetheless ate and sacrificed them. It was considered an honor if one slaughtered a cow for his guests, but the Brahmin's cow was under special protection, even then. The Atharva Veda says that to kill a Brahmin's cow is the same thing as killing a Brahmin. The ban on cow flesh stems from the period between 800 and 1200 C.E., just yesterday, in the long Hindu view of things.*

---

Cows are fed by the populace and are often festooned with bright flowery garlands. During special festivals, oil is poured upon their foreheads, and water is offered at their feet. There's even a cow holiday, Gopastami, when the cow is treated exactly as if she were a god.

"Cow protection is one of the most wonderful phenomena in human evolution."

—*Mahatma Gandhi*

## PILGRIMAGES

Pilgrimages are undertaken by all classes. A pilgrimage to the Ganges is the most popular of all, for to bathe in the holy Ganges River insures health and brings spiritual merit (sort of a point system). To gain further spiritual merit, many Hindus not only bathe in the sacred river, but read scriptures while doing so. It is considered most auspicious to die near the Ganges. The ideal Hindu funeral is to be cremated at the river's edge, and then have one's ashes scattered in this most sacred river. Therefore many Hindus try to come to Varanasi in their extreme old age, hoping to attain *moksha* by dying near the Ganges. Other pilgrimages are undertaken to mountain shrines.

Another very popular pilgrimage is to Mathura, where Krishna was supposedly born. Worshippers have been traveling there for more than a thousand years.

## FESTIVALS AND DEVOTIONS

As I mentioned before, Hindus practice countless rituals through-out the year. The greatest festivals are the annual ones, however. You may want to schedule your trip to India in connection with one of the following:

- *Holi:* In this late February festival, children throw colored water on each other. The origin of this custom is sexual and is connected with Krishna and his cowgirls. Others claim that on this day the god of sexual pleasure, Kama, was burnt up by Krishna's third eye and had to go around look-ing for a new body to inhabit.

- *Divali:* This is the Festival of Lights. It occurs in October and celebrates the return of Sita and Rama. Ganesha and Lakshmi are also given special veneration. People cleanse their homes and fill them with lighted candles. Shopkeepers whitewash their shops. They also place lamps in the local trees, to help spirits find their way to the land of bliss. Some people see connections between this holiday and All Souls Day in the Christian calendar. By the way, this is supposed to be a good day for gambling.

- *Ram-Lila:* In this North Indian festival, huge effigies of demons from the *Ramayana* are burned.

- *Durga Puja:* This powerful festival is held in December in northern India. It is sacred to Durga. The festival is cele-brated with street dancing. In Calcutta, statues of Durga are immersed in the river after the festival.

- *Habisha:* A thirty-five-day ritual in honor of Shiva, this important event takes place in the city of Puri (state of Orissa), at the temple of Jagannatha during October–November. The ceremony is for older women only, and perhaps 100,000 attend each year. The devotee first purifies herself by consuming the five products of the cow: milk, curds, *ghee* (clarified butter), urine, and dung. During this period, the woman undergoes severe ascetic practices, scarcely eating, taking a lot of purifying baths,

**THE DOUR BAULS**

*One group of Hindus, the Bauls, do not believe in celebrating any festivals whatever.*

but saying many prayers. Then she travels to Krishna's great temple, where she meets other women, dances, and sings. Curiously, women who make the pilgrimage are traditionally taunted by their fellow villagers when they return home.

- *Snana-yantra:* At this festival, a statue of a god is ritually washed with milk and paraded around town in a huge cart, more than forty-five feet high and with seven-foot wheels. Devotees often got so excited they flung themselves in front of the great wheels and got squashed in the process. The spectacle gave rise to the English word *juggernaut,* which refers to a course of events (or a person) who crushes everything in its path.

## MODERN REFORMERS AND REFORM SOCIETIES

Just as Christianity has spawned numerous reform movements, so has Hinduism.

### The Society of Brahman

The Society of Brahman (Brahmo Samaj) was formed in 1828 by Ram Mohan Roy (1772–1833), a prominent Brahmin from Calcutta. This was the first movement to try to find common ground between Hinduism and Westerns religions and hence is important to Westerners. Its aims were to promote monotheism and combat social and caste abuses. Roy relied on the Upanishads as his scriptural authority.

Roy traveled widely in the west, and even before that, knew several British Christian missionaries who influenced him with respect to the one-God concept. Roy felt that festivals, pilgrimages, and image worship were unnecessary and harmful. His movement gained some momentum in the nineteenth century, but largely due to internal conflicts, it faded at the end of that period and eventually split into three groups, all of which still exist. It is also probable that Westerners gave the society more importance than it ever possessed in India.

## The Noble Society

In 1875, Swami Dayananda (1824–1883) founded the Noble Society (Arya Samaj) to restore Hinduism to its Vedic roots and to form a universal Hinduism. Dayananda believed the Vedas contained all truth—even scientific ones. He also said the Vedas taught monotheism, a claim even harder to make. Although the society did encourage some social change like the emancipation of women and religious reforms (discarding image worship and the caste system), the movement staunchly defended cow veneration (and the cows were getting out of hand).

The society abjured most rituals and said our guide to behavior should be love and justice. We should think about society as a whole, not just ourselves. It also encouraged formerly Hindu Muslims and Christians to turn back to Hinduism, provoking some serious religious squabbles.

The society has a set of ten beliefs, none of which seem revolutionary. These beliefs include faith in a God who is the personification of existence, knowledge, and bliss; assurance that the Vedas are the word of God; belief that we should be ready to accept truth; and that our deeds should be in accord with righteousness and love. All people should help others and obey the laws of society.

## Sri Aurobindo

One important name in modern Hinduism is that of Sri Aurobindo (1872–1950), one of Hindu's greatest yogins. This native of Bengal (whose original name was Aravinda Ackroyd) lived all over the world in his youth, but returned to India at the age of twenty, when he began to study the Vedas and the Bhagavad Gita. In his earlier days, he was a political activist and was arrested, jailed, and placed in solitary confinement. Later, however, he abandoned political activism for spiritual activity.

This scholar-mystic called his brand of yoga, integral yoga *(purna yoga)*, directed at the liberation of the entire being. He believed that the result would be not only a spiritual liberation, but a total transformation of life on earth. He believed that through integral yoga, disease and even death could be conquered. According to Aurobindo, all human and natural life will, eventually, reflect the

**A GREAT YOGIN**

*For some of his followers, Sri Aurobindo was an incarnation of God himself.*

divinity within us. "Perfection has to be worked out," he said. "Out of imperfection we have to construct perfection, out of limitation to discover infinity, out of death to find immortality, out of grief to recover divine bliss, out of ignorance to rescue divine self-knowledge, out of matter to reveal spirit."

He established an ashram in Pondicherry and wrote a great deal. At the time of his death, he was revered as a poet, scholar, and philosopher. His most famous work, *The Life Divine,* develops a theory about spiritual evolution. He also wrote a very long poem, *Savriti: A Legend and a Symbol,* which he worked on until the time of his death. Altogether he produced more than thirty works, some of which were devoted to explaining the symbolic significance of many Rig Veda hymns, especially those to Agni.

---

### THE EVOLVING ASHRAM

*Often you hear the word* ashram *in connection with Hinduism. Today an ashram is a center for religious study and meditation; spending time in one is supposed to hasten enlightenment. Most ashrams offer a vegetarian menu and a rather Spartan atmosphere, which is believed to be more conducive to spiritual development. In classical times, gurus established ashrams for their own disciples, but today many people of different faiths, especially Westerners, "vacation" at ashrams for rest and renewal.*

---

Aurobindo believed that the cosmos evolved from matter into life and mind. Eventually it will evolve further into spirit and truth-consciousness. Human beings can reach this state through what he called the triple transformation, a rather complicated process.

A city, Auroville, touted as being the first "planetary village on earth," was established in his honor. This village, which is recognized by the Indian government, is an interesting experiment, although it has recently run into financial problems. Its charter asserts that it belongs to humanity as a whole. Cars, tobacco, drugs, alcohol, and extramarital sex are prohibited there, and all crops are grown organically.

### The Ramakrishna Movement

Ramakrishna (1836–1886) was a Bengali temple priest and famous mystic who understood the divine as form, formless, and transcending both. He experienced God, he said, in all religions and through all ages. It is said that he worshipped as Jain, Buddhist, and *bhakti* Hindu. He recognized all religions as leading to the divine. Ramakrishna began as a worshipper of Kali (or Devi), but later "converted" to the *Vedanta* school. Still, his great passion was to see the goddess Kali face-to-face.

Ramakrishna also experimented with Tantra. He is considered the head of the modern "Indian Renaissance," for instead of either trying to make Hinduism conform to Western ideas or rejecting those ideas outright, he sought to incorporate relevant Western concepts into orthodox Hinduism. His followers called him Paramahamsa, "the Ultimate Swan." This was a great compliment.

Swami Vivekananda (1863–1902) was the favorite disciple of Ramakrishna and founded the Ramakrishna movement. It is not only the largest monastic order in India, but also the first real "missionary" movement of Hinduism to the west. (In 1893, Vivekananda gave a speech at the First World Parliament of Religions in Chicago and was a great hit.) Vivekananda played down Ramakrishna's image worship and ecstasies and emphasized the more intellectual approach of the Upanishads. He formed the Ramakrishna Mission, named, of course, after his beloved guru. One of its centers has been located in Hollywood since the 1930s, and many noted British writers, including Christopher Isherwood, Aldous Huxley, and Gerald Heard were members at one time or another.

"All our strength is the strength of God."

—*Ramakrishna*

### The Swadhyaya Movement

This *bhakti* social reform movement, which began about fifty years ago, is based on the Bhagavad Gita. The word *Swadhyaya* means "self-study." The founder was Sri Pandurang Vaijnath Athavale Shastri. His followers called him "Dada," which means "older brother." The group's basic principle is "work is worship," and devotees travel from village to village, without government backing, to help people learn to manage their lives better. They also teach farming techniques. The movement has no hierarchy and no paid staff, and has been remarkably successful in transforming lives. The group builds nonsectarian temples out of local materials and has also undertaken a tree-planting program; the trees are referred to as Tree Temples and are dedicated to God.

## ALTERNATIVE AND SPLINTER MOVEMENTS

No consideration of Hinduism would be complete without a mention of a few of its interesting offspring.

### *Madame Helena Petrovna Blavatsky and Theosophy*

Madame Blavatsky (or HPB, as she was always called) was the founder of the Theosophical Society. HPB believed that she was a psychic, and as a child, she claimed to know the thoughts of all objects, including the thoughts of inanimate things. Blavatsky went traveling around the world as an adult, and, according to her own account, she spent two years in Tibet learning mystical secrets. Eventually she went to New York, where she performed psychic shows that included levitation, table lifting, and out-of-body projections.

In 1875 HPB and Colonel Henry Stell Olcott founded the Theosophical Society, although they traced its roots to the third century C.E. According to HPB, the original founders were the spiritual masters, whose names were Koot Hoomi, Lal Singh, Djwal Kul, and Morya. Koot Hoomi was the most sociable of the masters, frequently communicating with his disciples, often by letter. The society was billed as nonsectarian and nonpolitical. HPB's most famous works are *Isis Unveiled* (1877), which outlines her main ideas, and *The Secret Doctrine* (1888), which explains her conceptions of how the universe is evolving. HPB claimed that she learned her arcane knowledge from an ancient text, *The Book of Dyzan*.

According to Blavatsky, beings she called Devas (not the Hindu goddesses, but something between angels and gods) existed on earth before human beings. They are dormant, however, and will not become active until humans have reached a certain stage of development.

Blavatsky died in 1891. Her body was cremated and the ashes divided and scattered in Europe, America, and India. Theosophists still commemorate the day of her death: May 8, which they call White Lotus Day.

### *Krishnamurti*

Annie Besant and C. W. Leadbeater led the Theosophical Society after Madame Blavatsky. They discovered the young Jiddu Krishnamurti (1895–1986), a South Indian of the Brahmin caste.

Believing that Krishnamurti was the Lord Maitreya, the final incarnation of the Buddha, they had him sent to school in England and gave him a new name, "Alcyone," similar to "Halcyon," a brilliant star of the Pleiades. He was initiated into the Esoteric Section of the Society by the invisible spiritual Mahatma Master Koot Hoomi, and thus joined the Great White Brotherhood.

In 1911, Krishnamurti began the leadership of his own order within the society: the Order of the Star of the East, and the Krishnamurti Foundation was created in Ojai, California. Then, a personal tragedy affected Krishnamurti (and the society) in a serious way. His beloved brother, Nityananda, died after a long illness, despite the prayers of Krishnamurti. As a result, Kirshnamurti lost faith in the powers of the masters and in the society. He resigned officially in 1930, but continued to teach, although he never accepted followers. In fact, he rejected all formal religion and philosophy. To find truth, he taught that one must become fully aware of the mind and its psychological processes, which he divided into nine parts:

HERE AND THERE

*Although the Theosophical Society was founded in New York, its headquarters have indeed been in India since 1878.*

- Awareness

- Thought

- Imagination

- Conditioning

- Knowledge and learning

- Fear, memory, attachment, and dependence

- Conflict

- Relationship

- Intelligence

When Krishnamurti died in 1986, his ashes were scattered in three places: England, California, and the Ganges River in India.

## Transcendental Meditation

Transcendental Meditation (TM), also known as the Spiritual Regeneration Movement, was taught by the Maharishi Mahesh Yogi. He learned it from his own guru, Guru Dev, which means "divine teacher." After Guru Dev died, the Maharishi lived in a Himalayan cave for a couple of years. In 1971, he founded the Maharishi International University, now located in Fairfield, Iowa. He also founded other organizations dedicated to perfect health and world peace.

TM can be taught only through a personal master. The practitioner is given a secret mantra, which has no special meaning. In contrast to other Eastern traditions, the mantra is not chanted—it is "thought." No special postures are required for TM (although the most auspicious times for practice are morning and evening), and no renunciation of the world is required.

### The Hare Krishnas and Krishna Consciousness

When most people think of Krishna Consciousness, they think it's one of the stranger inventions of the 1960s. This is completely wrong. The movement is 500 years old. This form of *bhakti* Hinduism was actually founded by Chaitanya Mahaprabhu (1486–1534), a Bengali saint, who believers adore as an incarnation of Krishna.

Krishna, an avatar of Vishnu, has always been one of the most popular of Hindu deities. Krishna is a fighter and teacher, a child and a lover. The International Society for Krishna Consciousness (ISKCON), the Hare Krishna Movement, brought Krishna devotion to the United States in 1965. This is actually a pretty conservative revivalist form of *bhakti* Hinduism, Vaishnavite style (adoration of Vishnu). It is monotheistic in nature—believing in only one God, in this case Krishna. It celebrates Krishna as the "supreme personality of godhead" and believes that the words ascribed to Krishna in the Bhagavad Gita are his literal words.

Mahaprabhu believed that incessant chanting of the mantra "Hare Krishna" would bring its devotees to a state of infinite bliss. Although this may sound silly to some people, chanting has long been an Eastern meditation practice. Correct chanting brings one to

---

**THE DEMISE OF MAHAPRABHU**

*Several accounts exist of Mahaprabhu's death. In one story, the saint danced himself blissfully into the sea and drowned, maybe intentionally, maybe not. Another authority says he hurt his foot dancing (notice the same leitmotif here) and it got infected—whereupon he died. A simpler but less believable story than either of the others claims that he simply absorbed himself into the image of the god at the temple of Jagannatha.*

a heightened state of consciousness. Far from being a monopoly of Eastern traditions, chanting has found its way into Christianity, Islam, and Judaism. Still, Hare Krishnas are more serious than most about chanting. Modern devotees chant the Hare Krishna mantra 1,728 times a day. Like Roman Catholics, they have a rosary to keep count of the prayers. The rosary consists of 108 beads, and the Krishnas chant the mantra once per bead. That means sixteen rounds of the 108 beads. It takes about two hours every morning.

Male devotees who live in an ashram shave most of their hair, and ashram women wear a traditional sari. This is not a requirement for those who live elsewhere. All Hare Krishnas are strict vegetarians.

### Krishna Comes to the United States

The Society's international popularizer was A. C. Bhaktivedanata Swami Prabhupada (1896–1977), who, although dismissed as a charlatan by those who don't know any better, was a fine Sanskrit scholar as well as an important *bhakti* leader. Prabhupada was born in Calcutta; his birth name was Abhay Charan De. In India, he worked as a sales executive in a pharmaceutical company. He also made some highly regarded translations of the Hindu classics. In fact, his followers believe that his is the only perfect translation of the Bhagavad Gita.

Prabhupada arrived in the United States in 1965, when he was seventy years old. Having renounced his family and possessions years before, he brought with him to New York lit-

**CHANTING STYLES**

*A special form of chanting, known as cantillation, uses musical modulations to create special energy patterns and power channels. Zen Buddhism makes use of a peculiar monotonic, fade-away-at-the-end kind of chant.*

---

**TAKE NOTE**

*George Harrison wrote "My Sweet Lord" in honor of Krishna. Harrison was a fan of the Maharishi Mahesh Yogi and helped out by buying The Krishna Society a country estate in Hertfordshire, England. This estate, now known as Bhaktivedanta Manor, is the still the headquarters of the movement in England.*

---

tle more than his begging bowl and a pair of sandals. He lived in the Bowery, where he attracted his first American following. Later on, he moved to the Haight-Ashbury district of San Francisco.

The movement spread to Europe, Japan, and Australia, and its vegetarian followers became famous for living a communal lifestyle and selling flowers in airports. But the Hare Krishnas are best known for their chanting of a sixteen-syllable maha-mantra: "Hare Krishna, Hare Krishna/Krishna Krishna/Hare Hare/Hare Rama

Hare Rama/Rama Rama/Hare Hare." (You may be familiar with the chant from the musical *Hair*.) The chant may be done either privately in meditation *(japa)* or as a group activity *(kirtana)* with hand-clapping and musical instruments. Today the ISKCON headquarters are in Los Angeles.

### Osho

"I am not against anything. I am for all. I am utterly for all...I don't belong to any tradition, all traditions belong to me."

—*Osho*

Another interesting Eastern group that landed in the West is the Rajneesh Foundation International. The founder, Bhagwan Shree Rajneesh, was born in India in 1931. Originally Rajneesh was a Jain. It is believed that he achieved *moksha* at the age of seven.

Rajneesh taught philosophy at the university in Jabalpur, India, but soon gave it up and began lecturing to wider audiences. His teaching is an eclectic amalgam of several religions and philosophies:

- God is everywhere, and God is in communion with all life.

- There are no real contradictions, just complementaries.

- Truth should be experienced rather than just understood.

- Sexuality affirms spirituality.

One of Rajneesh's trademark practices is called the Mystic Rose. In this meditational exercise, one laughs for three hours a day during the first week, cries for three hours a day during the second week, and sits in total silence for three hours a day during the third week. He also advocated what he called "dynamic meditation." Here one jumps up and down yelling, "Hoo! Hoo! Hoo!"

Rajneesh set up his foundation in 1974 and established an ashram in Poona, India. He came to the United States in 1981 and moved to a large ranch near Antelope, Oregon. He was not treated favorably by many Americans and eventually left the country. Rajneesh died in 1990 at the age of fifty-eight. Shortly before he died he changed his name to Osho. His compound in Poona still exists, and his teachings are widely read in India and in the United States.

### Ram Dass

One of the most famous exponents of Hinduism in America is Ram Dass, who was born Richard Alpert in 1931. Dass, who has a Ph.D. from Stanford University, was involved with Timothy Leary and the LSD scene in the sixties, but renounced it all by 1967. He headed east to India and became a disciple of Maharaji. It was Maharaji who gave Alpert his Hindu name, which means "servant of God." His most famous work, *Be Here Now*, was published in 1971. Ram Dass continues to teach in this country and he is currently involved in many social causes, including prisoner welfare, AIDS hospices, and others.

## ECKANKAR

Considered on the fringes of traditional Eastern thought is a movement called ECKANKAR, which was officially founded in 1965, although its adherents claim it's the "oldest religion" on earth. Its first known leader was Paul Twitchell (?-1971). Twitchell claimed that his real name was Peddar Zaskq and that he was the nine hundred and seventy first Living ECK Master. ECK is ECKANKARese for Holy Spirit. Twitchell (or Zaskq) said he learned his secret wisdom from his father, who learned it from an Indian holy man, Suddar Singh. Later on, Twitchell met Singh in Paris and spent a year studying at his ashram in Allahabad. Twitchell served in the Pacific during World War II, where he met with a Tibetan Master named Rebazar Tarz, who taught him the true mysteries of ECKANKAR. The true mysteries of ECKANKAR mostly involve Soul Travel, wherein the soul travels back to its true home, God.

## Deepak Chopra

Deepak Chopra is a very popular person from the Hindu tradition who has won a worldwide following. Although his book *How to Know God* combines a religious theory with self-help advice, Chopra is more famous as a proponent of the ancient Indian system of Ayervedic medicine than as a religious figure.

Still, the American fascination with both makes Chopra an almost irresistible figure to many. According to Chopra, human beings can actually change their age by resetting their biological clocks. The way we eat, think, and behave all influence our life span. Chopra's Hindu roots are apparent when he says, "There is a part of yourself that is not subject to change; it is the silent witness behind the scenes. This is essentially your spirit."

## CHAPTER RECAP

- *Bhakti marga* is the yoga of love or devotion.

- Many *bhakti* Hindus worship a member of the Hindu "trinity": Brahma, Vishnu, or Shiva.

- Brahma is the creator god, Vishnu the preserver god, and Shiva the destroyer god.

- Some Hindus worship divinity in the form of the eternal feminine.

- The famous Hindu cow veneration is an expression of *bhakti marga.*

- Transcendental Meditation, Hare Krishna, and other movements popular in the West are really outgrowths of *bhakti* yoga.

*Recommended Reading*

Brockington, J. L. *The Sacred Thread: Hinduism in Its Continuity and Diversity.* New York: Columbia University Press, 1981.

Brown, Mick. *The Spiritual Tourist: A Personal Odyssey through the Outer Reaches of Belief.* London: Bloomsbury Publishing, PLC, 1998.

Courtwight, Paul B. *Ganesa, Lord of Obstacles, Lord of Beginnings.* Oxford: Oxford University Press, 1985.

Dimmitt, Cornelia, and J. A. B. van Buitenen. *Classical Hindu Mythology: A Reader in the Sanskrit Puranas.* Philadelphia: Temple University Press, 1978.

Fischer, Louis, ed. *The Essential Gandhi.* New York: Random House, 1983.

Gonda, Jan. *Vishnuism and Sivaism.* International Publication Service, 1970, 1976.

Huyler, Stephen P. *Meeting God: Elements of Hindu Devotion.* New Haven, CT: Yale University Press, 1999.

Jayakar, Pupul. *The Earth Mother.* New Delhi: Penguin Books, 1989.

Kramrisch, Stella. *The Presence of Siva.* Princeton, NJ: Princeton University Press, 1981.

Mitchell, George. *Hindu Temple.* New York: Harper and Row, 1978.

Nikhiananda, Swami, trans. *The Gospel of Sri Ramakrishna.* New York: Ramakrishna Vivekananda Center, 1952.

O'Flaherty, Wendy. *Shiva: The Erotic Ascetic.* Oxford: Oxford University Press, 1981.

PART

*2*

# *Buddhism—*
# *Compassionate Wisdom*

More than half the population of the world lives in areas where Buddhism is now (or has recently been) the dominant religion. At present, there are more than 250 million Buddhists, about 90 percent of them in Asia. Buddhism, with its practicality and compassion, attracts new converts to it every day.

Sadly, however, Buddhism is currently suppressed and persecuted in some of the very areas where it attained its greatest development. Still, new Buddhist movements are springing up in Japan, South Korea, Taiwan, Indonesia, and even in India—the land of its birth. Buddhism has even come to America. It first arrived during the 1830s, when the New England Transcendentalists became enthralled with Eastern traditions.

It's easy for Westerners to get Hinduism and Buddhism mixed up. Both religions use some of the same key terms, such as *dharma* and karma.

*Seated Sakyamuni, the Historial Buddha*
*China, Liao dynasty 907–1125 C.E.*
*(cast bronze with gilding)*

Both seek liberation from suffering and ignorance. Both believe in reincarnation and the endless cycle of rebirth and redeath. Both use gurus or teaching masters to help disciples find truth. Both value meditation as a way to enlightenment. Both see the phenomenal world as essentially unreal or untrue. Despite their similarities, though, they proceed from entirely different bases. In fact, they are mirror images of each other.

For Hindus, God (and gods) is everywhere and everywhere there are gods and God. For Buddhists, there is no ultimate god. For Hindus, the visible world conceals the Undying, Immutable Eternal Brahman. For Buddhists, the visible world conceals a great emptiness. For Hindus, the soul is immortal. For Buddhists, there is no soul. There is not even any inherent "self," at least not in the way the word *self* is usually employed.

To many, Buddhism seems totally negative, for it rejects both selfhood and godhead. It asserts that the very core of life on earth is suffering. Yet Buddhism has captured the Western imagination as has no other Eastern school of thought.

It's a religion that prizes emptiness, yet it has brought fulfillment to millions. It's a philosophy that contends we have no soul, but it offers salvation to everyone. It's all due to one man, Siddhartha Gautama, whom we call the Buddha, the one who is Awake.

# The Life and Teachings of Buddha

*T*he story of Buddha is the story of a heretic. (In fact, Buddhism is still considered a heresy by orthodox Hindus.) It's a heresy that enlightened the world.

Siddhartha Gautama, the man who became the Buddha, was born a Hindu in Kapilavastu, a city located in the mountainous border region between India and Nepal. He was the only son of a royal family.

## THE BIRTH OF THE BUDDHA

The year of the Buddha's birth is argued among Buddhists; most Indian and Western scholars date him from 566 to 486 B.C.E., or possibly 563 to 483. Southeast Asian Buddhists prefer 624 to 544 B.C.E., while Japanese and Chinese Buddhists choose a later period, 448 to 368 B.C.E. (This latter date may be more accurate, according to the newest evidence.) That he lived to be eighty years old is fairly certain, though.

It was a time of prosperity, trade expansion, and material wealth, at least for the upper castes. During this same period, however, the ancient *Vedic* religion had become rigid, unyielding, and legalistic. Bloody sacrificial rites took the place of ethics and spiritual development. In response to this unhappy state of affairs, religious seekers, wandering philosophers, and spiritual reformers, of whom the Buddha was the most noted, began popping up all over the place.

The Buddha's mother was named Maya—the Sanskrit word for "illusion." It is almost certain that her name was symbolic, meaning that the Buddha was born to lead humankind from illusion into light. As befitting a savior of the world, the Buddha's conception and birth were unusual. He was conceived when his mother was taken up to a Himalayan heaven, where a six-tusked white elephant painlessly pierced her side. It wasn't a real elephant, of course, but Avalokiteshvara, a Bodhisattva, or future Buddha.

If all this seems a bit confusing, don't worry about it. It's just a legend, and few Buddhists take the tale (or tusks) literally. The story gets even more elaborate. The Buddha-fetus was not nourished by his mother the way normal fetuses are; instead it was fed a drop of elixir from a magical lotus that opened at his conception. (In Buddhism, the lotus symbolizes the true nature of things.)

Siddhartha, the future Buddha, was born ten lunar months later, in the beautiful Lumbini Gardens, painlessly delivered from his mother's right side (the one gored by the ersatz elephant). Legend says Maya held on to a tree branch to support herself during the birth, an interesting detail that may be based in fact.

When the Buddha was born, he stepped on to an eight-rayed lotus (also magic), and from there looked into the ten directions of space, represented by the eight rays of the lotus, plus "up" and "down." This gesture signifies that enlightenment will eventually come to all beings everywhere, through the work of the Buddha.

Sadly enough, Maya died only a week after bearing the child, but she got into heaven immediately. Legend says that she just couldn't bear the joy of being mother to the Buddha for one more minute.

## THE BUDDHA GROWS UP

The future Buddha was raised by his aunt, Mahaprajapati, who married the king in her sister's place. As the eldest son and member of the Kshatriya caste, Siddhartha was expected to inherit his father's throne. There was a snag in the state of affairs, however.

**REFORM RELIGIONS**

*It is widely believed that the development of Buddhism forced Hinduism to re-examine and reform itself, becoming a richer and more humane religion in the process. An interesting parallel can be drawn to events in the Western Renaissance during the Catholic Counter-Reformation.*

According to the story, Siddhartha's father, Suddhodana, had been warned by an old Brahmin astrologer that a special, although as yet undetermined, fate awaited his son. This priest had just happened to notice the special thirty-two primary marks and eighty secondary marks that indicated a world savior. He then predicted that the boy would become either the king of a fabulous empire or else a great teacher of salvation for human beings.

Naturally, the king didn't want to take any chances. He wasn't interested in raising a world savior. He figured that if he kept the child from all dark knowledge of the world, compassion would not awaken in him, and he'd never realize that the world even needed to be saved. To this end, the king did everything he could to ensure his child a pain-free existence. He built him a fabulously beautiful (and walled) pleasure garden, provided him with every form of earthly delight, and ordered all elderly, sick, and disfigured people to keep away. He hired the best tutors and masters of martial arts. He then married his handsome son off at age sixteen or seventeen to a beautiful woman, Yasodhara. Soon the young couple had a son. Curiously Siddhartha named the child Rahula, which means "fetters." It seemed an odd, but prophetic choice.

Later the Buddha confessed that although he had enjoyed his happy though illusory youth, he always felt as if he were an elephant in a cage. (Elephant imagery keeps cropping up in Buddhist lore. In fact, in his account of the Buddha's later enlightenment, Ashaghosha mentions that the Buddha's gait was that of an "elephant in rut." It's hard to say what that means, exactly.) At any rate, the Buddha knew there was more to life; he just didn't know what.

When he was about twenty-nine years old, Siddhartha bribed his charioteer, Channa, to take him out for a ride around town—his first excursion from his royal gated community. (Tradition locates the place as Lumbini Park.) He had the shock of his life.

### The Four Sights

As they wandered about the bazaar, enjoying the colors, the music, and entertainment, an elderly man, leaning on a stick, hobbled past. Siddhartha was astonished and asked his charioteer what he was looking at. "Simply an old man, Highness," replied the charioteer, with what must have been a wry smile. Siddhartha demanded an

**THE MAIDENLY MAYA**

*Although the earliest accounts don't say so, later writings about the Buddha's birth assure us that Maya was a virgin when she gave birth to the future savior.*

explanation. "Highness, we all get old. It's part of the nature of things." Siddhartha frowned.

The next day, he saw a sick man, possibly leprous, being carried past on a pallet. The man was suffering terribly and cried out in agony. "Another old man?" guessed Siddhartha. "No," answered his charioteer. "Just a very sick one. Sickness can strike anyone at any moment. There is no escape."

Then, a funeral procession wound its way past. Pallbearers held a stinking corpse aloft, while the mourners wailed. "A very sick man, I suppose," murmured Siddhartha sorrowfully. "Indeed, he is past all sickness, Highness," responded the charioteer. "He's dead." And the charioteer explained death to Siddhartha, adding, "Everyone dies. There is no escape. Soon they will burn his body on the funeral pyre."

"This whole world is nothing but a funeral pyre!" cried Siddhartha, who was torn at the heart.

Distraught, he cast his eyes about and noticed another older man, dressed as an ascetic in rags. Yet he seemed full of strange purpose. "Who is that man," demanded Siddhartha, "who walks unmoved in the midst of anguish?" "Why, Highness, that is a *sannyasin,* a wandering ascetic, a holy man who has renounced this life to find inner peace."

And Siddhartha fell into deep thought.

### The Great Renunciation

That night, or soon after, the Buddha awoke after a night of partying. The legend says that he looked with sudden distaste at the dancing girls who lay snoring all around him, their makeup smeared and their clothes stained with who knew what. He realized that even the pleasures of life had their nasty side. He decided to leave and took one last glimpse of his wife and son. He kissed his wife on the toe so as not to awaken her and went off to find his new life.

He discarded his rich clothing and handed his servant his horse and jewels. He cut off his long black hair, following the custom of one who has renounced the world. This moment is known in Buddhism as "The Great Going Forth." Siddhartha traveled south and eastward.

> "While the rest of the human family suffers and starves, enjoying false security and wealth can only be seen as a form of insanity."
>
> —*Thich Nhat Hanh*

First he visited Alra Kalama, a great sage, but he acquired no special knowledge. He had no better luck with Uddaka, another noted pundit. Siddhartha's questions about suffering and ultimate reality remained a puzzle. This was an important lesson in itself. Siddhartha gave up trying to learn from others and started off on his own quest, along with a small company of fellow seekers.

## QUEST FOR TRUTH—THE SIX-YEAR SEARCH

During this period, Siddhartha Gautama tried everything he could to achieve release from his suffering. He amazed everyone by his feats of asceticism. He almost stopped sleeping and eating. For a while he was living on a grain of rice a day and got so thin that when he touched his stomach, he could feel his backbone.

Asceticism was all the rage in India at the time. (To some extent it still is.) Indian holy men sat staring at the sun till they went blind, held up their arms till they withered and stiffened, and slept on beds of nails. None of this

### IMAGES OF THE BUDDHA

*The idea of a thin, ascetic Buddha is a far cry from the "fat and happy Buddha" (Mi-lo fo) image we see everywhere, which, by the way, is really a Chinese innovation, developing around 1000 C.E. In Japan, the same image is called Hotei. He represents joy and prosperity. If you're not used to them, the images of an emaciated, starving Buddha can be pretty unnerving.*

stuff helped as much as one might think, Siddhartha noted. He decided to start eating and blessed a milkmaid, Sujata, for providing a bowl of curds for him to ease his incessant hunger.

Apparently he had some degree of success in trying the traditional methods of salvation. Under one teacher he reached the "Sphere of No-Thing-Ness." Under another he achieved the "Sphere of Neither-Perception-nor-Nonperception." But this wasn't his idea of enlightenment. He visited temples, but was disgusted by the cruelty of the animal sacrifices then practiced there.

After six years, Siddhartha was no closer to enlightenment than before, and he had had enough of it. "That's it," he told himself. He sat down beneath a fig tree (the Bo tree) and faced east. "I'm sitting here and I'm not moving. Not until I achieve enlightenment." It was the May full moon, a time still celebrated by Buddhists.

## TEMPTATIONS OF THE BUDDHA

Mara, an Indian version of the devil, tempted Siddhartha. He was scared to death that if the Buddha-to-be succeeded in his task, the whole world would be saved and he, Mara, would have no one left to torment. The Buddha had made a seat of Kusha grass, whatever that is, but Mara claimed the grass throne belonged to him, not the Buddha. Siddhartha, who didn't have much else in life, called upon the earth to witness that the throne was his. Artistic representations of this moment are popular in Buddhist cultures.

Mara then sent out an army of demons to tempt Siddhartha, to no avail. He tried fire and darkness. He actually came pretty close to succeeding by sending out his three daughters, Lust, Greed, and Restlessness, but Siddhartha withstood it all. The Buddha said later that if the girlie temptation had lasted just another night, he would have given in.

## THE SUPREME AWAKENING

During the final trip to enlightenment, Siddhartha went through several stages of consciousness. During the first watch of the night, he recalled all his past lives. During the second part of the night, he understood the entire chain of causality and was able to look upon the entire world. His compassion grew and deepened. Then, in the third watch, he developed the design for understanding and living life that has come to be called the Four Noble Truths and the Noble Eightfold Path.

At this point, Siddhartha Gautama achieved perfect knowledge and became the Buddha. The word *Buddha* comes from the Sanskrit *budh*, which means to awaken. Our English word *bud* is cognate to this, for buds are also in the process of awakening. (Henry David Thoreau is famous for saying that he had never met a man who was fully awake. Of course, he never met the Buddha.)

The very moon smiled upon him then, and a rain of sweet flowers fell gently from the night heavens, as the Buddha sang his great song of victory. For seven days he stayed in that spot, glorying in his enlightenment *(Bodhi)* and looking deep into his own mind.

---

**SAMMA SAMBUDDHA**

*Gautama Buddha was not the only Buddha-Being. Many others have existed over time, but only he is designated with the title* Samma Sambuddha: *the Supreme Buddha. He often referred to himself, however, as* Tathagata, *the "one who has gone before."*

He understood suffering and death in a new way, a way that led away from them both, not by escaping them, but by transcending them.

It is worth noting that the Buddha discovered absolute truth on his own, through meditation, rather than from learning at the feet of a guru. Reliance upon one's own efforts has become a hallmark of modern Buddhism. Although most Buddhist schools also make use of the guru method, the Buddha himself never advocated it.

Even after the Buddha's enlightenment, the evil Mara had a few tricks up his sleeve, none of which were very effective. Once he tried hurling a powerful thunderstorm at the Buddha, but a great cobra arose from the lake and spread his hood protectively over the Buddha.

There was just one last temptation, however—and it didn't come from Mara. It came from the Buddha's own inner self and was therefore the most terrifying (and tempting) of all. "Why don't I," he thought, "now that I'm enlightened, just enter into Nirvana right this minute? Surely I don't want to waste any more time on the cloddish humans. They won't get it, anyway." Buddha was really tempted by his thoughts, but his Buddha-Heart of compassion knew that he was needed here. Some sources say that the great god Brahma himself (who was also subject to rebirth and re-death) had to beg the Buddha to save all beings. So he relented and stayed with us a while longer.

## THE DOCTRINE OF THE MIDDLE WAY

The Buddha left the site of his great awakening and traveled west to the city of Benares, where he delivered his famous first sermon. This discourse took place at a deer park on the outskirts of the city, on the full moon of July. His small but knowledgeable audience consisted of the five ascetics who had left his company when Siddhartha abandoned asceticism.

His first sermon is called the "Sutra of Setting in Motion the Wheel of Righteousness." The title needs some editorial work, but it apparently got his point across to his audience of five, who were pretty sophisticated. In it he preached the doctrine of the Middle Way, wherein he explained that neither self-indulgence nor severe asceticism served the purpose of finding enlightenment. But the Middle Way, he said, leads to bliss.

**THE FIRST DISCOURSE**

*Today a domelike stupa (memorial monument) marks the spot of the Buddha's first sermon. Stupas dot all Buddhist lands. Most of them house a relic or statue of the Buddha.*

## FOUNDING OF THE SANGHA

### NIRVANA

*Nirvana is not an earthly paradise, but a state in which one has no desires. If one has no desires, according to Buddhist thought, one is happy.*

Apparently everyone was mightily impressed by this strange Middle Way concept, and his disciples quickly increased in number. Buddha called his disciples by merely saying, "Come, O monk," and they followed him. (The comparison with Jesus is rather striking in this regard, as in several others.) For the rest of his long life, the Buddha traveled throughout northeastern India, going from village to village, with his message of release from suffering.

He sent his disciples abroad with these words: "Go forth, O *Bhikkus* (monks) for the benefit of many, for the bliss of many, out of compassion for the world." He also gave them the power to accept converts on behalf of the new religion.

The rainy season was just beginning, and the Buddha then went to Uruvela to hole up for a while. (Traveling during a monsoon isn't as much fun as it sounds.) While there, he met up with some fire-worshippers. Buddha merely shook his head at their religious rites and told them, "The whole world is on fire. The eye is on fire, the forms of existence are on fire, and all sensations are on fire. The fires are the fires of anger, lust, and illusion." These words struck the devotees of fire, and they decided to become Buddhists instead.

A local king, Bimbisara, was so impressed with the Buddha's teaching that he gave him a plot of land, the Bamboo Grove, to establish his first *sangha*, or spiritual community. (The *sangha* is still the basis of Theravada Buddhism.) It became the custom to build Buddhist temples in a grove around a Bodhi tree, the tree of enlightenment. Thus it was possible for Buddhist monks to enjoy a stable abode, as opposed to the *sannyasin* tradition of wandering around the countryside. Inevitably, this bound the monks closer to the community in which they lived.

### The Sangha Grows

From the beginning, it is plain that the Buddha wished his monks to form a universal community, not just another sect. He reiterated this over and over in his instructions to them, saying that they were to serve "for the gain of many, for the welfare of many, out of compassion for the world." It was just after this that the Buddha's long-suffering father, Suddhodana, finally tracked him down and begged him to come home. The Buddha agreed, and when he reached the door of the palace, his son, Rahula, met him and asked for his inheritance. At that point, the Buddha received his son into the holy order. (It's not clear that this is exactly what Rahula had in mind, but that's what he got, nonetheless.) Even the Buddha's father became a lay disciple.

We really should mention Buddha's cousin (or maybe half-brother) and greatest disciple, Ananda, whose name means "bliss." Although Ananda wasn't the smartest of the disciples, or the most enlightened, he had a lovely personality and was clearly the Buddha's favorite. One story goes that he told the Buddha that he was soon getting married and that there would be a big feast. "Well," the Buddha responded, "for me, all life is one great feast, since I have overcome all desires." That was enough for Ananda. He decided not to get married after all, but spend the rest of his days as a disciple sleeping in the forest with the Buddha at night.

Ananda made an unprecedented plea for the rights of women when he suggested to Buddha that they be permitted to form their own order of nuns. Nothing of the kind had ever been dreamed of before, and the Buddha wasn't too sure about the wisdom of the plan. He is reputed to have mumbled something about women being a lot of trouble and so on and so forth. He even suggested that an order that excluded women would last a thousand years, but one that included them was good for only half as long. Ananda argued the women's case well, however, and the Buddha finally relented.

In fairness, we should add that the women themselves did a good job of persuading the Buddha. Foremost among them was Mahapajapati, the Buddha's own aunt and foster-mother. After having been refused admission three times, she shaved her head and followed around after him with a group of other women, weeping. The Buddha gave up, and the first religious order for women was established. Under the Buddha, nuns and monks had equal privileges. Discrimination against nuns began later on. Oddly enough, after the Buddha's death, at the First Council, Ananda was censured for persuading the Buddha to accept women, and for another reason as well—for his failure to request that the Buddha live longer.

**A SPECIAL APPEAL**

*For some reason, members of the Kshatriya, the Buddha's own rich caste, seemed especially attuned to his message. They showered the infant movement with many gifts of land and buildings.*

Just as the Buddha had his "beloved disciple," Ananda, he also had the Buddhist version of Judas Iscariot. This was Devadatta, another cousin. Devadatta had developed ominous psychic powers, and after he was denied permission to lead the *sangha,* he made various plans to murder the elderly Buddha. The Buddha, however, had a few psychic powers of his own and always managed to defeat Devadatta.

Devadatta unwittingly added a major principle to Buddhism. One day the evil disciple shot down a swan that was flying overhead minding its own business. The Buddha saw the cruel act and patiently removed the arrow, cleaned the wound, and bound it up. The furious Devadatta demanded his swan back. When Buddha refused to yield the animal to certain death, Devadatta took his cousin to the council court for a legal opinion. Buddha successfully argued that because he cared for the bird, it belonged to him rather than to the one who tried to kill it. From this the Buddhist principle of property was born: "A living being belongs to the one who loves it." (The story of King Solomon and the two women arguing over the baby is remarkably similar.)

---

**BUDDHIST NUNNERIES**

*Although* sanghas *for nuns were established in several Theravadan countries such as Sri Lanka and Burma, they have since died out. None ever existed in Thailand. Still, Theravadan women sometimes attempt to take nuns' vows and follow the nun's life without the support of a* sangha. *A movement is underway to revive the sanghas.*

---

## THE DEATH OF THE BUDDHA

The Buddha died when he was nearly eighty years old, after a brief illness that may been brought about by food poisoning—or just plain poisoning. His last meal was either deadly mushrooms or rancid pork, depending on one's source. In both cases, the cook was a low-caste blacksmith named Cunda.

Just as the Buddha's whole life was an exemplar for all people, his last moments on earth were filled with compassionate wisdom. He thanked the man who had poisoned him, because it released him from his earthly bonds. He comforted his disciples who wept because they would have no master to teach them. "You have the *dharma,*" he told them. "That's all you need. We all follow the *dharma.*" By "*dharma*" the Buddha was probably referring to the Noble Eightfold Path. He also counseled them to accept the inexorable flux of the universe with good grace. Even today, Buddhists call their own religion "*dharma*," not Buddhism, which is a Western term.

"Remember," he told his grieving disciples, "all compound things must dissolve. Work out your own salvation with diligence!" And so he died and passed into nirvana.

At the moment the Buddha died, a terrible earthquake shook the earth, and a fearsome storm ripped the sky, as if both the earth and heaven mourned his passing. Some of the disciples, too, wept copiously and tore their clothes and hair in bitter grief. The wisest of them understood the final lesson, though: that every single individual, even the Buddha who appears on earth, is a compound being and must be separated into its component parts and pass from this existence.

---

### A JOYFUL MOMENT

*According to one account, the Buddha managed to die in the lotus position. Other accounts claim that Buddha died quietly on his right side, his palm tucked neatly under his chin. Statues of the Buddha support both theories.*

---

After the Buddha's death, the community was at a loss, because no successor had been appointed. A council convened in 483 B.C.E., to decide difficult points of doctrine and policy. The council model became a paradigm for handling future controversies. All together there were four such early councils.

Perhaps because the Buddha appointed no successor, the disconsolate Buddhist community became dependent upon Buddha icons and various collections of teachings to help them remember their master. Whether or not the Buddha would have approved of this practice is difficult to say. Like Socrates and Jesus, he wrote nothing himself and nothing in his work suggests that he wanted any statues or paintings of himself created. It was inevitable, though.

**THE BUDDHA'S ASHES**

*The Buddha's body was cremated and the ashes divided into ten parts. (Some of them ended up in the Victoria and Albert Museum in London for a while, but they were later returned to the place where they had been stolen from.)*

## BUDDHA'S ETHICAL TEACHINGS

Although the Buddha founded a new religion, that wasn't his intent, which was merely to purify and reform current Hinduism. Two divergent schools developed competing traditions about his teachings. Members of the Theravada school believe that the Buddha taught everything he knew for us to follow. Those in another group, the Mahayana school, claim that the Buddha had a secret store of wisdom, which he revealed in a highly selective way. Both groups can point to the voluminous Buddhist scriptures to back up their point.

**EARLY BUDDHIST SCRIPTURE**

*Not only did Buddha leave behind no writing, neither did his first disciples. The earliest Buddhist writings we possess were composed several hundred years after the death of the Buddha. Yet they were based upon what we hope are reliable oral traditions.*

## The Four Noble Truths

The Four Noble Truths are the core of the Buddhist message. Each one follows directly from the one preceding, thus giving moral form to the Buddhist idea of causality and the concept that all life is deeply interconnected. According to Buddhist teaching, the Buddha revealed the Four Noble Truths during his first sermon at Benares. The word *noble* is instructive. The word the Buddha used was *aryan,* but instead of meaning noble in a racial or aristocratic sense, he meant noble as an ethical property. This is a tremendous step forward in the history of ethics—the idea that there is not one path for the well-born and another for the lower classes. Instead, there is one noble path for all people.

Instead of talking directly about ethics, however, the Buddha talked about suffering. He made a connection between suffering and sin that Jesus was to make half a millennium later.

Here are the Four Noble Truths:

1. Suffering *(dukkha).* Living means suffering. Birth is suffering. Life is suffering. Death is suffering. For Buddha, this suffering existed in three forms: pain (either physical or mental), change, and rebirth. Even when we are in the midst of enjoying something, we suffer when we fear we may lose it.

2. Cause of suffering *(tanha).* Suffering, like everything else, has a cause. It comes from desire. (Literally, the word *tanha* means "grasping" or "thirst.") Still another way Buddhists talk about suffering is to use the word *attachment.* When we become attached to a particular thing, we lose equilibrium and perspective. The object of our desire becomes too important in our lives. It doesn't really matter what that object is: money, fame, life-partner, chewing gum, or strawberry shortcake. If our whole happiness and well-being

become focused on that object, our life is thrown out of balance.

3. Cessation of suffering. Suffering can be ended by extinguishing desire. This is the state of Nirvana, in which all desire is extinguished. This is a goal that Buddhist monks aim for, although laypeople are simply encouraged to keep their wants as few and light as is reasonable.

4. The path out of suffering. Because there is a state free from suffering, there must be a way to attain it. And there is: the Noble Eightfold Path *(Ashtapatha)*.

Suffering, then, is at the core of Buddhist thought; but what is meant by suffering is far from clear. This ambiguity is illustrated by a dialogue the Buddha had with a certain Kassapa, a naked ascetic. (Kassapa's nakedness has nothing to do with the rest of the story, but I thought it was an interesting note.) At any rate, Kassapa asks the Buddha what causes suffering, offering some leading questions of his own in case the Buddha gets stuck. (Buddha tried to avoid the entire conversation by telling Kassapa he was busy on house visits, but Kassapa refused to take no for an answer.)

He starts out: "Is suffering caused by oneself?"

"No," responds the Buddha.

"Well, then," rejoins Kassapa, "is the suffering caused by someone else?"

"No, it is not."

"Okay," says Kassapa, taking another stab, "Is it caused both by oneself and by someone else?"

"No, it is not," returns the Buddha (whether smugly or not, I can't say).

Kassapa is clearly running out of options. "Does it arise spontaneously?" he asks, although he must know that can't be right either.

"No," says the Buddha.

"Then," Kassapa says desperately (or sarcastically perhaps), "suffering must be non-existent!"

"No, suffering exists," said the Buddha. Finally Kassapa decides to ask the Buddha to explain suffering in his own words, rather than trying to wring an answer out of him.

DEFINING *DUKKHA*

*Literal translators prefer to translate* dukkha *as "unsatisfactoriness," but although this word is technically more accurate, it doesn't carry the punch of "suffering."* Dukkha, *however, does include minor aggravations as well as extreme agony or metaphysical despair.*

**HOW TO BE HAPPY**

*The Buddha teaches that happiness comes from cherishing others; suffering comes from cherishing ourselves.*

This seems like a good idea on the face of it, but with the Buddha it could be a mistake. At any rate, he responds promptly enough, just as if he had been thinking about it for years, as indeed he had. "Conditioned by ignorance are karmic constituents; conditioned by karmic constituents is consciousness; conditioned by consciousness is individuality; conditioned by individuality are the six senses; conditioned by the six senses is contact; conditioned by contact is feeling; conditioned by feeling is desire; conditioned by desire is clinging; conditioned by clinging is becoming; conditioned by becoming is rebirth; conditioned by rebirth are old age, death, sorrow, grief, depression, and dismay. In this way the whole heap of suffering originates." If you ask me, this answer goes into the "you-asked-for-it" category. Kassapa's responses are not recorded. Perhaps he just got dressed and went away.

One good thing about suffering, though: It lets us see things the way they really are (instead of the way we like to pretend they are). So even suffering leads us, eventually, to truth and bliss and freedom.

## *The Noble Eightfold Path of Liberation*

The Noble Eightfold Path is the working heart of Buddhism. It provides a practical guideline to enlightenment, not just theoretical conjectures. (It is true, though, that the Noble Eightfold Path has been traditionally more important in monastic than in lay Buddhism.) Although the path has eight elements, all can be practiced at the same time. It doesn't have to be a linear process. The steps are:

- Right views

- Right intent

- Right speech

- Right action

- Right livelihood

- Right effort

- Right mindfulness

- Right concentration

## The Steps of Wisdom

Right views and right intent are known as the wisdom *(prajna)* part of the Noble Eightfold Path. Right views means to have the intuitive knowledge that all existence is indeed suffering; all existence is impermanent; and there is ultimately no "self" or "soul." Right views means to see through illusions, and right intent, or right thought, means to remove emotional blocks that keep us chained to those illusions. The mind of right intent is a mind of pure motives, not oppressed by sensual, ugly, or malicious thoughts.

## The Steps of Moral Conduct

Right speech, right action, and right livelihood all refer to moral conduct. One should live in such a way as to do no evil, to do good, and to purify the mind. This is the ethical *(sila)* branch of the Noble Eightfold Path and is the part that is especially practiced by laypeople, not just monks and nuns.

Specifically, right speech means not to lie, spread rumors, exaggerate, hurt people's feelings, or chatter aimlessly. Right action is exactly what it sounds like: no killing (including animals), no stealing, no illicit sexual practices, no gambling, and no intoxicants. Monks take additional vows. They promise not to engage in sexual behavior, to abstain from eating after noon, not to sleep on luxurious bedding, and not to handle money or view entertainment. In some countries monks and nuns "cheat" on the "no food after noon" requirement by eating an evening "medicinal meal."

**AN EIGHT-SPOKED WHEEL**

*The symbol of the Noble Eightfold Path is an eight-spoked wheel, which in turn has become a general Buddhist emblem.*

**KILLING CATEGORIZED**

*The Buddhist philosopher Buddhaghosa, who wrote in the fifth century C.E., said that some kinds of killing are worse than other kinds. Killing a person is a bigger sin than killing an animal, and it is worse to kill big animals than small ones. He also thought it is worse to kill good people than it is to kill bad ones.*

Right livelihood means certain occupations are forbidden: those involving killing or harming others (a military career, hunting, fishing, butchering) and those involving trickery or occult powers.

## The Steps of Mental Discipline

Right effort, right mindfulness, and right concentration are the mental disciplines one needs to achieve enlightenment. This is the meditative *(dhyana)* branch of the Noble Eightfold Path. Right

**DO NO HARM**

*Like Hinduism, Buddhism follows the ancient Indian ideal of ahimsa, or nonviolence. Buddhists vow to refrain from causing both physical and psychological suffering. Why add more pain to what is already inherent in life?*

effort means valiantly avoiding actions that can result in bad karma, specifically by cultivating a healthy state of mind. This isn't easy. "The mind," says the Buddha, "is subtle, invisible, and treacherous." That's a bad combination. Right effort means always striving to improve. Right mindfulness (meditation) means something rather different than it does in yoga; the aim is to awaken the mind rather than to still its activity. One is to become aware of one's breathing and body movements. Right concentration or contemplation *(samadhi)* is the unification of the mind. Some of the meditation practices to accomplish this goal are listed in the section on Theravadan Meditation Practices.

The Buddha was renowned for his ability to teach whatever his listeners most needed to hear. Later legends record that he could just utter one word (or even one letter), and each member of his audience would receive a whole discourse specifically designed for him or her.

The Buddha also taught by action-parables. In one famous case, a woman whose son had died came to the famous teacher and asked if he could restore her son to life. The Buddha agreed, but told the woman he needed a secret ingredient. "Go and bring me some mustard seed," he told her, "from a house in which no one has ever died." The woman scurried off; she looked high and low. And, as might be expected in a country with rampant smallpox, snakebite, cholera, plague, starvation, and ordinary old age, she drew a blank. Every single house had known death. Her search was not fruitless, however; for it taught her the first of the Noble Truths, the same one the Buddha had learned for himself years before in the marketplace: that suffering and death are ubiquitous. They cannot be avoided.

Another story tells of how the Buddha picked up a bunch of leaves and held them in his hand. He then asked the disciples which were more numerous: those in his hand or those in the forest. After giving the correct and obvious answer, the Buddha reportedly said, "In the same way, what I have not taught you is greater than what I have." This is a fairly late story, by the way, told by Mahayana Buddhists to justify the development of many ideas that Theravada Buddhists consider nonorthodox. Theravadas say the Buddha did not leave any "hidden teachings."

In general, the Buddha avoided metaphysical discussions, although plenty of them crept into Buddhism over time. He maintained what came to be known as a "noble silence" about matters beyond the grave and on abstruse philosophical subjects. Instead of being grateful to him, his disciples kept pressing him for answers to unanswerable questions. It was very annoying. The Buddha wanted only to find the answers to practical questions such as "how to be happy." One would think that would be enough, but then some people can't be happy until they know everything.

## THE NONTHEOLOGY OF BUDDHISM

Buddha denied the existence of a creator god, and he also denied (apparently) the existence of an absolute unchanging reality beyond the world of change we see every day. Part of Buddha's problem with the concept of god may have been philosophical, but his conception of Nirvana does suggest that something endures beyond the world we see and think we know. It's just not clear what. What is clear is that the Buddha replaced the notion of a supreme being with the idea of a supreme state beyond being and nonbeing: Nirvana.

But Buddha probably had another reason for denying reality to any god. He knew from experience that people long to throw off responsibility for their fate onto some higher force. It's easier to pray for favors or blame divine will for misfortune than it is to seek one's own liberation. Buddha knew that asserting the existence of a deity was only a step away from temples, chanting, prayers, saints, and dogma. Because all these eventually appeared in Buddhism anyway, he may have been wasting his time.

## THE EXPANSION OF BUDDHISM AFTER BUDDHA

The most important figure in the expansion of Buddhism across India and into the wider world was King Ashoka (273–232 B.C.E.). Ashoka started out as a warrior king, and after he had expanded his empire about as far as it could go, he converted to Buddhism and professed sorrow for all the suffering his campaigns had caused. Apparently he felt some remorse while touring a battlefield and observing the results of a particularly nasty battle.

> "As on a heap of rubbish cast upon the highway, the lily will grow full of sweet perfume and delight. Thus the disciple of the Buddha shines forth by his knowledge among those who are like rubbish, among the people who walk in darkness."
>
> —*The Buddha*

He then renounced violence in all its forms (including the sacrifice of animals). He opened hospitals and veterinary clinics throughout his lands, and appointed "*dharma* ministers" to watch over everybody's morals. Ashoka made something of a big deal over his tolerance and forgiveness, but warned that people who did not repent would be executed. They almost all repented.

Legend says that he erected 84,000 *stupas* or memorials throughout his empire. That seems like a lot. He also erected the Seven Pillars of Wisdom, later a book title. The real Seven Pillars of Wisdom

---

**A BRANCH OF THE BODHI TREE**

*In addition to his son, King Ashoka sent his daughter Sanhamitta off as a missionary to Sri Lanka. She took with her a branch of the Bodhi Tree under which the Buddha was enlightened, and she planted it in Sri Lanka upon her arrival. It's still there.*

---

is a series of metal posts with words of good advice etched on them. And there are nine of them, not seven. Don't ask me to explain all this. I couldn't if I tried.

Ashoka apparently thought that because he was a moral king, the gods themselves would manifest themselves on earth during his reign. But they didn't. Whether this can be chalked up as a failure of Ashoka or of the gods is a matter of debate. He sent Buddhist missionaries throughout the known world, and they traveled as far as Syria, Macedonia, and Egypt. Many scholars think that these missionaries had an influence on developing religious traditions in those areas, but it's hard to prove. One of the most ardent missionaries was King Ashoka's son, whose name was Melinda. (To be fair, it might have been Menander. Or Mahendra.)

As mentioned earlier, Sri Lanka quickly became a Buddhist country. In fact, Buddhism became the state religion, and eventually only a Buddhist could be accepted as king. Supposedly the palace had 60,000 monks and the king could feed 5,000 of them at once, if he wanted to.

Tradition also claims that Buddhism came to Burma during Ashoka's reign, but this is historically doubtful. What is known is that a form of Tantric Buddhism arrived before the more orthodox forms that eventually drove it out. The king of Burma conquered Thailand, and so Buddhism came to that country also, where it remains a dominant force.

## CHAPTER RECAP

- Buddha lived his early life as a pampered prince.

- He escaped from his palace and saw the four sights that made him renounce his life of pleasure to seek truth.

- Buddha wandered for six years, until he achieved enlightenment under the Bodhi Tree.

- With his awakening, he discovered the Middle Way, the Four Noble Truths, and the Noble Eightfold Path.

- During his long life, the Buddha taught all over northeastern India and established the first Buddhist monasteries.

- Later, especially under the Emperor Ashoka, Buddhism expanded over the entire region.

*Recommended Reading*

Ambedkar, B. R. *The Buddha and His Dharma.* Bombay: People Education Society, 1957.

Burtt, E. A., ed. *The Teachings of the Compassionate Buddha.* New York: New American Library, 1955.

Conze, Edward. *Buddhism, Its Essence and Development.* New York: Philosophical Library, 1954.

Jayaillike, K. N. Ninian Smart, ed. *The Message of the Buddha.* New York: The Free Press, 1975.

Kalupahana, David and Indrani. *The Way of Siddhartha.* 1982.

Lester, Robet C. *Buddhism.* Hagerstown, MD: Torch Publishing Group, 1987.

Robinson, Richard H., and Willard L. Johnson. *The Buddhist Religion: A Historical Introduction.* Belmont, CA: Wadsworth Publishing Co., 1997.

Thomas, E. J. *History of Buddhist Thought,* 2nd ed. New York: Alfred A. Knopf, Inc, 1951.

# *Buddhist Metaphysical*

# *Concepts*

$B$uddhism is more than a religion—it's a philosophy too. And, like any self-respecting philosophy, it has developed a complex body of thought regarding the nature of reality, the structure of the universe, and the concept of the self. All in all, this kind of thing is called "metaphysics." (It sounds as if "metaphysics" means "beyond physics," and thus deals with spooky, weird supernatural stuff, but actually the name came about because of Aristotle. His unnamed book on things metaphysical just happened to be placed on a shelf next to his work on physics, so his students called the book *Metaphysics* ["with" physics].)

## IMPERMANENCE—ANICCA

The doctrine of *anicca* declares that nothing in the universe is permanent; all is fleeting. We are all aware of the changing hours and days, the passing seasons, and swift-flying years. Given long enough, the Great Pyramid will crumble to dust, Niagara Falls will wear away to mere river, and Everest, which is presently growing taller, will erode down to plain. Eventually the sun will burst and the earth stop spinning. The whole universe is in constant flux. Although things may appear the same from moment to moment, they have changed and are always changing. In fact, things change so that even in the act of perceiving them, the objects of perception have changed again—they are always one step ahead of the observer. "Regard this world," counsels the Buddha, "as bubbles on a fast-moving stream, or like the vanishing stars of dawn."

The Buddhist concept of interdependent arising *(pratiya samutpada)* states that what we see—or think we see—is largely dependent on its context. We see a bunch of leaves waving around, a black trunk, and some gnarly roots sticking out of the ground, and we think "oak," but the name *oak* is just a convenient short-hand way of identifying a collection of perceptions occurring at that moment. As Gertrude Stein might have said, "There's no there there."

**PARLEZ-VOUS PALI?**

*The Buddha's own language was probably Pali, and some of the earliest writings about him are written in this language. Today Pali is purely a literary language. Other sources use the sacred language of Sanskrit, a related tongue.*

## NO SELF—ANATTA

The doctrine of *anatta* is closely allied with that of *anicca*. Also known as *anatman* (the Sanskrit form of this Pali word), *anatta* is the opposite of the Hindu doctrine of *atman,* the soul. As long as one believes in the illusion that the self exists, one will be tormented by suffering. (Obviously, if there is no self, there is no one to desire and no one to suffer thereby.)

Buddhism, especially the conservative Theravadan school (discussed in the next chapter), denies the existence of such an entity as the soul. The key to the universe is not permanence, but impermanence. If there is indeed anything called a "soul," it must be part of the universe, and therefore cannot be permanent and changeless.

The human person is merely a collection of things: arms, thoughts, feelings, legs, phlegm, memories, and so on. None of these stays the same; they are merely conjoined for a certain period. Some hang around longer than others, but none stays precisely in its present state. Certainly the conglomerate doesn't stay the same. What we think of as "I" is merely a bunch of things reacting to similar stimuli pretty much the same way over a period of time.

Buddhist philosophers have analyzed human beings this way: We are all made up of five "bundles," or "heaps" *(skandas).* A fancier term is *aggregates,* but it means the same thing. The five *skandas* are: form, sensation, perception, predispositions, and consciousness. The word *bundle* is instructive, for the Buddha wanted us to think of ourselves in a normal state as bearing these bundles like heavy burdens; they weigh us down and cause us suffering. When we die, the aggregates scatter. At our rebirth (a concept Buddhism shares with Hinduism, its parent religion), the aggregates reassemble in a new way for another brief period. We have no essential, permanent "soul"; it's merely a linguistic convenience and a psychological convention.

Curiously enough, only when you truly and fully realize that you have no soul and are no self can you reach Nirvana, or salvation. (Clinging to the notion of soul creates *tanha,* or grasping desire, just what the Buddha wanted to get rid of.) The relentlessness of this doctrine caused some people to wonder, in this case, what exactly was to be saved and for what purpose. The "liberal" school of Buddhism, Mahayana, softens the doctrine of *anatta* quite a bit, replacing it with the concept of Buddha-nature or emptiness. The Buddha nature of each of us lies within us. We need only to awaken to its presence. (I'm not sure this is much of a simplification of doctrine, but there you are.)

> "To be in any form,
> what is that?
> Round and round we go,
> all of us, and ever
> come back thither."
> —*Walt Whitman*

## KARMA AND SAMSARA

In Buddhism, karma refers to the "fruits of action." Karma, as it is in Hinduism, is responsible for *samsara,* the ceaseless wheel of birth, death, rebirth, and re-death. For Buddhists, there are several possible modes of existence, including existence as a god, a person, a "hungry ghost," or a demon. Curiously, the best state is that of a human being, even though it is not the highest state. For only in the human state can one achieve enlightenment. It is only in the human state that we can follow the Noble Eightfold Path.

## NIRVANA

Nirvana, the final goal of Buddhism, is the absolute and unconditioned. It is the ceasing of becoming. For Theravadans, Nirvana is a state contrasted with the phenomenal world and is achieved when one has extinguished all desires.

For Mahayanists, who believe that there is no ultimate difference between the phenomenal world and any other, Nirvana is the state of enlightenment within oneself. It is peace and bliss, a state in which all passions are extinguished. Technically, it is possible to reach Nirvana while still alive, although Buddhists usually consider Nirvana as a state beyond both life and death.

The word *Nirvana* literally means "blowing out," "cooling," or "extinguishing." It is sometimes said that what is extinguished are desires and passions, but the Buddha probably meant something more than this.

The Buddha declared, "There is an unborn, a not-made, a not-compounded. If there were not, brethren, this that is unborn, not-become, not-made, not-compounded, there could not be made any escape from what is born, become, made, and compounded." He left it for his disciples to figure out what he was talking about. The Buddha was often not quite as explicit as one would like.

Although many Westerners find Buddha's concept of Nirvana a lot like death, the Buddha insisted that Nirvana was not nonexistence. Nor was it existence. Part of the problem seems to be that unlike Western ideas, Buddhism doesn't regard death as a permanent state, because, unless one has found Nirvana, one is doomed to rebirth.

**DAY-TO-DAY** *DHARMA*

Dharma *is sometimes used in another, more "mundane" sense: the laws of cause and effect. Or even just "law" in a more legalistic sense, although this usage didn't become common until the nineteenth century.*

## DHARMA

It is often said that Buddhists don't follow Buddha—they follow *dharma.* Although this important word is impossible to translate exactly, it means something like truth or order or path or righteousness. It is the principle that upholds the universe. It is the purpose for which every single person is born. For some people the word *dharma* became another way of expressing the whole Buddhist tradition, the teachings of the Buddha himself.

**KARMA FROM** *DHARMA*

*Karma can be thought of as "dharma in action." If your actions are in accord with* dharma, *the karma that inevitably develops will be "good" karma. If you act evilly and in opposition to* dharma, *the inevitable karma will be painful.*

The Four Noble Truths of Buddha express the supreme *dharma. Dharma* can be destroyed, however, by three "poisons" or defilements: hatred, ignorance, and greed. These are the very states of mind that cause *dukkha* (or suffering), and thus force one into the round of rebirth and re-death.

## THE NATURE OF THE BUDDHA

Who was, or is, the Buddha, really? Every Buddhist sect, and every individual practicing Buddhism, will have a different answer, which is as it should be, since Buddhism asks its adherents to think for themselves. For Theravadans, Buddha was merely a man, the historic Siddhartha Gautama, who lived well, found enlightenment, and taught others to do the same. For Mahayanas, Buddha was a wondrous miracle worker. Others regard the historical Buddha as a manifestation of a universal, even transcendent, Buddha-Being. For still others, Buddha is their personal savior. In some traditions, there are many Buddhas, some of whom visit the earth periodically.

"'He abused me, he beat me, he defeated me, he robbed me.' In those who harbor such thoughts hatred will never cease."

—*The Buddha*

## BUDDHA NATURE

Buddha nature is absolute reality (suchness, thatness, or *tathata*). Yet, like all reality, it is ultimately transitory. Each moment in time reveals itself and then passes. It's the ultimate wonder that flashes through all existence. *Tathata* reveals itself ultimately in Buddha nature.

Human beings all have Buddha nature. According to some schools, that nature has been contaminated by ignorance, greed, and hatred. These schools believe that one must work continually at removing these pollutions from the mind. Other schools, notably Zen, contend that nature can never be contaminated; it is always pure and perfect. Our job is merely to discover its shining existence within us.

## CHAPTER RECAP

- *Anicca* is the doctrine of impermanence: All things in the world are constantly changing.

- *Anatta* is the doctrine of soul-less-ness: There exists no essential, permanent self or soul.

- The ultimate goal of the spirit is to find Nirvana, a state of peace and joy.

- Hatred, ignorance, and greed prevent us from realizing Nirvana.

- Some Buddhists consider Buddha to have been merely an enlightened man, while others consider him one of a series of supernatural beings whose mission is to save the world.

*Recommended Reading*
*Some Sayings of the Buddha.* New York: Oxford University Press, 1973.

Kalupahana, David J. *A History of Buddhist Philosophy.* Honolulu: University of Hawaii Press, 1992.

Rahula, Walpola. *What the Buddha Taught.* New York: Grove Press, 1959.

# *Theravada Buddhism — The Way of the Elders*

*T*heravada Buddhism is the dominant kind of Buddhism practiced all over southern Asia, but its center is probably Sri Lanka. In some cases, merchants carried the new religion to trading outposts; in other cases, rulers adopted the faith on behalf of their people. Theravada Buddhism has a decidedly conservative bent, strongly focused on preserving the original teachings of the Buddha.

## THE PATH OF MINDFULNESS

In Theravada Buddhism, if one has completed the Noble Eight-fold Path, he may be known as an *arhat* (worthy one). Such a person has attained freedom from rebirth. Gautama Buddha was the original *arhat*, the rest merely his followers. To attain *arhat*hood, the aspirant must overcome these four major mental/emotional/spiritual obstacles: sensuality, speculative views, spiritual ignorance, and attachment to existence. (That last one is a toughie.) The Abhidamma, part of the Theravadan scriptures, has a more extended list.

An *arhat* may be recognized by five criteria, all of which are rather difficult to test in actual practice. If a master recognizes the five criteria in his disciple, however, he may be declared to be an *arhat*. Having achieved this position, one is freed from all grief and is liberated from all ties. Those in the Mahayanan tradition often accuse *arhats* of being "selfish," only looking out for their own salvation and heedless of the needs of others. This is probably a gross exaggeration. Theravada Buddhists likewise accuse Mahayanans of having abandoned the Buddha's dying dictum, "Be a light unto yourselves" and replacing self-reliance with baseless faith. This is probably a gross exaggeration also.

## THE MONASTIC COMMUNITY

Theravada emphasizes the life of the monks rather than that of laypeople. In fact, the best way to attain salvation is to become a monk and make it your life's work. Many Theravadans begin their career as monks very early in life. The monastery or *sangha* is the very soul of the Theravadan community. Theravadans believe that the *sangha* is responsible for the direct transmission of the Buddha's words from his day until our own.

Theravadan monks are easily recognized by their orange robes; this is just one more reminder of the strong cultural connections between Buddhism and its parent religion, Hinduism. The Hindu *sannyasins* also wear orange robes (when they wear anything at all).

To help achieve cohesiveness, Theravadan monks observe a special ritual *(uposatha)* every new and full moon. During this fortnightly ceremony, the rules of the order *(patimokkha)* are recited, and confessions are heard. Serious offenses can be punished by expulsion from the order.

Monks earn their daily bread by begging for it, but because they are often the best-educated persons in the community, they also run schools for the village children and give advice on various matters. For this reason, Theravadan monasteries are often located in the middle of town.

## THE LAITY

Laypeople in Theravadan countries assume that Nirvana will not be theirs in this life. It's a state reserved for those who decide to become monks. Laypeople, however, can improve their chances for Nirvana next time around by leading a moral life and helping the

---

**DUAL PURPOSES**

*Theravadan monks often carry an umbrella. Not only is such an implement a boon in the monsoon season, but it has a symbolic value as well, for it represents the Buddha's authority. Notably, the Buddha himself would have denied he had any authority.*

**DUAL INTENTS**

*While the chief virtue in Theravada Buddhism is wisdom, and that of Mahayana is compassion, they are twin goals, for neither is possible without the other.*

monks all they can. In this role as providers *(dayaka)* they achieve great merit (karma) for their next life.

## THE TRIPLE GEM

The ancient formula known as the Triple Gem goes back to the time of the Buddha himself, and even today is recited by millions of Buddhists the world over. It is simply: "I take refuge in the Buddha; I take refuge in the *dharma;* I take refuge in the *sangha."* *(Buddham saranam gacchami; Dhammam saranam gacchami; sangham saranam gacchami.)* Although all schools of Buddhism honor the Triple Gem, Theravadan practitioners give it much more emphasis than others.

These are the three jewels *(tiratana)* of Buddhism. One does not "take refuge" in the Buddha by praying to him for assistance, but by using his life and teachings as a model. Likewise the *dharma* must be experienced and followed to be effective—it's not good enough merely to say one takes refuge in it. Some work must be done on the part of the seeker. Obviously the same is true for the *sangha,* the monastic community.

> **A TRULY EASTERN FAITH**
>
> *Because the West has no sangha tradition, Theravadan Buddhism never really caught on here. Those interested in it have had to go to Theravadan countries.*

## THE PALI CANON—THE TRIPITAKA

Theravadan scriptures are written in Pali, unlike Mahayanan texts, which were originally composed in Sanskrit and written on palm leaves. The dates of any of these texts are very uncertain.

The Pali canon consists of three "baskets" *(tripitaka)* or groups of discourses, forming altogether thirty-one texts. (The palm leaf texts were apparently originally stored in baskets.) Each sutra begins with the words, "Thus I have heard..." These discourses were compiled soon after the Buddha's death by a council of 500 monks who had studied directly under the Buddha.

### Vinaya Pitaka

The first basket is the Vinaya Pitaka, the book of discipline. It consists of five works all together and contains 227 rules for the monasteries and nunneries. (All Theravadans follow the same rules no matter where they live.) It is also a treasure trove for scholars seeking to learn more about the historical and economic conditions of early Buddhism.

### Sutta Pitaka

The Sutta Pitaka is the second basket, containing the basic discourses and sermons of the Buddha. They are divided into five collections. The most honored is the Dhammapada (*dharma* path), a short collection (423 verses) of the Buddha's words gathered by an anonymous admirer. Four versions of this work are currently in existence.

"Those who have not obtained discipline, and have not gained treasure in their youth, perish like old herons in a lake without fish."

—*The Buddha*

The key verse is number 183: "Give up evil; do good, and cleanse your mind: this is the teaching of the Buddha." Theravadans feel these words go right to the heart of Buddhism. The opening words are equally famous: "All that we are is the result of what we have thought: It is founded on our thoughts, it is made up of our thoughts. If one speaks or acts with an evil thought, pain follows, as the wheel follows the hoof of the ox that draws the wagon.... If one speaks or acts with a pure thought, happiness follows him like a shadow that never leaves one."

No one is certain how much of the Sutta Pitaka reflects the actual words of the Buddha, however. The Sutta Pitaka also contains stories from the life of Buddha, although it is not a complete biography.

### Abidhamma Pitaka

The third and latest of the three baskets is the Abhidamma Pitaka, seven treatises of technical, metaphysical, psychological, and scholarly material. It contains no lively allegories or interesting stories. It doesn't even mention a specific person or actual events. Its main purpose is to organize Buddhist knowledge and to refute the views of other schools. This basket, though dry and uninteresting to the casual reader, has great stature in Theravadan countries, especially in Myanmar. (One Buddhist theory is that the Buddha preached this last basket to the gods in heaven, who are not easily bored.)

According to the Abhidamma, there are ten imperfections *(kilesa)* that keep people from achieving enlightenment. The three big ones are greed, hate, and ignorance. These give birth to the other seven: conceit, speculative views, useless doubt, mental laziness, restlessness, shamelessness, and lack of conscience.

## THERAVADAN MEDITATION PRACTICES

Theravada Buddhism recognizes two kind of meditation: that which leads to tranquility and that which leads to insight. Although Hindus also practice meditation, the orientation is different. In Hinduism, the idea is to find the true self, while in Buddhism, the orientation is outward—ultimately toward Nirvana.

### Tranquility Meditation

The meditation that leads to tranquility is known as *samatha*. According to Buddhaghosa, author of The Path of Purification (found in the Abhidamma), there exist forty objects of meditation. Each disciple should choose those objects best suited to his own character and temperament. Buddhaghosa further divided the characters of people into six sorts: the lustful, the hot-tempered, the easily deluded, the self-assured, the quick-witted, and those of the discursive mind.

Before meditating, the practitioner finds a comfortable, isolated spot and sits in the lotus position, the classical posture for meditating. People of the East find this position very natural, as they have been doing it from childhood. For Westerners, it's a different matter. If you can't manage it, any comfortable position will do, so long as the back is kept straight, the hands folded in the lap, and the eyes remain half-closed and unfocused. You should focus your attention on some spot like the tip of your nose, or your forehead, perhaps.

At any rate, a listing of the some of these forty meditation objects is extremely interesting. Some, the so-called "Ten Devices," seem harmless enough:

- Earth device: a circle made of dawn-colored clay

- Water device: a bowl of clear water

- Fire device: a bright flame seen through an opening

- Air device: the breeze shaking the branches of a tree

- Blue device: a circle of blue cloth

- Yellow device: a circle of yellow cloth

- Red device: a circle of red cloth

- White device: a circle of white cloth

**THERAVADA'S DETRACTORS**

*Critics of Theravada Buddhists complain that they are sticklers for rules, but Theravadans see nothing wrong with rules. They believe they keep people out of trouble.*

- Light device: a shaft of light falling through an aperture

- Space device: a limited space seen through an opening

Buddhaghosa, more ominously, also lists the "Ten Impurities" (not for the faint-hearted):

- A swollen corpse

- A discolored, bluish (or greenish) corpse

- A pus-filled corpse

- A split open corpse

- A corpse mangled by dogs

- A dismembered corpse

- A partly dismembered corpse

- A bloody corpse

- A worm-infested corpse

- A skeleton

**TRUE COMPASSION**

*One exhibits true compassion when one equates the suffering of others (human and animal) with one's own pain.*

Most Buddhists practicing this meditation simply imagine a corpse, but a few prefer to practice on the real thing.

Other objects of meditation include the "Ten Recollections." These are: the Buddha's virtues; the merits of the *dharma;* the holy *sangha* (all these comprise the three refuges); the merits of the precepts; the merits of liberality; the equality in virtue between oneself and the gods; death; the body; breathing; and peace of mind. One might meditate on the "Four Sublime States of Development": universal love, compassion, the happiness of others, and equanimity. Or one might select the "Four Immaterial States": infinite space, infinite consciousness, nothingness, and neither perception nor nonperception.

If that's not enough you can meditate on the "One Notion": the loathsomeness of food. Or the "One Analysis": the four primary elements.

Students begin by attempting to reach through what are called the eight states of concentration. Once these have been achieved, they may begin insight meditation. (There's no rule that says one kind of meditation has to be undertaken before another one, but that's the usual practice.)

### Insight Meditation

Insight meditation *(vipassana)* may be used with tranquility meditation, or separately, according to the desire of the practitioner. In this practice, there are three meditations: the meditation on impermanence *(anicca)*, the meditation on suffering *(dukkha)*, and the meditation on no-soulness *(anatta)*. The Noble Eightfold Path is also a part of insight meditation.

The meditator works on the four states of mindfulness (body, feelings, mind, and mind objects). As the student progresses, he passes through the state of pseudo-Nirvana, and finally into true Nirvana, which may last only a second or so. With each practice, however, the meditator can achieve the state more easily and for longer periods.

One begins *vipassana* training by observing the breath and keeping careful note of what is happening. Likewise one should calmly note body sensations such as "itch," "cramp," "splitting headache," and so on. When things get too bad, you can alternate sitting meditation with walking meditation.

**INSIGHT IN AMERICA**

*Vipassana meditation has really taken hold in the United States. There is an Insight Meditation Center in Barre, Massachusetts, among other places.*

## CHAPTER RECAP

- Theravada Buddhism, the Way of the Elders, is popular in southeast Asia.

- Theravada Buddhism emphasizes the life of the monks more than the lives of layfolk.

- The primary virtue of Theravada Buddhism is wisdom.

- Theravada Buddhists find the refuge in the Three Gems: the Buddha, the *dharma* (teachings), and the *sangha* (the monastic community).

- Theravada Buddhists practice two kinds of meditation: *samatha* meditation, which aims at tranquility, and *vipassana*, which aims at insight.

*Recommended Reading*

Bunnag, Jane. *Buddhist Monk, Buddhist Layman.* Cambridge, England: Cambridge University Press, 1973.

Collins, Steven. *Selfless Persona: Imagery and Thought in Theravada Buddhism.* Cambridge, England: Cambridge University Press, 1982.

Dharma Publishing Staff, ed. *Dhammapada.* Berkeley, CA: Dharma Publishing Company, 1985.

King, Winston L. *In the Hope of Nibbana: Theravada Buddhist Ethics.* Chicago, IL: Open Court Publishing Co., 1964.

————. *Theravada Meditation: The Buddhist Transformation of Yoga.* University Park, PA: The Pennsylvania State University Press, 1980.

Levine, Stephen. *A Gradual Awakening.* Garden City, New York: Doubleday, 1979.

Swearer, Donald K. *Buddhism and Society in Southeast Asia.* Anima Books, 1981.

# *Mahayana Buddhism —*
# *The Great Vehicle*

*M*ahayana Buddhism offers not one but many paths toward liberation. It is a rich and colorful tradition that many people find more emotionally appealing than the somewhat austere practices of Theravada Buddhism. Many people also find it more life-embracing, more available to the common person, and just more fun.

Mahayana developed about five hundred years after the death of the Buddha, although its adherents claim that its teachings go back directly to his precepts, correctly understood. Today Mahayana Buddhism is dominant in China, Japan, Korea, and Vietnam. (In fact, Buddhism became the state religion in Japan by 594 C.E.)

The word *Mahayana* means "great vehicle." The implication is that it not only has a broader vision and more sweeping view than Theravada, but also that its greatness can accommodate everyone—not just monks.

## THE PATH OF COMPASSION

It is often said that the central virtue of Mahayana Buddhism is compassion (as opposed to the Theravada ideal of wisdom). The sanskrit word for compassion is *karuna*, which can also be translated by the English word *kindness*. And kindness is one very good way of thinking about Buddhist *karuna*, for the root sense of

**IN THIS CHAPTER**

- Sunyata: *the concept of emptiness*

- *Bodhisattvas—heavenly and otherwise*

- *Buddha nature à la Mahayana*

- *Mahayanan scriptures*

- *Buddhism in China and Korea*

ANOTHER FAMILY
SQUABBLE

*Mahayana Buddhists,
especially Tibetans, call
Theravada hinayana, which
means "small vehicle."
Theravadans rightly consider
this a pejorative term and
refuse to use it.*

"kindness" is "kin." And in the Mahayanan view of things, all sentient beings are kin; we are all connected by the bonds of empathy and compassion, which in turn means "feeling with" someone. Mahayana Buddhists believe that compassion, kindness, and faith are the keys to salvation, for until all of us attain salvation, none of us will. This makes perfect sense. How can there be any true joy for a virtuous person unless all are virtuous and all share in that joy?

## MAHAYANAN PHILOSOPHY AND METAPHYSICS

Hold onto your brain—it's going to get a workout. If you have studied Plato, Descartes, or indeed any Western philosophy (and understood it), Mahayanan thought may strike you as strange and paradoxical. Even as absurd. It will remain absurd until you give up attachment to the habit of thinking in the old way.

### The Concept of Emptiness and Freedom

Mahayana Buddhists affirm that ultimately there is no difference between liberated bliss (Nirvana) and the world of appearances *(samsara)*. Both are emptiness *(sunyata)*. There is an important, although subtle difference between Mahayana Buddhists and Theravadans revealed by this concept. For Theravada Buddhists, the world is real, although it is transitory and impermanent. What gives the impression of stability is the way things are held together through the laws of cause and effect *(dharmas)*. Mahayana Buddhists disagree. They hold that even the *dharmas* possess no "self" and are thus empty and "unreal." Once a person fully understands this, he is free from them and achieves enlightenment.

It's important to understand that in the Buddhist view, *sunyata* is not a negative concept at all, but an opportunity to achieve both fulfillment and liberation. This sounds paradoxical, perhaps, but that's the way it is. Because reality is empty, it can be "made" into anything. Western existentialists just caught on to this idea in the twentieth century.

### Nagarjuna—The Philosopher of Emptiness

The most brilliant philosopher of the doctrine of emptiness was Nagarjuna (c. 150–250 C.E.), whose Stanzas on the Middle Path

(Madhyamika Karika) is the authoritative text on the subject. For him, the Middle Path was to avoid getting entangled in controversies, dogma, over-wrought emotional experiences, and naïve perceptions. He reiterated the basic Buddhist position that there is no real "self" and no ultimate ground of being. His school is called Madhyamika, and varieties of it became popular in China and Japan.

For him, even the concept of *sunyata* was empty. If it were not empty, it would be a real object, and thus capable of drawing attachment, which is just what Buddhists want to avoid. Each chapter of the book deals with a separate issue, including cause and effect and Nirvana. For Nagarjuna, nothing is eternal, but neither does anything have an end. Nothing is different, and nothing is identical. He said, "No production nor destruction; no annihilation nor persistence; no unity and no plurality; no coming in nor going out." These are called the "Eight Nos," reasonably enough.

He refused to be trapped into a kind of Western, Aristotelian either/or mentality. "Words are not cops," he complained. All this, of course, is in the old *neti, neti* tradition of Hinduism where philosophers could define the Brahman only by negatives. The same principle seems to be at work here.

To clarify or befuddle further, Nagarjuna offered what logicians call the *tetralemma*. (This is twice as difficult as a dilemma.) Choose any entity at all. Let's take widgets. On the face of it, there seem to be four and only four possibilities about the existence of widgets. (1) Widgets exist. (2) Widgets don't exist. (3) Widgets both exist and do not exist. (4) Widgets neither exist nor do they not exist. But Nagarjuna refused to assert the truth of any of these claims for any item of existence, because, as he said this "very assertion would be form and form is emptiness." Actually Nagarjuna wasn't talking about widgets. He was talking about Nirvana. Not that there's any essential difference between them. There now. Once you get used to thinking about things this way, it's hard to stop.

Nagarjuna also decided to tackle the problem of time. "If the present and future exist presupposing the past, the present and future will exist in the past. If the present and future did not exist in the past, how could the present and future exist presupposing the past?" Well?

"No bird soars too high if he soars with his own wings."

—*William Blake*

## BODHISATTVAS (HEAVENLY AND EARTHLY)

*Bodhisattva* is a word with a multitude of meanings. Literally it means "enlightenment being" and refers to one who is destined for full enlightenment, especially one who has postponed his entry into Nirvana to help other sentient beings attain enlightenment. Originally the word was used to describe the Buddha in his previous lives, before his enlightenment, and Theravada Buddhists today generally restrict the word to this meaning. However, the word's meaning has expanded among other Buddhists. In the Mahayana view, for instance, we are all bodhisattvas.

Some bodhisattvas are regarded as earthly beings who have achieved perfection in this life, while others are celestial types who are aspects of the Buddha himself. The next Buddha is currently a bodhisattva.

In the Mahayana understanding, the bodhisattva has achieved the six perfections *(paramitas):* wisdom *(upaya)*, morality *(shila)*, patience *(kshanti)*, strength *(bala)*, meditation *(dhyana)*, and generosity *(dana)*.

Usually, however, a bodhisattva "specializes" in one or another of these virtues. Avalokiteshvara is the bodhisattva of compassion; Manjusri, whose name means "sweet splendor," is the bodhisattva of wisdom and memory. Some Buddhists believe he founded culture and learning in Nepal.

Avalokiteshvara, Manjusri, and Maitreya are all celestial Buddhas. Maitreya is "the friendly one" who lives in his heaven *(tushita)* now, but will become the next Buddha to appear on earth. (He is thirty feet tall, so he should be easy to spot.) Maitreya will inaugurate a new age and lead us all into salvation. This will take another three or four or five thousand years, so don't hold your breath. Maitreya traditionally wears a stupa, or ceremonial mound, in his hair. He also carries a flask of ambrosia in one hand and a lotus in the other.

There are stages to becoming a bodhisattva—it doesn't just happen all at once. In some traditions there are seven stages, in others ten. Here are the ten:

1. Joyful

2. Stainless

**THE GIFT OF GIVING**

*Generosity is highly prized in Buddhism. It brings with it many gifts, including happiness, long life, and rebirth in heaven.*

3. Luminous

4. Radiant

5. Hard to conquer

6. Face to face

7. Going far

8. Immovable

9. Stage of the good

10. Cloud of *dharma*

**THE FRIENDLY BUDDHA**

*Both Theravada and Mahayana Buddhists believe in and love the Maitreya. In China he is called Mi-lo-fo, and in Japan Miroku. He is popular in Korea under the name Miruk.*

It takes a long time to accomplish all these stages. Some say it takes $384 \times 10^{58}$ years, minimum. Most commonly it is said to take three immeasurable *kalpas*. It all amounts to about the same thing.

Since everyone will get to be a bodhisattva sometime, at least theoretically, Mahayana Buddhists sometimes take the bodhisattva vows, first compiled in the sixth century C.E.: "Beings are infi-

**MOST WONDROUS AVALOKITESHVARA**

*Even if you are thrown into a fiery pit, just thinking of Avalokiteshvara will release you. Basically the same thing happens if you are drowning, about to have your head cut off, surrounded by enemies, attacked by witchcraft, ambushed by goblins, or get thrown off a mountain.*

nite in number; I vow to save them all. The obstructive passions are endless in number; I vow to end them all. The teachings for saving others are countless, but I vow to learn them all. Buddhahood is the supreme achievement. I vow to attain it."

Avalokiteshvara, "the Lord who sees in all directions," is an androgynous bodhisattva, the spiritual son of Amitabha, the Buddha of Infinite Light. The birth occurred when Amitabha was going through some particularly heavy meditation. A beam of white light zipped out his right eye. That was Avalokiteshvara. His first prayer was "*Om mani padme hum,*" which of course became famous all over the world. Avalokiteshvara has vowed not to enter Nirvana until all beings can join him there.

Avalokiteshvara is revered in China, Korea, Japan, Tibet, and Mongolia. In China, he is known as Kuan-Yin (or Guan-yin) and

REVERENCE FOR
KANNON

*In the temple city of Kyoto
is the longest wooden building in the world. It is filled
with more than a thousand
statues of Kannon, all lined
up neatly.*

is female. Kuan-Yin dresses entirely in white and holds in her hand the jewel of wisdom. She also has an eye in the palm of each hand; this helps her find people in need. She is extremely popular, for she hears the suffering of all beings and never refuses to help. The compassion of this bodhisattva can be aroused by the recitation of powerful mantras. (Her statues often depict her as having many, many arms, a symbol of her far-reaching compassion.) Her symbol is the bamboo plant, whose "hollow heart" means modesty. (In Japan the same deity is called Kannon, and she has many temples.) Kuan-yin is also a rice goddess.

## THE MAHAYANAN VIEWS OF THE BUDDHA

Mahayana Buddhists generally consider Buddha as a divine figure, sometimes manifesting himself as a savior. He has not postponed his absolute Nirvana-empowering enlightenment, but is sharing it with others. How the Buddha came to his divine status differs from school to school. In some Mahayanan thought, the Buddha began as an ordinary human being, who by his saintly actions gradually achieved enlightenment, and who is now available to pass on his saving grace to others.

Another Mahayanan school of thought considers that Buddha has always existed on an absolute plane, and that earthly Buddhas are the manifestation of this absolute reality. These are the bodhisattvas, sort of replacement Buddhas for the earthly Gautama Buddha who lived and died. Many of the bodhisattvas never do either. (Some schools claim there were at least 214 other Buddhas before the advent of Gautama Buddha. It took 120,000 years for Gautama to show up.)

### The Three Bodies of Buddha

Because the concept of infinite Buddhas (some divine, some not) got a little confusing, later Mahayanan tradition developed a doctrine called *trikaya*, or the "Triple Body" theory. According to this doctrine, Buddha has three bodies. One body is the *dharmakaya*, whose qualities are pure and uncontaminated. This is the historical Buddha as a visible manifestation of the divine reality. The word *dharmakaya* means "law or form body." A second body is the Buddha in the aspect of spiritual bodhisattvas, *nirmanakaya*, also called the "mind-made," "transformation," or "emanation-body." (He needed this for a celestial visit to his dead mother.) The Buddha can have more than one transformation body. A third body is the Buddha as an earthly being(s), *rupakaya*, visible to ordinary persons.

Other Mahayanans came up with a slightly different, but no simpler, twist on the three-body concept. According to them, the *dharmakaya* is more than uncontaminated, it is the ultimate reality that is the foundation of all Buddhas. It underlies all earthly reality. The *rupakaya* was traded in for the *sambhogakaya*, or "enjoyment body." This Buddha exists in the heavens teaching boddhisattvas.

The emanation body, *nirmanakaya*, is the one that appeared in the world to teach the *dharma*, but it was not a real flesh-and-blood body. Apparently, the Buddha never really had one of those. The *nirmanakaya* was some kind of—well—not illusion exactly, since it's just as real or permanent as everything else appearing in this or any other world—but an emanation of sorts. It looks like a body, feels like a body, walks and talks like a body, and is in fact indistinguishable from a body. But it's not a body. All the Buddhas, past and present, make use of the *nirmanakaya* to teach the *dharma*. I hope this is all perfectly clear.

> "Hatred is not appeased by hatred—it is appeased by love."
>
> —*The Buddha*

## SCRIPTURES

The scriptural library of Mahayana Buddhism is vast, unlike the austere Pali canon of Theravada Buddhism. It is also composed in many languages: Pali, Sanskrit, Tibetan, and Chinese. In fact, if the Chinese Buddhist canon alone were translated into English, it would take up more than half a million pages in print. Mahayanans do not reject the Pali canon; they just add to it.

Some early *sutras* (c. 100 C.E.), are called the Prajnaparamita Sutras, the *sutras* on the "perfection of wisdom," or "wisdom that has gone beyond." These works show how the universe reveals itself differently to an ordinary person and to a person who has attained wisdom. In other words, Nirvana can be attained in the here and now.

Another important text is the Vimalakirti Sutra, which declares that one can be a good Buddhist without becoming a monk. Later, but very influential scriptures include the Heart Sutra and the Lotus Sutra.

## The Heart Sutra

The Heart Sutra reports the words spoken by the bodhisattva Avalokiteshvara to Sariputra, a member of the Theravadan sect. It focuses on the critical Mahayanan doctrine of emptiness. Avalokiteshvara explains, "In emptiness there is no form, no feelings, no consciousness, no mind, no sound, no phenomenon...There is no ignorance, no aging, no death, no suffering, no source of suffering, no cessation of suffering, no path, no exalted wisdom, no attainment, and no non-attainment." It closes with a mantra, the mantra of the perfection of wisdom: "Gone, gone, gone beyond, gone completely beyond: AUM."

## The Lotus Sutra

The Lotus Sutra *(Saddharma Pundarika Sutra)* is one of the most beloved of all Mahayanan texts, and in east Asia, by far the most influential. Originally written in Sanskrit, it was translated into Tibetan, and thence into Chinese. It is the most sacred text of the T'ien't'ai (Japanese Tendai) and Nichiren sects of Buddhism. Part of the Lotus Sutra is a defense of Mahayana Buddhism against its "rival," Theravada Buddhism. Devotees divide the Lotus Sutra into two parts of fourteen chapters each. The first part, the "Shadow Gate," deals with the historical Sakyamuni and his law. The second part, the "True Gate," discusses the "eternal Buddha of original enlightenment." Here the Buddha is revealed as a universal divine figure.

Not surprisingly, the Theravadans claim their practices and beliefs are more in accordance with the teachings of the Buddha himself. The Lotus Sutra sweeps these claims aside, saying that the Buddha taught what was most appropriate at the time to his disciples, but not the ultimate truth. It hinted

**THE SUTRAS**

*Mahayanan scriptures are called* sutras, *which means "thread." Our word* suture *comes from the same source.*

---

**COMPARISON OF THERAVADAN AND MAHAYANAN BELIEFS**

- *Theravada Buddhists consider the Buddha a human being. For Mahayana Buddhists, Buddha is much more.*
- *For Theravada Buddhists, the ultimate virtue is wisdom (prajna). For Mahayanans, it is compassion (karuna).*
- *The final goal for Theravada Buddhists is Nirvana. For Mahayanans, it's salvation for all.*
- *The model for Theravadans is the arhat, the enlightened human being. For Mahayanans, the model is the bodhisattva, the being who will bring enlightenment to all.*
- *Theravada Buddhists put their emphasis on strenuous effort; Mahayanans put theirs on grace.*
- *Theravadans place emphasis on the monastic community; Mahayanans on the laity.*

that they were too stupid to hear the real truth as now proclaimed in the Lotus Sutra. It suggests that some of the Buddha's teachings were useful lies, the famous concept of "skillful means." The Lotus Sutra provides this parable as an example:

A house is on fire, with children inside, and the father of the house wants to get them out. Perhaps the children are too young to understand the concept of fire. The father would be completely justified in offering them toys and treats to get out of the house, even if he doesn't deliver on them afterward. He is saving their lives, and that is the greatest gift of all. Just so, explains the Lotus Sutra, Buddha may not have told his disciples the exact truth, but the important thing was to save their lives by setting them on *dharma* path, even if they thought they were going somewhere else.

Just as the father lied to save his children, so the Buddha fibbed now and again to save souls, to get disciples to take the right path. Eventually the disciples will understand the truth. The Lotus Sutra says all earlier teachings were likewise "skillful means" to show early followers the right path.

## BUDDHISM IN CHINA

Many historians believe that Mahayana Buddhism arrived in China during the first century C.E., when Buddhist monks accompanied merchants along the trade routes. Soon regular two-way traffic between India and China was established, with many Chinese visiting the birthplace of Buddha to collect sacred texts. Buddhism reached its peak in China during the seventh century C.E., and it was during this period that Japanese scholars came to China to study the faith and bring it back to Japan.

The twice-removed nature of this transaction may partly explain why Japanese Buddhism is so different from the original version. (Additionally, once it arrived in Japan, Buddhism partially absorbed all the aboriginal gods.) Oddly enough, the Japanese were first introduced to Buddhism, not by the Chinese, but by the Koreans. In the sixth century a Korean version of Buddhism reached Japan; this version of the faith, however, was much more concerned with the magical, protective qualities of the Buddha on behalf of the secular leadership than Buddhism's ethical beliefs.

**IN THE FOOTSTEPS OF THE BUDDHA**

*The Lotus Sutra declares that the billions of bodhisattvas, past and present, are all disciples of the one eternal Buddha.*

In some ways, Buddhism is foreign to traditional Chinese culture. Instead of celebrating the family, it urges celibacy, at least for monks. It had no use for ancestor worship or genealogy. It made up for these shortcomings, however, by adapting readily to Chinese norms wherever possible and offering a rich metaphysics and a peaceful, gentle philosophy that appealed to many people. Buddhism never replaced indigenous Chinese religions; it merely lived beside them and added to the complex mix of Chinese tradition.

## Ch'an Buddhism

The Ch'an school of Buddhism developed what became known as the "abrupt doctrine," the idea that enlightenment is achieved suddenly, rather than over a period of many years. It is called Zen in Japan and is discussed in chapter 12.

The founder of this doctrine was Hui-Neng (638–713 C.E.), the so-called Master of the Mirror and Sixth Patriarch of Ch'an Buddhism. He called his school the Southern school to differentiate it from the Northern school, which taught that enlightenment came gradually. In his most famous treatise, the Platform Sutra *(T'an Ching),* he said that meditative concentration *(samadhi)* and wisdom *(prajna)* were of one substance. *Samadhi,* he said, was the substance of wisdom, and wisdom the function of *samadhi.* One did not "follow" another; they arose together.

## Bodhidharma

Although some picky scholars insist that Bodhidharma (486–593 C.E.) was a mere legend who never existed, they have no real proof. After all, somebody brought Ch'an Buddhism to China, and it might as well have been Bodhidharma as anyone else. Therefore I do not apologize for the precision of the dates. If he lived, he had to live sometime. Supposedly he was the son of King Sugandha of India, but there's no proof of that either.

At any rate, this Indian missionary supposedly showed up in Canton around 520 C.E., where he had a visit with the Emperor Wu. Not the soul of tact, Bodhidharma informed the emperor that the imperial program of building temples and copying holy texts was a waste of time. Then he went off and sat in front of a wall for nine years, staring at it. Somehow this strange being managed to attract a disciple, a certain Hui-K'e, but only after Hui-K'e proved he was serious by chopping off his own arm.

Bodhidharma wrote six treatises that explained his basic ideas. These became the essential principles of Zen:

- Special transmission outside scripture

- No dependence on words

- Direct pointing at the soul

- Seeing clearly into one's own nature (Buddhahood)

Bodhidharma has been a popular figure in Chinese and Japanese art. In Japan, a Bodhidharma doll is a favorite gift for someone who has overcome many obstacles.

### Fa-Hsiang Buddhism

This classical, idealistic system of Buddhism was brought to China by Hsuan-Tang (596–664 c.e.), who had gone to India as a pilgrim. He started out as a Pure Land Buddhist, but changed his mind when he got to India. He learned his new style of Buddhism from the Yogacara school and brought the teachings back to China. Fa-Hsiang means "*dharma* characteristics," but the school he founded is also called Wei-shih-tsung, meaning "consciousness-only school." Fa-Hsiang Buddhism holds that the "real world" is an artifact of the conscious mind. Fa-Hsiang was popular during the Chinese middle ages but fell into disfavor during the ninth century.

## BUDDHISM IN KOREA

Buddhism reached Korea in 372 c.e. The ruling parties thought that Buddhism would protect them from the depredations of Mongols and other barbarians. During the Koryo dynasty, monks went busily to work and carved 80,000 wooden blocks for the printing of all known Mahayanan texts. The Mongols invaded and burned them. Luckily, the Koreans had a couple more sets lying around, one of which still exists. Evidently, Buddhism wasn't as

**KUNG FU**

*Bodhidharma is also credited with founding the martial art of Kung Fu boxing, a skill he developed to help the monks of Shao-lin monastery get some exercise. They were in terrible condition, apparently.*

good a Mongol-preventer as one might wish, and during the Yi dynasty (1392–1910) Confucianism became the state religion. Sadly, most Koreans didn't care for Confucianism.

**VASUBANDHU'S LEGACY**

*Vasubandhu, a great Yogacara philosopher, made a name for himself by refusing to admit that there was any distinction between one's own consciousness and the object of that consciousness.*

## CHAPTER RECAP

- Mahayana Buddhism is known as the Great Vehicle, and it concerns itself with everyday people as well as monks.

- The chief virtue of Mahayana Buddhism is compassion.

- The greatest philosopher of Mahayana Buddhism was Nagarjuna, who taught the doctrine of emptiness.

- Mahayana Buddhism developed the concept of the bodhisattva, a future or heavenly Buddha.

- The Chinese were introduced to Buddhism during the first century C.E. They were early followers of Ch'an (Zen) Buddhism.

*Recommended Reading*

Ch'en Kenneth. *Buddhism in China: A Historical Survey.* Princeton, NJ: Princeton University Press, 1970.

Conze, Edward. *Buddhist Texts Through the Ages.* Oxford: Oneworld Publications, 1995.

de Bary, William Theodore, ed. *The Buddhist Tradition in China, India, and Japan.* New York: The Modern Library, 1969.

Ellwood, Robert S. Jr., and Richard Pilgrim. *Japanese Religion: A Cultural Perspective.* Englewood Cliffs, NJ: Prentice Hall, 1985.

Eppsteiner, Fred, ed. *The Path of Compassion: Writings of Socially Engaged Buddhism.* Berkeley, CA: Parallax Press, 1988.

Welch, Holmes. *The Practice of Chinese Buddhism 1900–1950.* Cambridge, MA: Harvard University Press, 1967.

# *Tibetan Buddhism—The Way of the Thunderbolt*

*T*ibet is a huge, frigid, barren, oxygen-starved, remote clump of snow, rocks, and mountains. There are practically no trees. Nonetheless, for many people, Tibet (or at least the idea of Tibet) equals paradise on earth.

## A BIT OF BACKGROUND

Historically, the Tibetans were not exactly forward thinking, at least in the scientific sense. Although they had discovered the principle of the wheel, they used it only for "prayer wheels" and didn't figure out another use for their invention for a remarkably long period of time. One sixteenth-century traveler to Tibet, a certain Jesuit priest named Grueber, made a big deal about Tibetans eating raw yak meat and making medicine from the Dalai Lama's feces.

The country was too sparsely populated and too arid even to support cities, so monasteries served as focal points for the wandering nomads of the region. Eventually there were about 2,500 of them. This seems like a lot, but then Tibet is a lot bigger than you might think—about the size of western Europe, a fact few people stop to consider.

Although the Tibetans get a lot of favorable press nowadays for being attacked by the Chinese, one should never forget the fact that the Tibetans "started it" in 763 by attacking and ravaging Chang'an, the Chinese capital during the Tang dynasty. Then the Mongols attached Tibet to itself in a more or less friendly fashion. (It was the Mongol prince Altan Khan who came up with the inspired name Dalai Lama, or Ocean of Wisdom, for that spiritual leader.)

---

### DONKEYS AND DOGS

*Marco Polo was the first European to get anywhere near Tibet, and he was impressed with the huge Tibetan mastiffs used for guarding purposes. "Big as donkeys," he commented. This may in fact be true. I recently spent some time looking at American-bred yaks (who tend to be a bit smaller than the Tibetan types). I happened to be standing next to a Tibetan monk.*

*"At home, we have dogs bigger than those yaks," he told me somewhat contemptuously.*

*"Oh, you do not," I answered, not wishing to be trifled with by a man in an orange robe. We both stared in silence at the yaks for a few moments.*

*"Maybe not," he agreed reluctantly. "We have dogs as big as donkeys." I suppose he had been reading Marco Polo too, although it's hard to tell.*

---

Fortunately, the history of the ensuing centuries is too muddled to get into in this book, so I'll skip ahead to 1721 when the Chinese got their revenge and declared Tibet to be a vassal state. It remained so until 1911, when the Chinese, who were having enough problems of their own, gave up on the place for about forty years. The Tibetans did well for themselves during this period and created their own government, monetary system, postal system, and even a military. Unfortunately, in the light of later events, not one single country in the West helped out by recognizing Tibet as a sovereign nation, so the Chinese had no real opposition when they got their act together and took the place back in 1950. (Tibet begged the United Nations to help, but got nowhere.)

> "Tibetans are by nature quite aggressive people and quite warlike."
>
> —*The Dalai Lama*

## MYSTERIOUS TIBET

For some reason (see Orville Schell's *Virtual Tibet*), Tibet has captured the imagination of Westerners ever since the mid-1800s when we found out it was there. It served as the alleged venue for the paradise dubbed Shangri-La in James Hilton's *Lost Horizon*. And Western culture has used the country as an inspiration for numerous movies. *Golden Child* (with Eddie Murphy) put the first tender toe into the untouched waters of filmic Tibetan Buddhism in 1986.

*Golden Child* was followed in 1994 by Bernardo Bertolucci's *Little Buddha*. After the film was made, life imitated art in that a little kid from Seattle was declared the reincarnation of a high lama and was packed off to Nepal to study. The incident was remarkably similar to the story of *Little Buddha*.

A few other minor films followed, but the next significant release was Jean-Jacques Annaud's *Seven Years in Tibet,* the film version of Heinrich Harrer's memoir of the same name. The movie was shot in Argentina (Tibet is off-limits) and starred Brad Pitt as the central character.

*Kundun,* directed by Martin Scorsese, was the competition against *Seven Years in Tibet.* Scorsese decided to film his epic in Morocco and hired a lot of Tibetans to act in the film. Both movies were extremely expensive to make and, in spite of our fascination in all things Tibetan, performed poorly at the box office.

> **PARADISE TIBETAN STYLE**
>
> *It should be noted that the Tibetans have their own version of Shangri-La. Their paradise goes by several names: Shambhala, Zhang Zhung, and Olmulungring. Whatever you want to call it, it's been around since 16,017 B.C.E. And it looks nothing like Tibet. A few Buddhist texts survive that give directions for finding Shambhala, but scholars complain that the directions are "obscure."*

Television also bit into the Buddhist apple with *Dharma and Greg,* and even the world of rock is not immune. Beastie Boys' Adam Yauch is a sort of honorary Tibetan Buddhist and has added catchy numbers such as "Bodhisattva Vow" to his musical repertoire.

## THE ORIGINAL TIBETAN RELIGION

The original religion of Tibet was a shamanistic faith called Bön (pronounced, rather unbelievably, as "pern"). Its practitioners are the Bon-po, and in remote regions, which in Tibet are even more remote than elsewhere, it still exists. It is a religion of magic and priests, and includes an interesting mythology with characters called *lHa, aDre,* and *gS Hen.* These are easier to pronounce than they look, although not much.

## THE ARRIVAL OF BUDDHISM

Buddhism came to Tibet in 747 C.E. The weird missionary was a Kashmiri named Padma-Sambhava, which means "holder of the

**CLOSE UP**

*Although the outdoors scenes of Seven Years in Tibet were indeed filmed outdoors in the mountains, the director shot the indoor scenes in an old garlic warehouse.*

lotus." (The lotus in this case is a symbol of compassion and knowledge.) Trained in an occult branch of Buddhism called Tantra, Padma-Sambhava apparently achieved supernatural powers. He was invited to Tibet by King KHri Srong lDeu bT San on an interesting mission: to overthrow the demons who were opposing Buddhism in Tibet. He accomplished this feat with ease.

Today he is honored as "the second Buddha." He built the first monastery in 749 and won mastery over the traditional Bön religion by magical feats.

Still, things went a little wrong under Padma-Sambhava. There was all together too much drinking and sex going on for the establishment, so another missionary, named Atisha, was called in from Nalanda, India, to put things in order. Atisha explained that different people needed to follow different ways, and the way of Tantra was not right for everyone. He was right about that. (See chapter 22, Tantra: The Forbidden Treasure.) In addition to the traditional Theravadan (which Tibetans called Hinayana) and Mahayanan paths, Atisha set forth what Tibetans called Vajrayana, the Way of the Thunderbolt, or the Diamond Vehicle.

The Vajrayana path of Tibetan Buddhism is comprised of four sects:

- Red Hats (the Ancient Ones): The Red Hats trace their lineage directly back to the founder of Tibetan Buddhism, Padma-Sambhava, and use many Tantric texts in their practice. This sect also uses many elements of the old Bön tradition. For this reason, some other sects denounce them.

- Kagyupa: This school arose in the eleventh century and relies mainly on secret traditions orally passed from lama to disciple. It was founded in Tibet by Marpa (1012–1096). Marpa learned his Buddhism from Naropa, who learned it from Tilopa, both Indians.

- Sakyapa: The Sakyapa sect also developed during the eleventh century (it's good something was happening then). It focuses on Tantric practices designed to release the universal consciousness within each person.

- Yellow Hats (The Merit System Ones): The Yellow Hats compose a reform order currently headed by the Dalai Lama. It was founded by Tsongkha-pa (1357–1419), but really got going in the seventeenth century. Unlike some other sects, Yellow Hat monks are not permitted to marry.

## MILAREPA AND THE KAGYUPA SCHOOL

Milarepa (c. 1052–1135) is an important character in the development of the Kagyupa school of Tibetan Buddhism. This one-time sorcerer became known as one of the greatest Tibetan yogins, a fully enlightened one, and a national hero, besides. His psychic feats included the knowledge of *tumo*, the ability to turn up the body heat to such a pitch that one can live in complete comfort in the most bitter of Tibetan winters.

Unfortunately, Milarepa got off to a rather bad start for a fully enlightened one. He studied under Lama Yungtun-Trogyal ("The Wrathful and Victorious Teacher of Evil") and quickly perfected himself in the black arts. He started his own career in grand style at his cousin's wedding, by filling the room with vermin and then conjuring up a scorpion the size of a yak. The scorpion pulled down a pillar of the building, killing thirty-five people, but sparing his aunt and uncle whom Milarepa wanted to live (so that they could suffer more). To be fair, he did it only to please his mother, who disliked that side of the family.

Milarepa felt pretty bad about all this and decided to straighten out his life. He found another teacher, Marpa, the saintly founder of the Kagyupa school of Buddhism, and devoted himself to learning the *dharma*. (The Kagyupa school remained dominant in Tibet until the fifteenth century, when it was surpassed by the Yellow Hat reform movement mentioned previously.)

Not surprisingly, Milarepa chose the "Short Path to Enlightenment," a tricky blend of esoteric practices and Tantra. But Marpa took to beating Milarepa with boring repetitiveness, and even more annoyingly, had him build and rebuild a house for him several times. Milarepa was forty-four years old at the time and not getting any younger.

*OM MANI PADME HUM*

Om mani padme hum *is the great mantra used in Tibetan Buddhism. No one is sure precisely what it means, although the usual translation is: "Hail to the Jewel in the Lotus. Hum." Whatever it means, Tibetan Buddhists believe that the recitation of this formula spreads influences for compassion and goodness everywhere.*

**TWO TYPES OF TANTRA**

*Many Tibetan scriptures are called tantras, after one kind of Buddhism practiced in Tibet.*

At last, the surly saint was satisfied with Milarepa's carpentry and initiated his disciple in the mysteries. About this time, Milarepa dreamed his house was destroyed, and his mother too. He hastened home, found it was all true, and gathered up his mom's bones in a little brown bag, which he then used as a pillow for the rest of life. (Some accounts supply a different disposition of the bones, but this is the most entertaining one. It also sounds just like Milarepa.)

Milarepa then took up life as a hermit, living on nettle broth, which turned his skin completely green. Eventually, however, he transformed into pure intellectual light. At that point he forwent the nettle soup and dined upon ambrosia.

At the age of eighty-four, Milarepa died after knowingly ingesting some poisonous curds. (Curds are quite a comedown from ambrosia, but about on a par with nettle soup.) He was ready to die, he said, and entered Nirvana with a song. All accounts agree that Milarepa was a fine crooner, breaking into song at the oddest times.

---

**AN EARLY WESTERN SEEKER**

*One woman to explore the world of Tibetan Buddhism was Alexandra David-Neel (1869–1969), a Frenchwoman who became one of the first Westerners to enter the forbidden city of Lhasa. She became a Buddhist and studied with Gomchen of Lachen, a noted hermit and teacher of secret wisdom. She lived in a hut in the Himalayas and reportedly reached high levels of enlightenment through telepathy and other psychic arts.*

---

Milarepa is forever associated with Mount Kailasa, which is an important place of pilgrimage for Tibetan Buddhists. Mount Kailasa, located in the western Himalayas is, according to legend, the very center of the world. In Tibetan it is called Gang Rimpoche, and pilgrims walk clockwise around its base, the same way one would walk around a prayer wheel. (It is *very* important to walk in the correct direction. A few hardy spirits prostrate themselves completely at every step as they circumambulate the mountain, but that takes longer.)

## VAJRAYANA BASICS

Vajrayana Buddhism is a Tibetan form of Tantra, a special tradition discussed more fully in part 5. Because everything in Tibet takes on a particular life of its own, however, Tibetan Tantra no more resembles Hindu Tantra than it does Theravada or Mahayana Buddhism.

## Vajrayana Metaphysics

Tibetan Buddhism maintains that the phenomenal world we perceive is projected from our own minds. The only true reality is what Tibetan Buddhists called "clear light," a pure consciousness.

In Tibetan Buddhism, the disciple is responsible for the success—or the failure—of his training. The Buddha's dying words were, "Be a light unto yourselves," and Tibetan Buddhists take this injunction very seriously. The student spends most of his time meditating and often doesn't even lie down to sleep. His goal is to win the favor of his lama's *yidam,* or tutelary deity. After many austerities, he accomplishes this purpose. Then a strange suspicion overtakes him—perhaps the *yidam* is a mirage, part of his imagination. He confronts the lama with his suspicion. The lama informs him that he hasn't got enough faith and sends him back to work some more.

Eventually, the disciple decides for himself absolutely that the *yidam* does not really exist and stands stalwart in the face of the lama to inform him so. At this point, the lama says, "Gods, demons, the whole universe, are but a mirage which exists in the mind. It springs from the mind, and sinks back into the mind." And the disciple is free from all illusion.

Like all Buddhists and indeed Hindus (from whom they got the idea), Tibetan Buddhists subscribe to the idea of reincarnation, an essential component of karma. Unlike other groups, however, Tibetans believe that it is possible for one to know whom one was reincarnated from.

> ### A TIBETAN DEITY
>
> *One of the most beloved deities of Tibet is Tara, the compassionate mother of the world. In fact, Tara was born from a tear—the tear of pity. Often she is paired with Chenrezig, another favorite god. Like him, she has the power to forgive and save, and her name means both "star" and "savior." As one text puts it, "Even those whose limbs are being devoured by the worms that attach to their open wounds, stinking of pus, who devote themselves to you will find that their bodies become as beautiful as gold, and their eyes like the lotus." Tara comes in several colors: green, white, yellow, red, and blue. The first two are the most common.*

"It is an excellent thing to attain this vision of union in diversity, to feel others live in ourselves, and perceive ourselves living in others."

—*Alexandra David-Neel*

## The Mandala: Sacred Circle

A mandala is a mystical aid to meditation for both Indian and Tibetan Buddhists. The word *mandala* comes from the Sanskrit word meaning "circular." Roundness signifies perfection and completion. (Some mandalas, however, are square, triangular, or polygonal.) Whatever the shape, nearly all are symmetrical. The most elaborate mandalas are the Tibetan ones. Every figure within the design has a complex symbolic meaning.

In the center of the mandala is generally a Buddha figure. In this position, he is usually referred to as Adi-Buddha, the primeval Buddha, from whom all Buddhas emanate. Surrounding the central Buddha are four subordinate deities, each at a cardinal compass point. (The mandala is usually oriented to these four points, by drawing a square around the outside. It can also be done by the use of other designs within the circle.) Interspersed between the lesser deities are more divine figures, often female. The rest of the design represents the workings of the universe, and in one sense could be considered a "map" of the cosmos in space and time. The basic idea of every mandala is the same: to show how the universe was created from a perfect singularity and to explain the process by which it will return there.

## Prayer Wheels

Prayer wheels are unique to Tibetan Buddhism. These cylinders contain holy chants and mantras. A mantra represents a cosmic force, and the turning of the wheel is both an act of devotion and the release of power. Most prayer wheels are also inscribed with a mantra on the outside, usually *Om Mani Padme Hum.* Typically the worshipper turns the prayer wheel by hand, but wind and water are also sometimes utilized. One has to be careful to turn the prayer wheel clockwise, however. Counter-clockwise prayer wheel turnings can unloose demons.

## Mudras

Mudras are ritual hand gestures often associated with a particular deity. They are specific to Tibetan Buddhism. Many mudras are also standardized; for example, the right hand extended with the palm and fingers up means "blessing." If the hand is turned downward it means "generosity." Mudras are actually quite versatile, rather like sign language. There are mudras to depict twenty-seven philosophical states.

---

**MANDALA DESIGN**

*Mandalas can be painted, sculpted, embroidered, drawn, or drawn in sand. They can be danced. Some temples are even designed in the form of mandalas. In Tibet, lamas often create "mental mandalas." Mandalas exist in Hinduism also, where the central figure represents Brahman. Sometimes Hindus use Sanskrit symbols rather than actual figures.*

## THE TIBETAN BOOK OF THE DEAD

The Tibetan Book of the Dead, the *Bardo Thodol,* is a map of the afterworld. (The *Bardo* is a kind of middle state between this life and the next incarnation, a place of great uncertainty. The word *thodol* means "great liberation by hearing." The book instructs the dying how to reach liberation, the state beyond all states. A lama, seated near the head of the dying person, performs the rite.

The first state is *Chikhai Bardo,* where the person stays for four days, a place of bright, colorless light. It is sometimes called the Great Straight Upward Path. The trick at this stage is for the dying/dead person to realize that the luminosity he perceives all around is the *dharma* body of the Buddha and is identical to the luminosity within him. Those who perceive this are liberated and enter Nirvana immediately. The text urges the dying person to accept this revelation, even if he cannot understand it. Few and far between are those who succeed, however. Because of all the bad karma we have acquired, most people miss the point, even with the straightforward directions given in the *Bardo Thodol.*

For those who don't attain Nirvana, the next best shot is *Choyid Bardo,* the state of transcendent forms. Here dwell the *yidam,* other gods, and cosmic Buddhas. These are not really independent beings, however, but projections from the person's own mind. It is possible to attain Buddhahood by arriving at the realization that these beings are part of oneself. The deceased resides here for two weeks. During this stage, the subject is approached by the Judge of the Dead, who assesses the person's past deeds. If the dying person can recognize this being as a figment of his own mind, he may possibly achieve liberation. Most of us are too frightened to do so; however, one should never give up hope.

Those who miss the point are condemned to spend three weeks in the gray world of *Sidpa Bardo,* through which it is almost certain he will re-enter this world to be born, suffer, and die again. Still, the *Bardo Thodol* provides a series of meditations called "closing the womb," meant to keep the subject from being reborn. Apparently the deceased spends a lot of time in *Sidpa Bardo* watching couples have sex. In a weird permutation of Freudian psychology, the person in this state, if about to be reborn male, instantly desires the woman

**TIBETAN PRACTICE**

*Meditation comprises one of the three parts of Tibetan Buddhist practice. The other two are "hearing" (reading, studying, attending lectures) and "contemplation" (actively pondering the subject).*

"O nobly-born, the Great Glorious Buddha-Heruka, dark-brown of color; with three heads, six hands, and four feet firmly postured...the body emitting flames...the nine eyes widely opened in terrifying gaze...the protruding teeth glistening, giving vent to sonorous utterances of "a-la-la" and "a-HAH" and piercing whistling sounds—the red-brown hair standing on end, the heads adorned with dried human skulls, black serpents and raw human heads forming a garland for the body."

—*The Tibetan Book of the Dead*

(vice versa for girls-to-be-born). As he is "embracing" the opposite sex, however, all he can see is that person's sexual organ, which makes him angry and frustrated, and in this state he will be reborn into the world. To get there, the being must enter the father, emerge through the father's penis into the mother, and thus become the temporary resident of the mother's womb.

One might think this all a little prurient (not to mention the queasy feeling it might give living people to imagine a bunch of dead folk watching their sexual activities). Still, it's all for a good cause. The deceased might realize from his observations that men and women are just aspects of the Buddha. It's always possible, too (though very unlikely), that at the last second a person might become enlightened and achieve liberation.

A full ceremony occupies forty-nine days, not counting the three and half days afterward that it takes for the deceased to know that he's dead. At the end of the forty-nine days, it's assumed the person has either entered a new incarnation or found liberation.

In actual practice, most ceremonies are a lot shorter. If the person dies during the rite, which usually happens, he is tied to a sitting position for four days, while the reading continues. After this period, the corpse is disposed of. In Tibet, this usually means having the body chopped up by the "body butchers" and left out for vultures to devour. This is a sensible way to handle things, because the ground is usually too frozen to dig and wood is too precious to waste on burning bodies.

The Book of the Dead is more than a set of directions, though. It is also used as a meditation aid and philosophical guide for Tibetan Tantric Buddhists.

## TIBETAN LAMAS

The word *lama* means "superior." Not every Buddhist monk is a lama, for monks are still students, and only lamas may teach. Every lama is considered an embodiment of the Buddha. In common parlance, however, especially in America, all monks are called lamas. The word *tulku,* applied to some lamas, means "phantom body." Such a monk is the earthly incarnation of a bodhisattva. These monks are given the title rimpoche, "precious one."

Although disciples pay great reverence to their lamas as gurus, the devotion is not usually personal, and the disciples are quite able to separate the master's human faults from his sometimes suprahuman knowledge. One hears stories of lamas who are drinkers, fornicators, or given to various other moral misdemeanors. The wise disciple is not deterred, however, and merely waits for the inner truth he believes his master to exemplify to reveal itself. This doesn't mean that faults are excused; they are merely not judged.

### The Great Adepts of Tibet—Spiritual Athletes

Tibetan lamas are reported to have achieved remarkable feats. One of their best-known but mysterious abilities is that of *tumo*, a specialty of Milarepa. (If you're really good at *tumo*, you can throw a cold soaking wet sheet over your naked body and sit outside in the Tibetan winter. Your body heat will quickly dry the sheet, and you'll be fine. Alexandra David-Neel said that her practice in *tumo* kept her snug during her travels thorough Tibet.) Accomplished lamas are also reportedly able to levitate, go indefinitely without sleep, read minds, be in two places at once, and zip along through the Himalayan mountains really fast, a practice called *gompa*. Expertise in this field is called "relative achievement." The ultimate achievement is Buddhahood, of course.

### The Dalai Lama

Contrary to popular belief, the Dalai Lama is not the world head of Buddhism. He is not even the head of all Tibetan Buddhists, but only of the Yellow Hat *(Gelugpa)* school. The current Dalai Lama has achieved his worldwide esteem through the force of his own personality, not through an inherited office.

The first Dalai Lama took office in 1438. His given name was dGe-Dun-Grup-Pa (b. 1391). Another early Dalai Lama was a grandson of the Mongol leader Altan Khan. This made the Chinese very nervous, and they extended every effort to put the brakes on the whole Dalai Lama system. They haven't stopped.

The most famous early Dalai Lama, however, was the Great Fifth. (Actual name: Ngag-dBang bLo-bZang rGya-mTsho.) In 1650 or so, he revealed that he was the reincarnation of the god Chenrezig, the national deity of compassion. The Great Fifth was

**A DEVOUT PEOPLE**

*It's estimated that at one time lamas comprised one-fifth of the population of Tibet.*

so revered that his death was concealed for thirteen years and a monk who looked like him was trotted out for public appearances. The Great Fifth's successor, Melodious Purity, didn't exactly live up to his name. He spent a lot of time drinking and practicing Tantric sex rites. Somebody poisoned him after a while.

The present Dalai Lama, his Holiness Tenzin Gyatso (bsTan-dZin rGya-mTsho in Tibetan spelling) is the fourteenth of that title. He was born on June 6, 1935. The Dalai Lama is a truly great man, a charming human being, and a Nobel Peace Prize laureate (1989), not a bad combination. His current headquarters are in Dharamsala in northern India, although his traditional (until 1959) residence is a thirteen-story, 1,000-room palace in Lhasa: the Potala. The Potala still has tremendous symbolic significance for Tibetans, and is reputedly quite a sight with its fabulous gilt roof. Inside, it's supposed to be gloomy, dark, and cold. The Dalai Lama talks about sleeping under canopies dripping with mouse urine. He liked the mice, though. He said they were his friends.

As I said before, the Great Fifth stated that the Dalai Lama is an emanation of Chenrezig. In fact, the office of Dalai Lama is by special selection. When the Dalai Lama dies, a search is undertaken for his successor.

---

**IN THE FOOTSTEPS OF THE BUDDHA**

*The Panchen Lama, the "Gem of Great Learning," is second in stature to the Dalai Lama. His authority, however, is purely spiritual, not political. The Panchen Lama was an invention of the Great Fifth, who handed the title to his own teacher. He said he was the reincarnation of Amitabha, the Buddha of Light.*

---

For example, when the thirteenth Dalai Lama died, it was reported that his face turned eastward several days after his death. So a search was begun in that region. The searchers were guided by omens until they found the present Dalai Lama, still a toddler.

## Chogyam Trungpa (1939–1987)

Chogyam Trungpa (1939–1987) was one of the most important exponents of Tibetan Buddhism in the West. He was also a great *tulku,* an emanation of the bodhisattva, in this case the eleventh incarnation of Trungpa Tulku, and he acquired the honorific "rimpoche" or "precious one." In 1966 he wrote *Born in Tibet,* an autobiographical account of his youth, when he escaped (barely) from Tibet during the Chinese invasion. Unfortunately, Trungpa was in a car accident that left his left side paralyzed and prevented him from wearing his religious dress, a situation that had a bad effect upon him. In fact, he renounced his monastic vows, married a sixteen-year-old English girl, and started drinking. He continued to teach, however, and acquired such notable followers as William Burroughs, Allen Ginsberg, and John Cage. When he died (probably of cirrhosis of the liver), his body was packed in salt. This simple preservation enabled his students to meditate with the corpse for about two months. Then the late Chogyam Trungpa was wrapped in gauze, soaked in butter, and burned.

---

**THE TRAGEDY OF TIBET**

*Of course, the 1950 Chinese invasion of Tibet has largely eradicated Tibetan Buddhism in the land of its birth. The invaders destroyed many monasteries and also killed a great number of monks. The only silver lining to this horror is that this previously insular culture has now spread worldwide in a kind of Tibetan diaspora, bringing its own unique and powerful brand of Buddhism with it.*

---

## CHAPTER RECAP

- Tibetan Buddhism is officially known as Vajrayana Buddhism: the Way of the Thunderbolt.

- The original Tibetan religion was Bön, an animistic religion that became embedded in Tibetan Buddhism.

- Tibetan Buddhism makes use of mandalas, mantras, mudras, and prayers wheels.

- The most important Tibetan Buddhist text is the Tibetan Book of the Dead.

- The Dalai Lama is the leader of only one sect of Tibetan Buddhists: the so-called Yellow Hats.

*Recommended Reading*
Beyer, Stephen. *The Cult of Tara.* Berkeley: University of California Press, 1973.

Goodman, Steven D., and Ronald Davidson, eds. *Tibetan Buddhism, Reason and Revelation.* Albany, NY: Albany State University of New York, 1992.

Gyatso, Tenzin (Fourteenth Dalai Lama). *The Buddhism of Tibet and the Key to the Middle Way,* trans. Jeffry Hopkins and Lati Rimpoche. New York: Harper and Row, 1975.

Johnson, Sandy. *The Book of Tibetan Buddhism.* San Francisco: Harper and Row, 1995.

Rao, S. K. Ramachandra. *Tibetan Tantrik Tradition.* Atlantic Highlands, NJ: Humanities Press, 1978.

Waddell, L. Austine. *Tibetan Buddhism.* Mineola, NY: Dover Publications, Inc., 1992.

*Recommended Audiotape*
Gyatso, Tenzin (fourteenth Dalai Lama). *Opening the Eye of New Awareness.* Los Angeles: Renaissance Media, Inc., 1999.

# *Z e n   a n d   O t h e r*
# *J a p a n e s e   S c h o o l s*

$B$uddhism came to Japan in the sixth century, where it found soil for an unusually rich and complex development. To this day, Japan contains the most diverse traditions in all Buddhism. In addition to varieties of Buddhism, the Japanese mixed Buddhism with their native Shinto tradition as well as with imported Confucianism.

Buddhism was officially introduced to Japan in 552 B.C.E., when a Korean king asked Japan for some military aid. His messengers brought with them (besides the ordinary gifts) an image of the Buddha and a bunch of scriptures. The messenger promised that anyone converting to Buddhism would have good fortune. The new religion caught on like wildfire, at least among the elite, much to the dismay of the old guard who feared the native gods would retaliate.

During its earliest period, the so-called Nara era (628–784 C.E.), Buddhism was tremendously powerful. (Nara was an early capital of Japan.) During this time, at least six different schools of Buddhism flourished: Sanron, Jojitsu, Hosso, Kusha, Kegon, and Ritsu. These sects lost most of their prestige later on, however, with the development of Tendai and Shingon Buddhism. Three of them died out completely, but Hosso, Kegon, and Ritsu retain historical interest and still have temples open to the public. In the Nara period, there was a marked difference between the official, state-sponsored Buddhism, and Buddhism as it was actually practiced by the people. The Japanese government frowned on private devotions, perhaps feeling (rightly) that they couldn't be controlled.

The establishment of Kyoto in 794 C.E. as a new capital was partly an effort to free the country from official Buddhism, which many Japanese recognized as a foreign import. It also marked the beginning of the brilliant Heian period, which lasted until 1185. During this time, Japanese civilization made tremendous strides in architecture, literature, and art. The Japanese borrowed some of their ideas from China, but as usual, transformed them into uniquely Japanese expressions.

THE LONG
TENDAI PATH

*Tendai specifies fifty-two
stages to enlightenment.*

## TENDAI—THE HEAVENLY TERRACE

About 30 percent of Japanese Buddhists identify themselves as Tendai, a highly ritualistic school that has generally appealed to the aristocracy and royalty (the Japanese emperor thought it would protect his realm), although it began as a reform movement directed toward regular folk. Tendai reached its peak in the ninth and tenth centuries.

Tendai is also called the "lotus school," for it honors the Lotus Sutra above all others. Tendai originated in China, where it was known as T'ien-t'ai Shan, "Heavenly Terrace Mountain," its first center. In China, the greatest T'ien-t'ai philosopher was Chih-yi (538–597 C.E.) who took it upon himself to reconcile what some thought to be contradictory Buddhist teachings. He expanded on the Lotus Sutra's doctrine of "skillful means" by which the Buddha was able to adapt his ideas to listeners of differing abilities.

A Japanese monk, Saicho (766–822 C.E.), known posthumously as Dengyo Daishi, brought Tendai Buddhism to Japan from China. The Japanese Emperor Kwammu had sent him and another monk, Kukai, over there to learn something. Saicho was only a teenager at the time, but he was no slouch. He had been a priest ever since he was thirteen years old, and established his first monastery on Mount Hiei when he was eighteen. This later became a great Buddhist center, with more than 1,200 buildings. (In fact, it was so influential that a whole period, the Heian period, was named after it.) Most of the buildings in this complex were burned in the sixteenth century, although some have been restored recently.

In 805 C.E., Saicho began to expound his doctrine, which was essentially a mix of standard Mahayana fare, with an emphasis on meditation. Saicho believed that the Buddha has two simultaneous aspects: an earthly one and a heavenly one. In like manner, Saicho thought, the whole universe is present in every part of itself. This led Saicho to his most important doctrine: the Perfectly Harmonious Threefold Truth of the Empty, the Temporary, and the Middle. "Nonexistence is empty. Existence is temporary. They are both dependent on the 'middle.' When these three are in perfect balance, one can achieve enlightenment." I hope this is clear.

Saicho believed in the power of chanting the name of Amida (Amitabha) and was also fond of taking extremely long meditative walks. It helped him think.

Tendai Buddhism got a rather bad name during the Askikaga period, the so-called Dark Ages of Japan (1333–1568). This was because armed Tendai monks/thugs took to roaming the streets, challenging their religious opponents to duels, and in general terrorizing the populace.

> "Whether walking or standing, sitting or lying, only repeat the name of Amida with all your heart. Never cease the practice of it even for a moment."
>
> —*Honen*

## SHINGON—THE TRUE WORD

About 10 percent of Japanese Buddhists identify themselves as Shingon, which means "true or magical word." This esoteric school was established in Japan in 804 C.E. by the Japanese monk Kukai (774–835 C.E.). Like Saicho, Kukai imported his brand of Buddhism from China, where it was called Zhen-yan. Kukai opened many temples across Shikoku and the southern end of Honshu. His center was near Osaka, at Mt. Koya. This monastery, like the Tendai one on Mount Hiei, became an important teaching center for many centuries.

Like Tendai, Shingon appealed to the nobility, but it wasn't intended only for them, at least not at first. As court life became more and more important in Japan, however, both Shingon and Tendai abandoned their original missions to the ordinary populace, and over time their teachings were addressed to the elite alone.

Shingon derives from Indian and Tibetan Tantra practice, and like Tantra it has remained more practice-oriented than theory-dependent. In fact, my favorite Shingon monk is Shobo (832–909 C.E.), who formed a sub-sect of Shingon called Shugen-do. He and his monks spent most of their time subduing evil spirits of the dead.

Kukai taught three rituals for Shingon Buddhism: complex hand and finger gestures *(mudras)*, mystical vocalizations (mantras), and contemplation of celestial Buddhas. These represent the three functions of body, speech, and mind. In fact, Kukai taught that all existence was merely a manifestation of the Buddha's body, speech, and mind. He called this the three secrets, because he said ordinary people couldn't understand them. Once you understood the secrets, however, you would become identical with the Buddha himself.

**THE GREAT MASTER**

*After he died, Kukai was known as Kobo Daishi, the "Great Master."*

One of Shingon's most colorful practices includes a fire ceremony. For this purpose Shingon uses mandalas. Two of the most popular are the Kongo-kai (diamond world) mandala, which shows the universe from the viewpoint of wisdom, and the Tai-zo (womb) mandala, which looks at it from the viewpoint of compassion.

For Kukai, one ascended the ladder to Buddhahood in a ten-step process (quite a reduction from Tendai's fifty-two!) of gradual purification and enlightenment. You start thinking about food and sex, but at the end of the process you are absorbed with meditating upon cosmic glories.

The most important scripture in Shingon is the Mahavairocana Sutra (called Dainichikyo in Japanese).

One reason for the success of both Tendai and Shingon Buddhism is that both combine Buddhist precepts with the old Shinto gods. Kukai called this melding Ryobu Shinto (two-aspect Shinto). Thus it becomes very hard to draw a firm line between Shinto and Buddhism, and indeed, most religious Japanese don't draw such a line at all.

The Shinto deities and celestial Buddhas were very important in Shingon. Kukai believed that by invoking them one could attain health, wealth, and a good rainfall, although I suppose if one has health and wealth, it doesn't matter if it rains or not.

## PURE LAND BUDDHISM

About 18 percent of Japanese Buddhists identify themselves as Pure Land Buddhists, who worship Amida Buddha. Its offshoot, the True Pure Land sect or Jodo Shu, however, is the largest and most influential Buddhist sect in Japan.

Pure Land Buddhism was first established in Japan by Honen (1133–1212) in 1175. (Honen was apparently a rather prickly fellow, who got on the wrong side of the other Buddhists and the emperor too. He was banished from Kyoto, but he came back.)

Honen's most important disciple was Shinran (1173–1263), who, due to doctrinal differences with Honen, became the father of True Pure Land Buddhism (1224). Although Pure Land Buddhism and True Pure Land Buddhism are technically separate sects, the differences between them are so slight as to be indiscernible to most people. I'll treat them as one denomination.

Pure Land Buddhism addresses itself to laypeople as well as to monks. Shinran felt that although severe austerities were impossible for most people, love, faith, and compassion were within reach of all. He proved it too, by getting married, definitely not in the monkish tradition. The idea that austerities are not necessary became extremely popular in Japan. Pure Land doesn't ask people to be monks or sit for hours and meditate.

Amida is the Japanese Tathagata Amitabha, the Buddha of Infinite Light. In Pure Land Buddhism, he is Lord of the Western Paradise, but he is worshipped all over Asia under many names. Amida was a bodhisattva who swore that he would not enter Nirvana until the whole world found salvation. It was he, adherents believe, who became incarnated in Gautama Buddha.

Amida himself is of almost infinite height and brilliance. A tremendous halo surrounds him, and he bears upon his body 84,000 special marks, each of which manifests 84,000 virtues. These inestimable virtues enable everyone who sincerely believes in Amida to be reborn into the Pure Land. Symbolically, Amitabha represents the color red/gold, the summertime, and its fruits.

---

**GETTING TO THE PERFECT PARADISE**

*According to one story, Amida was originally a monk named Dharmacara, who spent five kalpas in very deep meditation. His object was to found the perfect paradise, the Sukhâvartî, or Pure Land, where he now resides and welcomes the faithful. To reach this paradise, all one needs to do is repeat his name in sincere faith. Dharmacara assured everyone in his Vow Number 33 that women who get to the Pure Land will be released from their womanhood upon entering, becoming—well—presumably men.*

The Pure Land (Saiho Jodo in Japanese) is filled with music, jeweled trees, fragrant rivers, magical birds, and varicolored lotus blooms. Showers of divine blossoms fall three times a day. People may remain in the painless, comfortable Pure Land as long as they wish—even until they reach Nirvana.

Pure Land Buddhism emphasizes the role of grace in reaching satori, or sudden enlightenment. Shinran believed that we are living in a dark age *(mappo)* that does not permit people to achieve salvation through their own power *(jiriki)*, either through discipline or the attainment of transcendent knowledge. We need help from elsewhere *(tariki)*. That help comes from Amida, the fountain of grace.

**THE ORIGINAL PURE LAND**

*Pure Land Buddhism was founded in China by Tan Luan (c. 476–542), where it was called Jingtu or Ching-t'u.*

## The Nembutsu

To receive this grace, Pure Land Buddhists recite the *Nembutsu,* a practice dating back to the introduction of Buddhism into Japan. *Nembutsu* is an abbreviation of *Namu Amida Butsu.* Honen had taught that if you said this chant ten times with perfect sincerity, you would be saved. This sounds easy, but I suppose it depends on how strictly you interpret the word perfect.

The idea of using a chant to get into paradise actually goes back to the Chinese Buddhist Hui-yüan in the fourth century. The phrase is especially potent if recited at the moment of death. Even today, in rural villages, there exist *Nembutsu* dances and drama, with the purpose of driving away the spirits of the dead. There is even a legend that the founder of the popular Kabuki drama was a *Nembutsu* magic dancer.

Pure Land Buddhists generally practice their faith by worshipping at a statue of the Amida Buddha, which is usually accompanied by a statue of Kannon, the compassionate goddess and a statue of Daiseishi, the Buddha of wisdom. Sacred texts include the Sutra on the Buddha of Immeasurable Life, the Sutra on the Meditation of the Buddha of Infinite Light, and the Sutra on the Amida Buddha.

During the Tokugawa period (1615–1868), Buddhist temples and priests were controlled by the shoguns. They required everybody to register at their local temple as a Buddhist (this was to worm out any Christians lurking in the area). This policy eventually turned into a fairly good census system. The Tokugawa shoguns favored Pure Land Buddhism and undertook a policy of persecution against the Zen sects. The shogun period came to an end in 1868, when with the help of outsiders like Commodore Perry, the feudal lords regained control of their country and moved the capital to Tokyo.

## NICHIREN

Nichiren was founded by the Japanese monk Nichiren Daishonin (1222–1282), the son of a fisherman. It's one of the only major Buddhist schools actually founded in Japan rather than in China.

Nichiren began as a Tendai monk and was even trained at Mount Hiei, but he soon decided that Tendai was too ritualistic and corrupt. In fact, he believed that all other branches of Buddhism were corrupt and that only he had found the true essence of Buddhism. Even today Nichiren Buddhists are generally intolerant of other Buddhists, believing they have found the one and only truth.

### The Importance of the Lotus Sutra

Nichiren believed we are living in the dark age of *mappo,* and the way out was the Lotus Sutra. (Here he agreed with Tendai Buddhism.) But although Tendai Buddhists honor other *sutras* also, for Nichiren the Lotus Sutra is the one and only one. The Lotus Sutra has always been popular in Japan because it promises salvation to all people, something that earlier religion had not done. In it, Nichiren believed, the heart of the Buddha's teachings could be found. Devotion should be paid to it, and to nothing else, for it replaces all other Buddhist teachings. (Unfortunately for Nichiren's theory, the Lotus Sutra is full of ideas that Buddha never held, especially the idea of an "eternal Buddha of original enlightenment.") Nichiren also decided that he himself was the reincarnation of Bosatsu Jogyo, a disciple of Buddha's mentioned in the Lotus Sutra.

Nichiren excoriated the Kamakura regency government of his day, mostly because it refused to outlaw other sects. He seemed to harbor a particular resentment against Zen monks, whom he called "devils." He also offered his opinion that people who went about

**NICHIREN IN AMERICA**

*The United States has more than 150,000 members of this sect, called the Nichiren Shoshu of America. It was brought here by Japanese women who married American GIs.*

chanting the Pure Land chant would all go to hell. (Nichiren had its own chant, the Daimoku, but that was different. See following.)

He prophesied that disaster in the shape of a foreign invasion would soon arrive. (The Mongols did invade Japan in 1268.) No one likes a gloom-and-doomsayer, however, and soon both the authorities and the common folk were out to get him. He was attacked by an angry mob, imprisoned, and exiled—more than once. He was supposed to have been executed, but at the decisive moment lightning came out of nowhere and struck the executioner's sword. Things like that happen from time to time. Nichiren did eventually die; he was on his way to a hot springs near Tokyo at the time.

About 30 percent of Japanese Buddhists identify themselves as Nichiren. They are most famous for their sacred chant, the Daimoku: *Namu-myo-ho-renge-kyo.* This translates into something like "Devotion to the Sutra of the Lotus of the Wonderful Law." By chanting this phrase, Nichiren taught, one would implicitly be chanting the entire sutra.

## Nichiren Worldview

According to Nichiren, the universe is divided into ten worlds. They include: hell, the world of hungry ghosts, human beings, heavenly beings, the boddhisattvas, and the Buddhas. All realms exist at the same time, and each of the ten worlds exists in each of the others.

For Nichiren Buddhists, the Buddha is an eternal being, not just an historical personage. When Gautama Buddha was enlightened, it meant that all of the universe was also slated for eventual enlightenment.

Nichiren advocates worldwide peace and members of the faith have engaged in well-publicized events promoting it. In fact, in 1995 it sponsored a peace walk from Auschwitz to Hiroshima and Nagasaki.

## The Value Creation Society

A lay offshoot of traditional Nichiren Shoshu is Soka Gakkai (the Value Creation Society), which was founded in the twentieth century by Tsunesaburo Makiguchi (1871–1944) and Josei Toda. Both men were persecuted during World War II because they refused to install Shinto shrines in their homes as required by law. Although

---

**THE DAIMOKU**

*The Daimoku is inscribed on a holy tablet, the gohonzon. The original gohonzon is in a shrine at the foot of Mount Fuji, but other official gohonzons are hand-copied by priests on scrolls, one of which is given to each new member.*

Makiguchi died in prison, Toda survived the ordeal and after the war converted about 750,000 new members to his brand of Nichiren.

Unlike traditional Buddhism, Soka Gakkai teaches that "earthly desires are Nirvana," always a popular concept. Its members live and work in society, and the movement is extremely rich, partly because they are closely connected with Mitsubishi Bank. According to members, their goals are culture, education, and peace. The canonical text of Soka Gakkai is Kachiron, the collected writings of Makiguchi.

Today there is a rift between the religious (Nichiren Shoshu) and lay (Soka Gakkai) branches of the movement. The religious leaders of Nichiren have ex-communicated members of Soka Gakkai for refusing to change their ways. Today an estimated 20 million people follow Soka Gakkai.

Other new religions in Japan that owe their source to Nichiren are Reiyukai (founded 1925) and Rissho Koseikai (1938). Rissho Koseikai is also dedicated to the Lotus Sutra and believes the Buddha is present in all of us.

**HUNGRY GHOSTS**

*Hungry ghosts have tiny little pinheads and great big stomachs; thus they can never eat enough to satisfy themselves.*

## ZEN—THE GREAT WAY OF ENLIGHTENED EXPERIENCE

Zen Buddhism is completely different from all other Japanese schools of Buddhism. It is a mind-to-mind tradition, a tradition that scorns the use of texts and chants. As mentioned previously, Zen Buddhism began in China, where it is called Chan. The traditional founder was the inimitable Bodhidharma, who came to China around 470 c.e. The first real Zen master, however, was probably Hui-Neng (637–713). In Japan, Zen exerted great appeal among the military class, who ruled Japan until 1868.

More than other Mahayana branches of Buddhism, Zen is a philosophy. There is no worship in the practice of Zen, and in many ways Zen seems to harken back to the old Theravada teachings. Like Theravada, it places great emphasis on meditation.

Today only about 8 percent of Japanese Buddhists identify themselves as practitioners of Zen. Still, the Zen tradition is an extremely important one, both for its influence in Japan and for its impact in the West. In the United States, Zen is a dominant form of Buddhism—although its popularity has recently been challenged by

**IN THE FOOTSTEPS**
**OF THE BUDDHA**

*Ultimately the name Zen*
*comes from the Sanskrit*
*word* dhyana, *or meditation.*

other traditions. In Japan, nearly every form of artistic expression and daily life has been heavily influenced by Zen: painting, architecture, the tea ceremony, even bathing practices.

Zen reached its zenith in China during the Sung Dynasty (960–1279), and in Japan became the prevailing school of Buddhism by the fourteenth century. It even survived the so-called dark ages of Japan, when the native Shinto religion was almost forgotten altogether.

The goal of Zen is satori, or enlightenment. Satori is a new understanding, an intuitive lightning flash of insight into the true nature of existence. This insight bypasses all our ordinary logical or analytical ways of looking at things. The way to satori is through *zazen,* or sitting meditation. The Sixth Zen Patriarch said, "Sitting is the means to obtain absolute freedom." Through *zazen* one obtains freedom from the wild "monkey mind" that runs chattering about and reaches for the "sky-mind" of Zen emptiness. One sits in a *zendo*—a meditation hall. One of the first practices is being able to sit and count ten breaths without letting anything distract you from the exercise—no errant thoughts or feelings or states of awareness. As you might expect, this takes many months. When successful, you can go on to harder things. Personally, I was never able to get beyond "one."

Two major schools of Zen exist today (Soto and Rinzai), but both descend from the Southern Chinese Chan School, the school of sudden enlightenment.

## Soto

Soto (Ts'ao-tung) was founded by the Japanese monk Dogen (1200–1253) in 1244. He wrote the "Treasury of Knowledge of the True Law." He was originally ordained as a Tendai monk when he was thirteen, but, while on a trip to China with his teacher, discovered the Ts'ao-tung school of Chan. Dogen established the Japanese version in 1236.

The main emphasis of Soto practice is *zazen*—just sitting, their way of referring to meditation. This silent sitting is done for several hours a day, usually in both the morning and evening. Silence is very important, as Zen Buddhism teaches that words do more to conceal reality than to reveal it. There's definitely something to that. The goal of meditation is to achieve awareness of our oneness with the entire universe, a unity that underlies all phenomena.

### Rinzai

The other major school of Zen is Rinzai (Lin-chi), first introduced by Eisai (1141–1215) in 1191, and further developed by Hakuin Ekaku (1685–1768). Eisai had begun by studying Mahayana scriptures, but found nothing in them that would lead to enlightenment. Like the Buddha himself, he believed that liberation would not come about by reading or chanting.

Rinzai Zen uses both sitting meditation and the koan. This practice is called *sanzen.* The great popularizer of Rinzai Zen in the West was Daisetz Suzuki (1870–1966). He wrote more than twenty works in English discussing basic Zen principles and emphasizing a practical approach to Buddhism that appealed to many Americans. Contrary to what people think, however, Suzuki was not a qualified Zen master, a holder of lineage. In fact, Suzuki's *dharma* name means "great stupidity."

Suzuki never received the formal *dharma* transmission that authorizes one officially to pass on Zen teachings. In a way, this fact actually helped him spread Zen teachings to the United States, as it made him less formally bound to a particular school. Suzuki was especially important for his influence on critical European and American thinkers and artists: Alan Watts, Allen Ginsberg, Aldous Huxley, Arnold Toynbee, Carl Jung, Erich Fromm, Gary Snyder, Jack Kerouac, John Cage, Karen Horney, and Thomas Merton. Of course, as Zen developed in America, it changed in response to its new environment. The "Beat Zen" of the 1950s was a far cry from the original Japanese or orthodox American version.

Rinzai emphasizes sudden enlightenment primarily by meditating upon a koan or word puzzle. Rinzai Zen also emphasizes meditation as a means to achieve enlightenment, although it agrees that other methods are also productive, especially manual labor.

The Japanese warrior class (samurai) was particularly attracted to Zen. The ideals of sacrifice and single-pointed concentration appealed to its military spirit. The Japanese warriors thus developed

"The essence of Zen consists of acquiring a new viewpoint on life…"

—*Suzuki*

their own warrior code: *bushido,* which combines elements of Zen, Confucianism, and Shinto. The code is most famous in the West for its development of the concept of *seppuku,* or ritual suicide.

*The Koan*

The unique Zen concept of the koan originated in China during the T'ang dynasty (618–906 C.E.). A koan (*kung-an* in Chinese) is a paradoxical riddle whose "answer" will bring enlightenment, or satori. Of course, koans don't actually have any answers, which is what makes them so irritating. (Many answers to a koan are apparently neither verbal, nor sensible.) One is not supposed to think about a koan. One is supposed to experience it.

**A COMMON KOAN**

*Perhaps the most well-known koan to Americans is, "What is the sound of one hand clapping?"*

---

**ZEN BALL**

*Phil Jackson, basketball coach extraordinaire, uses Zen meditation with his players. He makes the point that in the constant flux and flow of basketball, one needs to "be in the moment" and think in the present, being always open to new possibilities. Just like life itself. To learn more about how Zen Buddhism meshes with professional basketball coaching strategies, read his book, Sacred Hoops. In this book, Jackson writes, in a paradoxical Zen strain, how his greatest challenge as a coach was to make Michael Jordan a worse player.*

---

In Rinzai Zen, the student is given a first, private koan by his abbot-master. This is called the *dharmakaya.* The most familiar of these beginner koan is this one: "A monk asks Joshu: 'Does a dog have Buddha-nature?' The student responds: 'Mu!'" (which means something negative like no or nothing). Well, that's it. It always seems to me that Joshu has already answered the riddle (even if the answer seems patently wrong), but that's just my opinion. I am not a Zen master. However, I have to give an example of my own favorite koan: "An ox walks by a window. First his head goes by, then his neck goes by, then his back goes by. Why doesn't his tail go by?" (I know the answer, but I'm not telling.)

To get the right answer, the student is supposed to meditate on the koan for many hours a day. He is also subjected to weeks of lectures about koan, which never seem to help all that much. At intervals he goes to his abbot, with his tentative answers, which are never right. This question and answer session is called *dokusan.* Then he goes back and meditates some more. The goal of all this is to get to a point called the "great doubt" a breakdown of all intellectualizing. The great doubt is followed by a "great death," wherein both body and mind are discarded. Only then does the student achieve a kind of unification with the koan. He is then enlightened. One's first enlightenment experience, *kensho,* is the process of seeing into one's own true nature. One has to be careful, however. Students who keep coming up with the wrong answers are liable to be slapped.

Several collections of classic koan exist, including *The Blue Cliff Record* and *The Gateless Barrier.*

### Zen in the West

Zen first came to the West, even if only briefly, at the World's Parliament of Religions in 1893. The emissary was Soyen Shaku, who arrived against the advice of his resident monks. "The land of the white barbarians is beneath the dignity of a Zen master," they complained, but it did them no good. Soyen Shaku came anyway.

Westerners were originally introduced to Rinzai Zen, and it was the dominant type of Zen Buddhism here for about fifty years. Nowadays, however, Soto Zen is much more popular. The famous San Francisco Zen Center is of the Soto School. The Western tradition welcomes women Zen masters, and many have achieved high positions within the movement. There's even a Zen school for gays, offered by Dorsey and Tundra Wind.

A major exponent of Zen in the West was Alan Watts (1915–1973), although he never formally accepted its teachings. Technically, he wasn't even a Buddhist, although his classic work, *The Way of Zen,* introduced millions of people to this way of thought.

Watts was born British, although he immigrated to the United States in 1936 and became a citizen in 1943. He had three wives, seven children, and a lot of fun with LSD, Timothy Leary, and Allen Ginsberg.

**ZEN MONKS**

*Another difference between Soto and Rinzai Zen is that Soto monks may marry, while Rinzai monks may not.*

## BUDDHISM AND THE ARTS IN JAPAN AND ELSEWHERE

In earliest Buddhism, there were apparently no paintings or sculptures of the Buddha—only symbols to represent him. Common symbols were the eight-spoked wheel, footprints, the lotus, and an empty throne. Actual images of the Buddha began to show up around the first century C.E. Theravadans prefer relatively simple statues of the Buddha meditating, reclining, or walking. Most are only two or three times larger than a normal human being.

Zen has had a much greater impact on Japanese art than any other Buddhist school. The purpose of all Zen art is to restore the mind to its original union with true reality.

### Poetry and Prose

A haiku is a poem that can be said in a single breath. (Considering the importance of breathing in Buddhist thought, this is fairly significant.) The classical haiku has seventeen syllables arranged in three lines of five, seven, and five syllables respectively. (This works pretty well in Japanese, but English doesn't break down this way very easily.) Traditionally, haiku were composed by wandering priests. Today this style of poetry is closely associated with Zen. Each haiku contains a "season" word and captures the essence of the passing moment. The greatest classical haiku poet was Basho (1644–1694) whose masterpiece was a poem about a frog jumping into a pond. It's not the *Iliad,* but one can do only so much in three lines, for example:

> The rattling bright wings
> Quick Autumn's pure sky moving
> Season of pheasants

Haiku has influenced such Western writers as Ezra Pound, e.e. cummings, Hilda Doolittle (H. D.), William Carlos Williams, and me (see previous sample). Buddhism (though not Zen in particular) also influenced Beat writers such as Jack Kerouac, Lawrence Ferlinghetti, and Allen Ginsberg, and later writers like Gary Snyder.

### Tea Ceremony

The Japanese tea ceremony *(sado)* originated in 1286. The founder is Shomei, a monk who imported the beverage and all its associated utensils. It is a Zen invention, and tea is considered a stimulus to meditation. Originally, like so much else in Japan, it came from China, where tea was used both as a medicine and as a means for keeping the monks up all night to meditate. The first tea master was the Zen monk Sen no Rikyu (1522–1591).

"In walking, just walk. In sitting, just sit. Above all, don't wobble."

—*Yun-men*

Ideally, the ceremony should be performed in a rustic teahouse *(chahitsu)* located in a garden *(roji)*, and approached by a stone path. Guests wash their hands in a stone basin and kneel at an alcove decorated with a scroll and flower arrangement. The tea should be drunk slowly with enjoyment. The green tea is served in simple but beautiful cups *(chawan)* of traditional design. The most popular are the black and red cups from Kyoto. Sweet cakes are also served, to "balance" the tea flavor. During the tea ceremony, conversation is strictly limited to talking about the tea, the cups, and the other objects in the teahouse. That keeps everyone calm.

Although the tea ceremony basically developed from Buddhist philosophy, it is now considered one of the arts in Japan and has no particular religious associations.

### Ceramics

Zen has also inspired the art of ceramics. The studied aim is to create objects of art that are natural and "spontaneous" looking. Of course, this is a lot harder than just pouring the stuff into a mold, but that's the way it is. In fact, aficionados prefer cups with cracks, bubbled glazes, and other "imperfections."

### Architecture and Statuary

The multistoried pagoda may be the most familiar type of Buddhist architecture, although stupas are more common outside China and Japan. Stupas are commemorative dome-shaped monuments originally designed in ancient India. There is a list of eight shrines that are singled out for special veneration. The earlier ones contain physical remains of, or objects used by, the Buddha or another holy person.

One famous stupa in Thailand reportedly contains a bone chip of the Buddha, carried there by a sacred white elephant. Pilgrims need to walk up 290 steps to get close to it.

Later stupas contain symbolic objects associated with Buddha, often tablets inscribed with these words: "The *Tathagata* has explained the cause of all things that arise from a cause. He has also explained their cessation."

Many Buddhist temples are guarded by stone lions—which resemble Pekinese more than lions. (Indeed, the Peke is known as

**THE DRAMA OF ZEN**

*Zen is the underlying influence behind the Japanese Noh plays, the classical theatre of Japan.*

the lion-dog of China.) These are famous *karashishi* and originally adorned Shinto shrines. The lion on the right, with his mouth open, is the male lion, the closed-mouth lion is the lioness. They symbolize life and strength.

Statues and paintings of the Buddha are everywhere in Buddhist countries, and they carry specific meanings. One of the most famous, a reclining Buddha in Bangkok, is a hugely popular tourist attraction. All statues of the Buddha are richly symbolic. The long ears of the Buddha are signs of his great wisdom, while his topknot symbolizes his higher consciousness.

In some areas, Buddhist statues dot the roadways, and worshippers often bring flowers and other offerings to celebrate the Buddha. For many, an image of the Buddha is a meditation aid, and looking at the image helps the subject recall the good qualities of the Buddha and strive to emulate him. There used to be some immense statues of the Buddha in Afghanistan, but they were blown up by the Taliban in 2001.

## Gardening

In Japan, garden architects are considered artists on a level with poets and painters. Buddhist gardening principles developed in China from traditional Chinese garden symbolism. In this system, natural objects symbolized gods. During the Han dynasty, the imperial garden in Chang'an was created to symbolize the entire Chinese nation. It supposedly had at least one sample of every native plant and included an artificial "ocean" (just a lake really) ringed by rocks (which symbolized mountains).

Gardens are an extremely important element in Japanese Buddhism. Some of the most popular ones are made of sand and rock rather than earth and flowers. The most famous Japanese garden is the rock garden at Ryoan-ji in Kyoto. It doesn't look like much compared to, say, a formal Italian garden, being just five clumps of boulders set in white gravel. Some of the boulders have moss on them, though.

You also can buy miniature "Zen gardens" consisting of some small rocks lined up on a little surface set on a long rectangular frame. They're designed to be enjoyed indoors, so the rocks are moss-free.

**BRINGING THE GARDEN INDOORS**

*Ikebana is the Japanese art of flower arrangement. The word means "living flower," and the art traces back to the composition of temple offerings.*

## CHAPTER RECAP

- Buddhism came to Japan in the sixth century.

- Japanese Buddhism combines elements of Chinese Buddhism, Confucianism, and native Shinto Japanese traditions.

- Some of the more important Japanese Buddhist schools are Tendai, Shingon, Jodo, Nichiren, and Zen.

- Soto Zen emphasizes zazen (sitting meditation), but Rinzai Zen also uses koans (riddles) to help practitioners achieve enlightenment.

- Zen Buddhism has had extraordinary influence on Japanese art.

- Zen Buddhism has become extremely popular in the West.

*Recommended Reading*

Anesake, Masaharu. *Nichiren, The Buddhist Prophet.* Magnolia, MA: Peter Smith Publisher, Inc., 1966.

Dumoulin, Heinrich. *Zen Buddhism: A History.* Trans. James W. Heisig and Paul Knitter. New York: Macmillan Publishing, Inc., 1988.

Fields, Rick. *How Swans Came to Lake: A Narrative History of Buddhism in America.* Boston: Shambhala Publications, 1992.

Foster, Nelson and Jack Shoemaker, eds. *The Roaring Storm: A New Zen Reader.* 1996.

Grimstone, A. V. ed. *Two Zen Classics: Mumonkan and Hekiganroku.* Trans. Katsuki Sekida. New York: John Weatherhill, 1977.

Inanda, Kenneth and Nolan P. Jacobson, eds. *Buddhism and American Thinkers.* 1983.

Moorale, Don, ed. *Buddhist America: Centers, Retreats, Practices.* Santa Fe, NM: John Muir Publications, 1988.

Reischauer, August Karl. *Studies in Japanese Buddhism.* New York: AMS Press, Inc., 1970.

Ryokan. *One Robe, One Bowl: The Zen Poetry of Ryokan.* Ed. John Stevens. New York: Weatherhill, 1987.

Statler, Oliver. *Japanese Pilgrimage.* New York: William Morrow & Co., Inc., 1983.

Suzuki, D. T. *Essays in Zen Buddhism.* New York: Grove Press, 1961.

————. *Manual of Zen Buddhism.* New York: Grove Press, 1960.

————. *Zen and Japanese Culture.* Princeton, NJ: Princeton University Press, 1973.

Tanabe, George J., and Willa Jane Tanabe. *The Lotus Sutra in Japanese Culture.* Honolulu: University of Hawaii Press, 1989.

Tonkinson, Carole, ed. *Big Sky Mind: Buddhism and the Beat Generation.* New York: Riverhead Books, 1995.

Tuck, Donald R. *Buddhist Churches of America.* Lewiston, NY: Edwin Mellon Press, 1987.

Tworkov, Helen. *Zen in America.* New York: Kodansha International, 1994.

*Recommended Audiotapes*
Herrigel, Eugen. *Zen in the Art of Archery.* Los Angeles: Renaissance Media. Inc., 1990.

Suzuki, D. T. *What Is Zen?* Los Angeles: Renaissance Media, Inc., 1995.

Watts, Alan. *Zen Practice, Zen Art.* Los Angeles: Renaissance Media, Inc., 1989.

# *Confucianism—*
# *The Power of Virtue*

Confucianism is a Western term for an Eastern tradition. The Chinese, in keeping with their scholarly turn of mind, call it *ju chia*, which means "school of the learned ones." To some people, Confucianism isn't a religion at all, for it doesn't deal directly with the spiritual or metaphysical realm. For example, when someone asked Confucius about death, he responded, "I don't even know about life—how can I talk about death?"

*Coins of the I Ching*

Although Confucius avoided discussing metaphysical things, Confucianism is more than just a humanistic philosophy. In the first place, Confucianism has absorbed many spiritual beliefs from Taoism, Buddhism, and ancient folk practice. Secondly, religion deals with this world as well as the other world. The whole question of whether or not Confucianism is a religion is a Western quibble that Easterners wouldn't bother with. Westerners often confuse "religion" with "church." On the other hand, philosophy is too a dry a word to describe Confucianism, which provides important ethical and ceremonial guidelines for living. As Confucius said, "The true moral law is not something far from the actuality of human life."

Confucianism is long on practice and short on theory. It has an almost pathological horror of abstractions. It has produced a pragmatic code for getting along in this world, a world that Confucians find enjoyable and worthwhile. That fact, more than any other, sets this Chinese-born religion apart from the Indian traditions of Hinduism and Buddhism, which emphasize getting out of this existence rather than getting along in it.

Confucianism deals with earthly problems that Buddhism avoids and Hinduism ignores, but which most people find pressing: What's the proper function of the government? How can families get along? How is society best run? Confucianism gives definitive answers to these concerns, which have shaped generations of Chinese people. This makes it important. One cannot possibly comprehend the Chinese without learning about Confucianism. In addition, Confucian influence has spread well beyond China; its principles are also honored throughout east Asia, especially in Japan, Korea, and Vietnam.

As a "this-worldly tradition," Confucianism is both sophisticated and civilized. More than perhaps any other religion, it pays honor to the human person and to the society we create. Confucianism doesn't aim at producing saints, hermits, priests, or magicians, but rather responsible family men and women, noble scholars, wise rulers, and prosperous subjects. It doesn't concern itself with transcendental beings, with past or future lives, or with arcane riddles. It disdains austerities and embraces the world. Like all Chinese traditions, Confucianism honors the idea of balance and harmony. Nature and cultivation, person and society, life and death, each has its place, and each is dependent upon the other. Society cannot exist without individuals, and individuals must come together to form a society. (A group of hermits meditating in the wilderness does not comprise a society, in the Chinese view.) A society, whether in the family, neighborhood, or nation, is where we live, grow, and learn. Confucians believe that to construct a peaceful, harmonious, and cultivated society is the highest goal we can achieve in this life.

# Essential Chinese Religious Concepts

*C*hinese religion did not begin with Confucius (552?–479 B.C.E.); it reaches far back into prehistory. As far as we can tell, though, the keystone of Confucian religion, the family, was also the basis of ancient Chinese religious practice.

The family makes itself felt in everything from the most elegant Confucianism to a primitive kind of ancestor worship. Although officially ignored or even denounced by Taoist, Confucian, and Buddhist intellectuals, folk religion held sway in China among the people right alongside the more "orthodox" traditions. Its values are the traditional ones of good health, long life, many children, and avoidance of disaster.

## THE HEAVENLY GOD AND THE CULT OF HEAVEN

The earliest Chinese, like most ancient peoples, were polytheistic folk who worshipped many spirits. The most important of these was Shang Ti, or sometimes simply T'ien, which means "heaven," or even "sky."

Interestingly enough, Shang Ti, although he rules heaven, is not considered the creator of the earth. He was honored during the early Shang dynasty (c. 1766–c. 1122 B.C.E.). In fact, many scholars

ANCIENT RELIGION
TODAY

*Traditional Chinese beliefs
are held much more strongly
today in non-Communist
Taiwan and Hong Kong than
in China itself.*

think Shang Ti was originally an ancestor of an important or royal family, perhaps the mythical Jade Emperor. At any rate, all Chinese emperors were called Sons of Heaven.

The Chinese thought of heaven as a place remarkably similar to the fabulous earthly court of the emperor—or perhaps it was the other way around; the emperor designed his court with an eye to his vision of heaven.

The Chou dynasty (c. 1122–265 B.C.E.) discarded the Shang Ti concept of the Shang rulers. They substituted their own idea of heaven (T'ien), a more impersonal divinity than Shang Ti. Sometimes, and even more abstractly, the word *tao* was used to refer to heaven, and the heavenly order was the *T'ien Tao.* Earthly emperors were expected to follow the way of tao themselves—their conduct was the *Wang Tao,* or royal way.

The major deities included gods of the stars, gods of the five regions (north, south, east, west, and center), nature gods, domestic gods, and divine patrons of the arts.

## HONORING ANCESTORS

The cult of one's ancestors is extremely ancient, going back as far as archaeology will take us. In early days, ancestor worship took place in temples, but later it occurred at the graveside, or in the homes of the family. Because China was a patrilineal society, the wife married into the husband's ancestors, so to speak. The Chinese did not pay veneration, however, to any but their own ancestors, feeling very rightly that it was hard enough to keep track of one's own forebears, let alone anyone else's. (Ancestral spirits might be found in three places—the ancestral home, the cemetery, or the temple.) The ancient Chinese set up shrines to ancestors, but that doesn't mean they worshipped them, precisely. It meant they respected and honored them.

Because of the great respect in which ancestors were held, Chinese genealogies are often very exact, particularly those of prominent families, like Confucius's. All of his descendants are documented right down to the present day, where they live in Taiwan. They are even accorded a title of nobility.

Although they didn't worship them, the Chinese felt that dead ancestors had the power to influence living family members and that the living could provide for the needs of the dead. (This is an early instance of the Chinese principle of reciprocity, which crops up over and over in all their philosophic thought.)

The Chinese paid homage to their ancestors in three ways: the funeral, the mourning period, and the continuing sacrifices. Each of these practices has two purposes—first to help the deceased and second to console (or protect) the living. Confucian rules provided for five degrees of mourning, and the greatest mourning was reserved for one's father. Death sacrifices, of course, are of very ancient origin; they were performed both by designated priests and by appropriate family members.

MORE MIX 'N MATCH

*Even Confucian Chinese use Buddhist and Taoist priests for funeral ceremonies. Death rites may last as long as seven weeks, at least for rich people. For the poor, it takes only two or three days.*

## HONORING EMPERORS

Closely allied to ancestor veneration is the great respect in which the emperor (the Son of Heaven) was held. Emperors were supposed to possess a special virtue *(tao)* that enabled them to perform remarkable feats of magic. The legendary emperor Yü, for example, drained the rivers when they threatened to flood the country by making an opening in the mountains for them to flow through. Obviously this is no job for an ordinary mortal. And Yü was not an ordinary mortal; he had no mother and was born directly from his dad. (His father had been lying around dead and rotting for about three years, though.) Yü could also change himself into a bear at will.

## HOUSEHOLD GODS AND ANCIENT DEMONS

In ancient Chinese religion, which predates both Taoism and Confucianism, the universe is populated by a raft of invisible, yet very real beings from the spirit world. Most, but not all, of these spirits were those of human beings. (This includes the ancestors, of course.)

Many of these entities were continually in a temper, usually because someone had forgotten or short-changed them on their sacrifices. Much early Chinese religion was oriented to keeping these spirit beings at bay. They erected "spirit walls" to keep them out of the house, sounded gongs or made other loud noises to frighten them, consulted various oracles, burned incense, and prayed like mad.

The benevolent spirits in ancient Chinese folk religion were deemed *shen,* while the evil demons were *kuei.* The *kuei* caused all kinds of problems, including madness and smallpox, but women in childbirth and tiny children are especially at risk from them.

**DEMON DETERRENT**

*The Chinese invented fire-crackers to scare off demons.*

## MEDIUMS

Ancient Chinese tradition also made use of mediums, persons who had cultivated such occult powers as communicating with the dead and speaking in tongues. Mediums are still popular in Chinese cultures, and people consult them for a variety of reasons, usually relating to sickness, bad luck, and evil spirit possession. Other problems on the top ten medium-consultancy list were: wayward spouses, childbirth requests, financial advice, gambling tips, problem children, insanity, and communication with the dearly departed.

## YIN AND YANG

Although both Taoism and Confucianism make abundant use of yin/yang symbology, the concept stretches back to more than a thousand years before the birth of Confucius or Lao Tzu. The concept of yin and yang is basic to both Confucianism and Taoism. These two traditions, which seem so antithetical in so many ways, both adhere to the idea of a fundamental dynamic interchange between complementary forces. That is what reality is made of, and that's how the universe works—through natural cycles.

Although commonly misunderstood, these words do not refer to good and evil. They are complementary, not opposite ideas. Both are absolutely necessary to the smooth functioning of the human being, the family, the country, and the cosmos itself. Yang represents the forces that are hot, male, dry, and light, while yin represents the female forces: dark, mysterious, feminine, and moist. The yang is logic, the yin is poetry. The yang is the sun, the yin is the moon. Each needs the other, another example of Chinese reciprocity and harmony.

## I CHING

The I Ching (Yi Jing) is part of the very ancient Chinese system of divination—the means whereby one can both read the future and keep in touch with the ancestors. Early techniques of divination involved reading bones and tortoise shells.

The I Ching is essential for a basic understanding of Chinese religion, for its philosophy pervades both Taoism and Confucianism. In fact, Confucius is reported to have said that had he had fifty more years of life, he would have devoted them to a study of the I Ching; that way, he said he would have avoided many errors. As it was, Confucius wrote ten commentaries to the ancient system; they are called the "Ten Wings" of the I Ching. These appendices, by the way, are what give philosophical significance to what at first was simply a means of foretelling the future.

The original system of I Ching is thousands of years old; it first consisted of eight "trigrams." Legend says it was first conceived during the reign of the mythical emperor Fu Hsi (c. 2852 B.C.E.). Those who maintain that Fu Hsi was not mythical must account for the fact that he had the body of a snake.

The trigrams are a combination of three broken *(yin-yao)* and/or solid lines *(yang-yao)*. Sometimes the solid lines are called "hard" lines *(kang)* and the broken lines are "soft" *(jo)*. Each trigram represents one of the eight basic elements in creation: heaven (three solid lines), earth (three broken lines), thunder (two broken, one solid), water (broken, solid, broken), mountain (solid, broken, broken), wind (solid, solid, broken), fire (solid, broken, solid), and marshes (broken, solid, solid). Don't ask me how the thunder got in.

Eventually the eight turned into thirty-two, then, into sixty-four different combinations or hexagrams. Properly read, they represent everything that can happen in the universe, but the I Ching is more than just a way of reading the universe. In some mysterious way, the I Ching, properly cast, can also influence future events, not just foretell them. Some of the hexagrams represent personal attributes, while others indicate family relationships.

King Wen, founder of the Chou dynasty (c. 1143 B.C.E.) doubled the trigrams into hexagrams, thus giving the I Ching twice the number of available symbols. In 213 B.C.E., however, the Emperor Ch'in ordered the I Ching to be burned, along with its

**NATURE WORSHIP**

*The ancient Chinese lived under the powerful and not always benevolent forces of nature. Floods, famines, earthquakes, bitter cold, and steamy heat controlled their lives. It was only natural that the powerful forces of nature should be incorporated into Chinese religious understanding.*

**THE EIGHT
TRIGRAMS OF
THE I CHING**

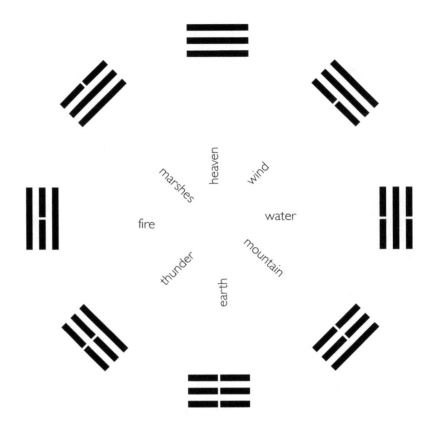

heaven

wind

marshes

water

fire

thunder

mountain

earth

**THE I CHING ABROAD**

*The I Ching did not reach the
West until the nineteenth
century, when it was translated first into German, and
then into English. The noted
psychoanalyst Carl Jung
showed great interest in it.*

commentaries. This was the infamous Fire of Ch'in. Fortunately, some copies survived.

The basic theory behind I Ching is this: Human fate is largely dependent on cosmic principles. To be successful, one should understand the order of the universe, then one can alter one's conduct accordingly.

The combination used for any reading is random, depending upon the throwing of three coins or fifty yarrow sticks. You can't use just any old coins or yarrow sticks you have lying around the house, however; they must be ritually purified first. In any case, using yarrow sticks to consult the I Ching is a complicated routine, properly performed only by an expert. (For one thing, yarrow sticks aren't so easy to come by as they might be.) The inquirer faces south and throws forty-nine yarrow sticks through incense while asking her question (one stick is kept aside). Most people just throw coins. In any case, the answer is never crystal clear.

Like Western Tarot cards, the I Ching doesn't give direct answers to questions; it merely suggests possibilities, leaving it up to the inquirer to choose the right one.

## MARTIAL ARTS

Although the martial arts are often associated with Japan and Korea, they were developed by the Chinese. The true founder, you will recall, is reputed to have been Bodhidharma, the missionary monk from India, who arrived in China around 520 c.e. He invented Kung Fu, a style of boxing. Later on, another Chinese monk, this one a Taoist, invented a "soft" or internal form of Kung Fu. The original "hard" Kung Fu supposedly has a special "death touch" *(dim mak)*. If this blow is applied, the victim will feel nothing—at first. Then he gets sick and dies.

## FIVE ELEMENTS

In the ancient Chinese metaphysics, the world is composed of Five Elements *(wu hsing):* water, fire, earth, metal, and wood. Interestingly, one of the Five Elements is alive (wood). What ties them all together is ch'i, which means energy or air. The word *hsing* is a verb meaning "to act." It is typical of Chinese religion that the basic "units" of reality are conceived as actions rather than as "blocks" of some inert substance. Thus, the "elements" are powerful and active. Water can conquer fire, and fire can conquer wood.

### Ch'i Gong

*Ch'i Gong (Qi Gong)* means "to work on *ch'i* (energy)" and is a combination of breath exercises, posture, and movement. There are three forms: Buddhist *Ch'i Gong,* Taoist *Ch'i Gong,* and Medical *Ch'i Gong.*

### Feng Shui

The term *feng shui* literally means "wind and water" and is the traditional art of situating buildings, graves, and cities at the most favorable locations, where they will receive beneficial energy. The most important forces to be aware of are the yin and yang.

---

**TIMELESS T'AI CHI**

*Something similar to t'ai chi was supposedly practiced by Huang Ti, the Yellow Emperor, back in 2700 B.C.E. The Yellow Emperor, on the advice of sages, devised an exercise program that not only granted him good health and peace of mind, but also made him immortal.*

**FORTUNE COOKIES**

*Fortune cookies are a Western invention that have nothing to do with Confucianism or any Chinese religion. I just thought you might like to know.*

In feng shui, the yin is symbolized by a white tiger, while the yang is an azure dragon. These, in turn, stand for the cardinal points of East and West. If you want a lucky spot, the tiger should be to the right, and the dragon to the left. The angle of their meeting is the ideal spot to situate a building. This is only the broadest generality, of course. You have to watch for other features as well, including which way the water is flowing.

Each of the so-called Five Elements has its place in space: wood in the east, fire in the south, metal in the west, water in the north, and earth in the center. One should take all these things into consideration.

In general, curved lines are favored over straight ones. Bad influences can to some degree be corrected by creating a pond on your property, the water of which will absorb toxic elements in the surroundings. Long winding paths to your doorway will also help keep away malign influences.

## CHAPTER RECAP

- Chinese religion did not begin with Confucius; he worked with a long-established tradition.

- Early Chinese worship included veneration of heaven, household gods, and ancestors.

- The ancient I Ching was used for divination purposes.

- The Chinese believed the world was composed of two complementary forces: yin and yang.

- Many other Chinese ideas, including the Five Elements, *Ch'i Gong,* feng shui, and the martial arts are blended into Confucianism.

*Recommended Reading*

Chang, Wing-tsit. *A Sourcebook in Chinese Philosophy.* Princeton, NJ: Princeton University Press, 1963.

Giles, Herbert A. *Religions of Ancient China.* Nashville: TN: Abingdon Press, 1970.

Kates, George. *The Years That Were Fat.* Cambridge, MA: MIT Press, 1960.

Moore, Charles. *The Chinese Mind.* Honolulu: University Press of Hawaii, 1974.

Smith, Howard. *Chinese Religions.* Austin, TX: Holt, Rhinehart and Winston, 1968.

Thompson, Laurence, G. *Chinese Religion.* Third Ed. Belmont, CA: Wadsworth, 1979.


*Recommended Audiotape*
Cohen, Kenneth. *The Way of Qigong.* Los Angeles: Renaissance Media, Inc., 1997.

# The Life of Confucius, the Master Teacher

Confucianism, of course, would be nowhere without Confucius (552?–479 B.C.E.). His importance lies in the fact that he was the first Chinese philosopher to develop a systematic, complete philosophy, much as Plato did for the West at about the same time.

Our best sources for the life of Confucius are the Analects (written by Confucius, supposedly) and the Mencius (written by Mencius). We know more about Confucius than about many other religious founders, but still not nearly enough.

## THE CHILDHOOD OF CONFUCIUS

Confucius was born in a poor but noble family in the small, but culturally with-it state of Lu (modern Ch'u Fu in Shantung) during the Chou dynasty.

Family tradition says that they were descended from the royal family of Shang; this is probably about as reliable as family traditions usually are. By the time Confucius was born, however, the family, whatever their origins, had come down in the world.

The time of Confucius's birth was one of great conflict and disruption, known in Chinese annals as the Spring-Autumn period *(Ch'un Ch'iu),* from 722–481 B.C.E. The Chou empire was beginning to collapse, and China was not really a single nation but a collection

CONFUCIANS SAY

*Confucius's Chinese name
isn't Confucius at all—it's
K'ung Fu-Tzu (Master
Kung). The word Confucius
is a latinized form of that
name given to him by Jesuit
missionaries in the
seventeenth century.*

of feudal states (and states feuding). As one might expect, the period immediately following it was called the period of Warring States (480–222 B.C.E.), when there was a complete breakdown in the political system. It's probable that living in this chaotic state made Confucius acutely aware of the importance of order in both personal and political affairs.

Confucius's soldier-father, K'ung Shu Liang-heh, died when Confucius was but a wee lad of three years. This made things that much harder for his mother, especially because she may never have been quite legally married to Confucius's father. One night before he was born, Confucian tradition tells us that his mother went into a cave and prayed for a son. The Black Emperor deity appeared to her and granted her wish. Just to make sure, however, when the time came, she decided to give birth in that very same cave. (She had to race to get there.) She baptized her newborn in a warm spring that gushed from the mouth of the cave.

Whether she was pleased with the appearance of her son is another matter. It is rumored that he was an exceptionally ugly baby with a big head. Chronicles of his life tell us that he had a wide mouth and the lips of an ox. It is also reported that he had a "dragon's back," whatever that is, a bulging forehead, and teeth like a rabbit.

Despite her poverty, Confucius's mother never faltered in her efforts to give her son the best possible education. This was probably because she knew he was special.

At any rate, Confucius was a strange child. The legends say that his favorite childhood games were imitating sacred rites, rearranging ceremonial vessels, and taking on various ceremonial postures.

His more conventional hobbies included riding in chariots, playing the lute, and practicing archery, all very gentlemanly pastimes, both then and now.

## CONFUCIUS'S EARLY WORK

Confucius's mother died when he was about twenty-three years old. During the prescribed three-year period of mourning, he studied ancient ceremonial texts and political institutions. When he was ready to enter the world again, Confucius began life as a teacher. (Before that he had served as a director of agricultural works. It is said that the cattle thrived.)

At age nineteen he married a woman from the state of Sung, and the couple had a son and a daughter, at least. When the son was born, the local ruler sent Confucius a congratulatory present of two carp. Confucius was so moved by this present that he named his son Carp (Li) in honor of it.

Because nothing in the historical record is stated about Confucius's wife, scholars have pretty much decided that the marriage was a failure. There isn't any evidence for this though. In fact, there's no evidence one way or another. Therefore, I feel equally confident in stating that Confucius and his wife had a lovely and harmonious relationship, which would have been in keeping with his own teachings.

I am somewhat more concerned by the fact that he married off his daughter to a certain Kung-yeh Ch'ang, who happened to be in jail at the time. "He's a good person at heart," insisted Confucius, "and it's not as if he's done anything really wrong." What the crimes of Kung-yeh Ch'ang were are never stated.

Confucius's great desire in life was to be a powerful government official, for he believed that if only he were given the authority, he could turn society around and make it comfortable and happy, but he knew that his own life and that the welfare of society also depended upon Providence.

At one time early in his career, Confucius was invited by Duke Chou to visit his imperial capital, Lo. It was a fateful trip, for there Confucius, in addition to studying many learned texts, was bitten by the political bug. Unfortunately, he was never able to gain a really important office, but he kept trying. He also became convinced while there that the study of the past was the key to understanding the present. "As we use a mirror to reflect the forms of things, so we study antiquity to understand the present," he said.

Confucius's life was one great search. In his Analects, he wrote: "At fifteen, I set my heart on learning. At thirty I became firm. At forty I had no more doubts. At fifty I understood Heaven's will. At sixty, my ears were attuned to this Will. At seventy I could follow my heart's desires, and know they were right." To live one's life so that the heart's desires are in accord with what is right is a wonderful

"I was not born with possession of knowledge, but being fond of antiquity, I ardently pursue it."

—*Confucius*

thing. So much of the time it seems that the heart's desires are not *at all* in accord with what is right.

Chinese writings contain many praises of Confucius's character. He was considered pleasant and good-natured, not hidebound or opinionated, no matter what the Taoists said. It is also reported that he never sang on a day in which he had earlier been crying. However, it must also be said that he complained from time to time that no one except heaven understood him. This is probably true.

**CULTURES CLASH**

*Confucius's rival, Lao Tzu, used to complain that Confucius spent too much time talking about dead men.*

## CONFUCIUS'S TEACHINGS

Confucius considered himself more a transmitter of culture and tradition than an original thinker, but he was both. And he wasn't just being modest. In the Chinese tradition, there was no great commendation attached to original thinking. It was better, thought the Chinese, to be in accord with the teachings of the great scholars of the old days. They knew what they were talking about. The most revered teachers guarded past teachings like great treasures. In fact, the more completely you could clothe new ideas in the cloak of the past, the more likely you were to have your ideas accepted. And Confucius excelled at this art. In fact, he managed to collect and organize hundreds of years of philosophical tradition into a coherent whole. His precepts have been followed for nearly three thousand years, and that's nothing to sneeze at.

Moreover, before Confucius, the treasure chest of Chinese literature, history, and philosophy was scattered about and unsystematized. Confucius's task in assimilating, ordering, and making sense of it all was enormous.

### Political Theory

Probably because of the political turmoil of his times, Confucius was a strong advocate of order in society. The way to obtain order, he believed, was for everyone to do his appointed job. This all sounds very much like the Hindu caste system, and indeed there are some similarities. It's a reasonable position, also. One cannot very well make out a case for an orderly society to come about by people *not* doing their appointed jobs. He was also probably the first person in history to advocate a one-world government, which he called a Great Commonwealth.

First, he said, there would be small and warring states. Then, there would be many peaceful, advanced states. Finally, everyone would see the light and form the Grand Commonwealth, a true utopia. Confucius described this world as one where brotherhood, honesty, and compassion would reign supreme. All the men would have good jobs, and the women would have nice homes. Doors could remain unlocked because banditry and theft would disappear. Despite all this fine talk, Confucius retained a realistic side. He said that one of the three essentials of good government were adequate arms (the other two being plenty of food and the confidence *(hsin)* of the populace). The last was the most important of all.

### Economic Theory

Money was essential too, but the most critical thing about funds was not their abundance, but their fair distribution. It does seem true that poverty is less grating on people's nerves than the perception of inequity. "Where there is harmony," he wrote, "there will be no complaint of shortage. Where there is contentment, there will be no rebellion."

## CONFUCIUS AS CIVIL SERVANT

In 517 B.C.E. or so, Confucius made a trip to the dukedom of Ch'i, just north of his own state of Lu. He was actually trying to get a government job there, but Duke Ching didn't offer one, so Confucius went home. While there, however, Confucius became enamored of shao music, reputedly composed by the Emperor Shun (2255?–2205 B.C.E.). He was so impressed with it that he couldn't taste his food for three months. At least, that's what he said.

At long last Confucius got his wish to be in charge. He was made chief magistrate, then chief justice, of Cheng-tu, which wasn't a whole province, just a town, but at least it was something. Legend has it that things just blossomed under Confucius's wise leadership. Everybody not only had enough to eat, but followed the correct diet for his or her individual needs. Sexual morality reached such a high level that men and women walked on opposite sides of the street. Merchants became completely honest. (Apparently, before this time, shepherds would load their sheep up with water to make them heavier before bringing them to market.)

In 497 B.C.E., however, Confucius quit his job. The proximate reason was that the Duke of Lu neglected to send Confucius an adequate portion of the spring ceremonial sacrifice. But Confucius took it as one sign among many others that the Duke was simply not attending properly to business. Confucius walked out of Lu, and took some hand-picked students with him. He wandered for fourteen years.

"Study without thought is vain; thought without study is dangerous."

—*Confucius*

## THE WANDERING SCHOLAR

It was as an educator that Confucius really shone. He accepted all worthy and capable students (male, of course), without regard for money or social position. His only requirement was that they should be possessed of intellectual curiosity. He divided them into four groups: those noted for their virtue, those skilled in speechifying, those adept in literature, and those knowledgeable in the ways of government.

Legend has it that he taught three thousand students altogether, but only seventy-two can be named with any certainty. And what did he teach? Primarily ethics, music, history, poetry, and ceremonial rites. Each discipline had a particular reason for being included in his curriculum. He believed that poetry was a moral force. It taught "ideals." Music restrained desire and was a "civilizing" force. History held a mirror up to the present. Ceremony regulated the mind and controlled conduct.

Contrary to common belief, Confucius didn't encourage people to accept his teaching without question. He wanted his students to think for themselves. He once wrote, "There are people who act without knowing why. But I am not one of them." He wasn't much of a debater, either. He lost a famous verbal duel with Lao Tzu, often credited with founding Taoism, but even ordinary people could outwit him. Whenever anybody asked him a hard question, he either wouldn't answer, got confused, or asked heaven to help him.

Despite his talents as a teacher, Confucius's real, never-ending desire was to be in control of the country. He thought that if only he had one good chance to run things, everything would get straightened out. It would never happen.

He wandered around, looking for some state where his advice would be welcome. The results were predictable. He first applied at the dukedom of Wei, but the duke preferred the company of his concubine. Another ruler, the minister of Sung, sent out an armed band to kill him. He and his students almost starved to death when they got lost in the wilderness. Another time, the citizens of the province of Kuang tried to kill him, mistaking him for somebody else, they said later. The Taoists made fun of him. Confucius tried not to let any of this bother him, but it had to hurt. He went about, he said, "living on coarse rice and simple vegetables. His only pillow was his bent arm." But he claimed to be happy nevertheless.

## OLD AGE AND DEATH

Confucius's life was in many ways sad and disappointing. He lost his only son, Yen Yuan, in 482 B.C.E. The following year, he lost his favorite student, Yen Hui. The funeral of the son is briefly discussed in the Analects. Apparently, it was custom for a loved child to be provided with both an inner and outer coffin. However, Confucius was a little short on funds and could apparently afford only an inner one. It was suggested that Confucius sell his carriage in order to pay for the outer coffin, but Confucius countered sensibly that in that case he, Confucius, would have had to walk, which was undignified.

One night he dreamed of his own death. These words came to him: "The great mountain crumbles. The strong man breaks. The sage withers away." He decided not to get up that day and died a week later. He was seventy-three years old and was buried at Chu-fu, his native town. His loyal disciples stayed for three years in the area, mourning his death.

Perhaps the gatekeeper of Shi-mên spoke Confucius's most telling epitaph: "Confucius? Isn't he the man who is always undertaking something even though he knows what he does is in vain?" Indeed.

## CHAPTER RECAP

- Confucius was an ugly baby born in poverty to an unwed mother.

- Confucius's great and unfulfilled desire in life was to obtain a high governmental post where his advice would be heeded.

- Like Buddha and Jesus, Confucius spent most of his life as a wandering teacher.

- Confucius considered himself a transmitter of culture rather than a creator of new ideas.

*Recommended Reading*

Confucius. *The Analects.* Trans. D. C. Lau. New York: Penguin USA, 1979.

Fingarette, Herebert. *Confucius—The Secular as Sacred.* New York: Harper and Row, 1972.

# *Confucian Values*

*C*onfucian values are the values of family, society, and culture. Although Confucius acknowledges that Heaven's Mandate is the ultimate guiding principle, he focuses his teaching on what that means in the real world of work, relationships, and responsibility. The primary concern is not our relationship with an overarching Heaven, but with our fellow human beings close at hand.

## CONFUCIAN ETHICS

The values of any religious system are expressed in its ethical theory, and here Confucianism is more richly endowed than almost any other tradition. The great thing about Confucianism is its attention to detail, and its ethical teachings seem to cover almost every conceivable situation.

### *Reciprocity*

The real key of Confucian values is the concept of reciprocity *(shu)*. "Do not do unto others what you would not have them do unto you" (Analects 15.23). This is merely the negative side of the Golden Rule. Many people think a negative formation like this gives people a wider margin for acceptable behavior, because it simply asks one to refrain from doing harm.

**ETHICAL TRIVIA**

*Jen is sometimes spelled ren, nowadays. However it's spelled, though, it is pronounced "run."*

For instance, let's say you want your Uncle Albert to give you a puppy. According to the Western version of the Golden Rule, you should give *him* one. (Maybe he'd take the hint.) It's very likely, however, that uncle Albert doesn't want a puppy. (With any luck he might give it back to you, but if he did he would be violating the Golden Rule, Western style.) Following the Eastern Golden Rule, you wouldn't get a puppy from Uncle Albert, because he doesn't want one, but at least you wouldn't be any worse off than you were before.

On the other hand, not giving a kid a lollipop because you wouldn't want one yourself isn't very nice either. Of course, this is too narrow an interpretation of this important rule, which is based on the universally held principle of reciprocity—the foundation of justice systems everywhere. Still, it appears to me that all principles based in reciprocity overlook the fundamental truth that all people don't necessarily want the same things.

At any rate, all the Confucian virtues flow directly from the principle of reciprocity.

### Human-Heartedness

The concept of human-heartedness comes from the Confucian ethic of *"jen." Jen* is a difficult term to translate and has also been called "benevolence," "love," and "humaneness." However it's translated, though, the quality of *jen* includes courage, kindness, empathy, and courtesy. This is the virtue of the superior person. One Chinese philosopher of the Sung Dynasty, Chu Hsi (1130–1200 C.E.), called it the "virtue of the soul," a beautiful phrase.

In fact, the Chinese ideogram for *jen* is the same as that used for "human being" and the sign for "two." The emphasis is on getting along. Thus the idea of harmony is built concretely into the written word. It is the principle of love itself. Virtue is impossible if one is the only being in the world.

Also included in the concept are "kindness" and "courtesy." To Westerners, the idea of connecting two terms like "kindness" and "courtesy" may seem odd, but Confucians know that some people just aren't naturally kind. They do, however, believe that everybody can learn the simple rules of courtesy, which also embody the principles of kindness. Offering a tired person food and rest comes under the rubric of both kindness and courtesy. Thus good behavior can be taught.

## Ritual

The virtue of propriety, of behaving correctly in all its aspects, is known as *li*. It refers to both public and private behavior, everything from the most solemn religious services to which chopstick to use.

*Li* means knowing what to say and do at the appropriate times, a skill we all need, sometimes desperately. It's not such a little thing. (Think what an advantage it would be to always know the correct thing to say and the best way to act in a given situation.)

---

### BRAINS VERSUS BRAWN

*Although the Chinese have prized scholarship for many, many centuries, this wasn't always the case. Originally, scholars were called ru, which means "a weak, cowardly person." Scholars were disdained because they were unskilled in manly martial arts and instead made their living through their knowledge of rites, ceremonies, and history. Later, however, this same word ru came to be an honorable term.*

---

The Chinese royalty had ministers of protocol to guide them in proper behavior, just as the White House does today. However, the system never works as well as it might, either then or now. In the beginning, *li* did not extend to commoners. Either they already knew how to behave or nobody cared. During the Han dynasty, however, when Confucianism became the state religion, everybody was supposed to use *li* as a guide to conduct. Interestingly, this word is originally connected with the word for "worship" or "rites." For some people, Confucianism thus became known as *lijiao*, the ritual religion.

"He who pares a melon for the Emperor should divide it into four parts and then into eight, and cover it with a fine linen napkin... A commoner will have to deal with it with his teeth."

—*Chinese Book of Etiquette*

## Culture

Confucius believed that the study of the arts and history was essential for the cultivated person. (He didn't use the word *cultivated* in the sense of "over-refined" but in a sense truer to its original meaning. A cultivated person is one who "works on himself" and who cultivates his abilities.) Education thus became a critical element in the Confucian ideal. Unlike the Taoists, who believe the best sort of person is the most natural one, Confucians believed that human nature needed to be developed to fulfill its great potential.

Confucius simply didn't agree with Taoists that the "natural" way is always the right way. He believed that "natural" human beings were capable of greed, deceit, and gross behavior. Cultivation and refinement are the tools we need to shape "natural" behavior into socially acceptable modes. The same argument goes on even today between those parents who think the best way to rear a child is to encourage his "natural" tendencies and those parents who feel that the "natural" tendencies are the ones that most need to be controlled. The debate goes to the heart of the Taoist/Confucian argument: What is the "true" nature of human beings?

## THE FIVE GREAT RELATIONSHIPS

Confucianism, more than any other Eastern religion, anchors what it means to be human in human society. It understands that the human spirit becomes most fully itself in relationship with other human beings; we are in a web of our own weaving. To attempt to "escape" or to deny our humanity is a silly and useless proposition. Although Westerners often speak metaphorically of the human "family," Confucius meant it in a literal, albeit extended sense. Everything is based on the concept of *hsiao,* or "filial piety."

The Five Great Relationships are not relationships of equality, but neither are they precisely unequal. They are best thought of as describing different, but reciprocal roles. Ideally, they are harmonious; each is dependent on the other. Obviously, one cannot be a father without having a son, a husband without a wife, and so on.

---

**FAMILIAL ROLES**

*In China, it was a capital offense to curse one's parents, and parents had the legal right to put "unfilial" children to death. Although our culture thinks that marriage is for the sake of the children, Chinese culture considered it as a means to support the older generation. Parents didn't live for their children—the children live for their parents. Children were not permitted to own their own property, even when adult, and were expected to live in the same home with their parents.*

We should note also that these relationships are built according to a definite hierarchical plan. Although the ruler has obligations to the son, and a husband owes his wife certain things, in Confucianism there is no question about who's the boss. The Chinese believed that order and hierarchy were necessary for the smooth running of society.

It may help to think of the Western concept of employer-employee as an analogy. Although the employer has power over his worker, the power is not unlimited. Nor is the employer "better" than the employee. All the relationships are reciprocal, and each person has both rights and responsibilities with respect to the other party.

> "Filial piety is the root of virtue."
>
> —*Confucius*

- Father-son. The father-son relationship is the essence of the concept of "filial piety," considered the source of all other virtues. This is because it's a family relationship based on blood and a kind of "natural" leadership. Even in the democratic West, most of us believe that the parent should lead the child and not the other way around. The parent's responsibility is to teach the child, support him financially, and be a moral guide. The child is to be obedient (no matter how old he is) and care for his parents during their dotage. In Chinese culture, any disobedience or misbehavior on the part of the children (no matter how old) brings shame to the parents. Young couples who are not able to have children also bring disgrace to their elders.

- Elder brother-younger brother. The age difference between siblings is so important in Confucian countries that a different word is used to designate an older brother or sister from a younger one. In many ways, the older brother takes the place of the father (and considering the likelihood of untimely death in those ancient cultures this was a good thing). The older brother is responsible for the care, control, and support of younger siblings, especially in the absence of a father. They are expected to obey him as they would a father.

- Husband-wife. The husband is expected to support his wife and direct her. She is expected to serve and support him. In ancient China, the son's parents chose the wife. He never actually met her until the wedding day. If a wife was unable to produce an heir, it was permitted for the husband to take another wife, but not the other way around.

- Friend-friend. Friendship held a critical place in Chinese culture, much as it did in the Renaissance period of western Europe. It figures much more largely than does the notion of romantic love. Because China was patriarchal, the friendships spoken of were almost always between men, but the same principles can be applied to friendships between women.

- Ruler-subject. The ruler-subject relationship is very similar to that of father and son. The only difference is that rulers are supposed to model their behavior upon the example of heaven.

The Confucian scholar Mencius summed it up this way (perhaps a bit oddly to Western ears): "Between father and son there is affection; between prince and subject there is integrity; between husband and wife there is proper distance; between older and younger there is proper precedence; between friend and friend there is faithfulness."

In capitalistic countries like Japan and South Korea, the concept of the Five Great Relationships has spread to the world of work, where corporations are seen more as family than as mere employers. In keeping with the hierarchical nature of Confucianism, promotions and salaries are based mostly on seniority.

Confucius offered an explanatory theory, which was a bit cryptic in its original formulation. "Rule, ruler; minister, minister; father, father; son, son." This, however, is what he meant: One should live up to the ideal description of one's office or position in life. If you are a father, you should *act* like a father, fulfilling a father's responsibilities and behaving in every way like the perfect father. And if you are a son, you should fulfill your obligations as a true son and behave accordingly.

This theory is called the Rectification of Names. Rectification means "make right" and Confucius's idea was that if people performed

the obligations of their estate in life by following the ideal definition of that function, things would go a lot more smoothly. That's
undoubtedly true. It is amazing, when one stops to think of it, how
many problems are caused by people doing something other than
what they should.

## CONFUCIAN THEORY OF HUMAN NATURE

One's system of ethics depends largely on what one thinks of
human nature—whether it's basically good or essentially bad.
Unfortunately, Confucius himself was not very clear on this point,
although he apparently believed that human nature had at least the
potential for goodness.

One Chinese philosopher, Mo-Tzu (c. 468–390 B.C.E.) had a
more optimistic view of human nature than Confucius did. Mo-
Tzu, who lived during a time of great violence and strife, rightly
decided that wars were
singularly uncivilized and
unhealthy to boot. How
could things be righted?
Simple, thought Mo-Tzu.
All we had to do was love
each other. In fact, if we
founded a society based
on the principles of uni-
versal love, wars would
cease and everybody
could get down to some
heavy-duty gardening.

> **HEART AND MIND**
>
> *The Chinese word for human nature is* hsing, *and Confucians spilled a lot of ink in their arguments over its precise nature. The character for hsing is a compound for mind and heart.*

> **MO-TZU BECOMES A MEMORY**
>
> *Mo-Tzu thought too much money and time were wasted on expensive cultural activities like elaborate ceremonies and fancy funerals. Even recreation, he complained, was a major waste of time. He thought people should be more productive. Neither the Confucians nor the Taoists liked this one little bit. It's not surprising, really, that Mo-Tzu's beliefs, with their rather un-Chinese nature, were doomed to die out. Still, the idea of universal love does seem to keep cropping up from time to time, no matter how often sensible people try to stamp it out.*

Lest you think Mo-Tzu was a romantic with his head in the air
and his nose in the clouds, this isn't quite the case. Mo-Tzu thought
that the practice of universal love is only common sense and enlightened self-interest. "If this weren't a practical idea," he asserted, "why,
even I would disapprove of it. But how can there be anything good
which isn't useful?" Perhaps he had a point. Hate, he maintained,
simply doesn't pay. "Whoever loves others is loved by others," he
argued, "and he who hates others is hated by them in turn."

## CONFUCIAN METAPHYSICS

For the most part, Confucius steered clear of metaphysical discussion. "If you don't know about life, how can you know about death?" he demanded. Still he apparently believed that heaven had ultimate control over human affairs, and probably agreed with traditional Chinese concepts about the soul.

In Chinese theory, the human person has not one, but two, souls. (Other religions give people even more. It depends on whom you ask.) One soul is the *hun*, an intellectual entity that becomes a *shên* or spirit when the person dies. The lower soul is *po*, which becomes a ghost when the human person dies and goes with him down into the grave.

Confucius himself tried to keep things on a more mundane level. He never spoke of "miracles, wonders, spirits, or chaos."

## THE CONFUCIAN MARRIAGE

Marriage had regulations of its own—at least for women. A famous female Chinese scholar, Pan Chao (c. 48–112 c.e.) wrote an influential work directed at teaching young married women how to behave. First, she extols the virtue of humility. "She should put others first, herself last," counsels Pan Chao soberly. "If she does something good, she shouldn't mention it, but if she does something bad, she shouldn't deny it." Pan Chao isn't finished yet, however.

Humility, apparently, isn't enough. "She should seem to tremble and fear at all times," she says firmly. As far as men and women are concerned, the wife should serve the husband. It is good to know, however, that Pan Chao believed men and women should both receive educations. Pan Chao wasn't crazy about the idea of conjugal closeness. "If husband and wife spend too much time together, following each other around the house, they will begin to lust after each other and take liberties."

Then there's the mother-in-law problem. Mothers-in-law are to be obeyed without question, whether they are right or wrong. For Pan Chao, harmony in the home was more important than getting one's way.

## CONFUCIAN POLITICAL THEORY

For Confucius, one way to make people better was to make society better. He is one of the first thinkers to understand how much influence society and culture have on the average person. It was fairly impossible, he thought, to raise an incorrupt person in a corrupt society. To this end, Confucius expanded his concept of *jen* (humaneness or human-heartedness) to include the government. The best government, so far as Confucius was concerned, was a genuinely *good* government, one that acted by moral persuasion, and the officials of which set a positive example for their subjects. He did believe that a strong military was important for a stable government, but not as important as food for the populace and the good will of the people. It is strange that this common-sense idea still hasn't caught on.

One way to do this was to encourage scholars and philosophers (namely himself) to participate in the workings of the state. Confucius originally wrote to persuade rulers themselves. Later, he sort of gave up on that idea and addressed his works to scholars, who he thought would positively influence the rulers. He wrote, "If you govern with virtue, you will be like the North Star. It remains steadfast while all the other stars swing around it."

> "In the study of poetry, one learns to serve one's parents and prince; besides, one is better acquainted with the names of birds and beasts, weeds, and trees."
>
> —*Confucius*

## CONFUCIAN LITERATURE

The amount of Confucian literature is vast, but I can at least touch on a few major works.

### The Five Classics

By tradition, The Five Classics were written or at least edited by Confucius, but the Confucian canon didn't become well established until the Song dynasty (960–1279). This literature became the basis for all learning for about 600 years—from 1313 until 1912. Confucius was very clear about the fact that he didn't write them himself. "I transmit," he said, "I don't create."

### The Book of History

The Book of History *(Shu Ching),* supposedly edited by Confucius, purports to be a collection of ancient royal speeches. It is also

**THE MISSING CLASSIC**

*There was apparently once a sixth classic, the Book of Music (Yao), which somebody lost. Part of it may be included in the Book of Rites.*

known by many as The Book of Documents. In addition to the speeches, the book includes some narrative material from ancient times until the Chou period (1122–256 B.C.E.). Originally there were one hundred such documents covering sixteen centuries, mostly the early dynasties. Confucius put them all into chronological order, no easy job in itself. Then he wrote introductions for them. Only twenty-eight documents remain.

The *Hung Fan* chapter of this work contains the philosophy of the Five Elements, mentioned in the first chapter of this part.

### The Book of Poetry or Songs

The Book of Poetry *(Shih Ching)* is an anthology of 305 popular songs, probably compiled about 600 B.C.E. The songs themselves may cover a five-hundred-year period from the ancient Chou dynasty all the way to Confucius's present in the Spring and Autumn period. The original collection allegedly contained over more than three thousand songs, but Confucius did some heavy editing. He realized that people can read just so many songs before they get tired of them. What we have left are poems of love and courtship, mournful poetry about being deserted (a kind of Chinese blues), as well as "banquet songs" meant to be recited during state dinners and such. Many of the songs have a moral lesson to them. (Perhaps one detects the hand of Confucius here.)

He also taught poetry for the purposes of cultural adornment, remarking that in past times it was customary to insert snippets of poetry in polite conversation. Fortunately, this practice has gone out of favor, at least in this country.

### The Book of Changes

As I mentioned in chapter 13, the Chinese used the Book of Changes (I Ching) to divine future events and to understand present happenings. It has been influential not only in Confucianism and Taoism, but has also attracted a large Western following. It was Confucius's own favorite book.

### The Book of Rites

The Book of Rites *(Li Chi)* has forty-nine sections dealing with ancient ritual and government, music and philosophy. Also included by tradition is the *I-li*, a Miss Manners for Chinese rituals such as marriages, funerals, and archery contests (no shooting the spectators). In this book, Confucius also suggests that widows, orphans, the sick, and the poor need to be cared for. If they have no family, then the government should do it. This was such a revolutionary concept that some people haven't managed to figure it out to this day.

The Book of Rites also includes the Institutes of Chou, which describes the ideal function of government officials.

"Without studying rites," Confucius explained, "one cannot get anywhere in society." The correct following of ceremony was thought to bring people into closer harmony with nature. Contrary to what is popularly believed, however, rites meant something more than empty ritual to Confucius. "As for mourning rites, there should be sincere grief rather than attention to trivial details."

### The Spring and Autumn Annals

The Spring and Autumn Annals *(Ch'un Ch'iu)* is a diary-like history of Confucius's own state of Lu and was for a long time considered to be the only original work by Confucius, but it probably wasn't after all, say modern scholars. The thesis is "Why Lu Declined" and covers the period from 722–481 B.C.E.

As I mentioned earlier, there is also a Spring and Autumn period in Chinese history, running from 770 to 476 B.C.E. During this period, the great feudal states arose. It was during this time that Taoism, Confucianism's philosophic rival, reached its classical stage.

## The Four Books

The Four Books, all Confucian texts, were systematized by the Sung dynasty scholar and philosopher Chu Hsi and other Neo-Confucians. They were the basis for the competitive Chinese civil service examinations that were mandatory for hundreds of years.

### The Great Learning

Originally this work was a short chapter of the Book of Rites, but is now placed separately as one of The Four Books. Supposedly it was originally written by Confucius, but scholars no longer buy this idea. It discusses the true character of a noble person. It represents the general principles of Confucian teaching, with little

**SEASONS SIMPLIFIED**

*The reason why only spring and autumn were mentioned is that in ancient Chinese reckoning there were only two seasons, spring, which included summer, and fall, which included winter. The Chinese wisely believed in simplifying things as much as possible.*

emphasis on ritual. (This is probably why it was removed from The Book of Rites. It has been printed separately since the thirteenth century.) The Great Learning is written for rulers and it gives basic guidelines in the art of statesmanship. It provides an eight-step program for reformation; the first five steps are for individuals, the last three for society as a whole. The eight steps are:

1. The investigation of things

2. The extension of knowledge

3. Sincerity of the will

4. Rectification of the mind

5. Cultivation of the personal life

6. Regulation of the family

7. National order

8. World peace

In classical China, the Great Learning was the first book to be memorized by keen students. According to this work, peace is obtained when each person cultivates the correct virtues. This will naturally extend first to the family, then to the neighborhood, and finally to society at large.

### The Analects

The Analects, or *Lun Yu,* a work of twenty chapters, contains the heart of Confucius's teaching. Some are sayings, other short stories. They usually begin with the words, "The Master says..." Obviously this is the source of all those "Confucius say" jokes.

Unfortunately, for analytical study, the chapters don't seem to be arranged in any particular order. Many of these sayings were carved into stone. Confucian followers sometimes make rubbings of the sayings and take them home.

### The Book of Mencius

This book *(Mêng-Tzu)* is a collection of the teaching of Mencius, whom I'll discuss in the next chapter. Much of it repeats the teachings found in Confucius's Analects. Its main emphases are that violence is counterproductive and that humans beings are really good at heart.

### The Doctrine of the Mean

The Doctrine of the Mean was originally part of the Book of Rites, but because it deals with the connection between human nature and the underlying principles of the universe (instead of rites and ceremony as such), it was excerpted and given its own place. Traditionally, the author is said to have been Confucius's grandson, although this is doubtful.

## CHAPTER RECAP

- The basis of Confucian philosophy is *shu,* the principle of reciprocity.

- Confucius also laid great stress upon the value of *jen,* or human-heartedness, and *li,* or correct ceremony.

- For Confucius, harmony depends on the Five Great Relationships: father-son; husband-wife; elder brother-younger brother; friend-friend; ruler-subject.

- Confucius believed that people had the potential for goodness and merely needed cultivation.

- Confucius thought that government would improve if more philosophers worked in the political arena.

### Recommended Reading

Chai, Ch'u. *The Story of Chinese Philsophy.* New York: Washington Square Press, 1961.

Tu Weming. *Confucian Thought: Selfhood as Creative Transformation.* Albany, NY: State University of New York Press, 1985.

# Confucianism

# Through the Ages

*C*onfucianism didn't stop with the death of Confucius. It was a developing tradition that absorbed the ideas of many later thinkers and philosophers. Two of these philosophers were Mencius and Hsün Tzu. Mencius and Hsün Tzu disagreed violently with each other about the true nature of people, but as is so typical of Eastern religions, Confucianism managed to reconcile their contradictory views into a sophisticated, yet understanding view of human nature. The result was a stronger, more tensile religion that has endured and prospered in the face of almost insurmountable odds.

## MENCIUS—THE "SECOND SAGE"

Without Mencius (Mêng-Tzu), there would be no Confucianism. For it was Mencius who popularized Confucianism and who made it accessible to the general public. Without him, Confucian ideas would probably have remained an elitist curiosity. This is why Mencius is known as the "Second Sage" of Confucianism.

The name Mencius is a latinized form of Mêng-Tzu, or Master Meng. He is commonly believed to have lived from c. 372 to 289 B.C.E., thus putting his life about a hundred years after Confucius, during the period of the Warring States, when life was even more disrupted and chaotic than it had been a century earlier. The title

*Warring States,* was, if anything, an understatement. Everyone was fighting everybody else. It was a nasty time to be alive, because in addition to wars (and as a result of them) there was oppressive taxation, poverty, and a bunch of miserable itinerant politicians whose job was apparently to help petty kings squeeze out every available grain of rice from their subjects.

Mencius was born Meng K'o; he came from Tsou in Shantung, a state adjacent to Confucius's Lu. Like Confucius, Buddha, Jesus, and a lot of other people, Mencius had a miraculous happening attend his birth. An angel announced the great event to his mother (who would have known about it sooner or later anyway) and at the critical moment, the whole area filled with brilliant, vibrantly colored light.

His mother kept moving around trying to find the perfect spot to bring up young Mencius. Her first choice was close to a cemetery, at least until she found out that her son's favorite game was to pretend to bury and mourn dead people. Rightfully worried about her son's choice of entertainment, she tried another location, this one near a market. Naturally, young Mencius played at being a merchant, and though you'd think Mother Meng would have been relieved, she wasn't. She didn't want her son mixed up in anything so ordinary and unrefined as the retail business. She finally chose a spot near a school, and predictably, Mencius took to imitating the teacher. That made her happy.

Mencius is considered Confucius's greatest disciple. He never actually met Confucius, but he did study under Confucius's grandson Tzu Ssu. Like Confucius, Mencius spent a lot of time wandering around and hoping that some king sooner or later would be smart enough to realize that he needed some good advice, rather than the self-serving flattery that was the usual staple of politicians.

## Mencius the Optimist

Mencius believed that human beings were essentially good and that evil comes from society. He got into a lot of heated arguments with philosophers who held different views. Some said that human nature was neither good nor bad, just neutral. Some said that human nature could be good or bad—depending on the environment.

Others claimed that some people were naturally good and some weren't, which is what I rather think myself.

Mencius believed that our inner goodness comes from our feelings. If you do something wrong, he said, don't blame your feelings. You've gone against them somehow. Everybody has compassion, he said. That leads to *jen,* or human-heartedness. Everybody has feelings of shame and dislike, and that leads to righteousness. (I can't follow this line of reasoning myself, but that's what he said.)

Unlike his master Confucius, Mencius loved to argue, especially when he could back someone into an indefensible position. One of Mencius's opponents, a man named Kao Tzu, argued that human nature was like water, and could thus flow anywhere. Maybe, answered the wily Mencius, but it doesn't *naturally* flow just anywhere. It *naturally* flows down. In the same way, human nature naturally inclines to goodness. This is a very good answer, although he didn't explain why human nature just *naturally* might flow toward being bad. He was just an optimist, I guess.

Human nature can be forced into evil, Mencius continued, but a bad environment destroys its nature, just as a beautiful, tree-covered mountain could be denuded of its forests by stupid, greedy townsfolk. The mountain is majestic and beautiful in its nature, but it can be forced into ugliness. Because we are basically good, all we need to do is to cultivate those good qualities. (His optimistic take on humanity may have come from rubbing elbows with Taoists.) At any rate, Mencius is considered an idealist. It is our job, he thought, to help our innate human goodness to flower. He thought education was the great key, because education helps us to develop our logical faculties. Without education, he said, we are prey to fatalism.

Mencius didn't go overboard on his optimism, however. He thought that universal love was neither achievable nor desirable. The concept of loving one's neighbor as oneself seemed ridiculous to him. "You should love your nearest and dearest first," he advised. "That's right and natural." After that, he thought that loving one's friends and neighbors was a good idea. Then we could love everybody else, if there's time.

Like Confucius, Mencius was interested in good government and a stable society. He thought a king's first job was to provide his

"What one upholds in one's heart is human-heartedness. What one upholds in his conduct is righteousness."

—*Mencius*

people's basic needs in food, water, and firewood, and he provided some specific instructions as to how to bring that about. He complained about the heavy taxes. Proper taxation, he said, should consist of cloth, grain, or personal service—but only one at a time, and not in any undue amount.

Rulers should govern by the principle of *yi,* or righteousness, not from a profit motive or greed. If the king acted from righteousness, he believed, then everyone else would do the same.

> "The people rank highest in a state; the spirits of the grain come next; and the sovereign is of least account."
>
> —*Mencius*

### Political Theory

Mencius's biggest contribution to political theory was completely his own, and it was a tremendous innovation. He believed that government should function with the consent of the people. Confucius had never proposed anything like this. In fact, Mencius was something of a revolutionary. He said that if a king became a cruel tyrant, it was perfectly all right to kill him, because he no longer had any mandate to rule.

In fact, good government should surge upward from the common people, not trickle down from the emperor to the people. He agreed that the emperor had the mandate of heaven, but maintained that heaven had the eyes and ears of the people. Confucius would not have agreed at all. When all was said and done, the greatest disciple proved he had a mind of his own.

## HSÜN TZU

Hsün Tzu (c. 312–c. 238 B.C.E.) was from north China, the state of Chao. (This was a fertile breeding ground of early Confucianism.) Hsün Tzu was a younger contemporary of Mencius but had no generation loyalty and disagreed completely with him about the nature of human beings. He thought we are corrupt and born bad. We are greedy and self-interested. In fact, by nature we actually hate other people.

Like Confucius and Mencius, Hsün Tzu had trouble finding a job as a state adviser, although he certainly tried hard enough. He wandered from place to place—Yen, Ch'I, and Ch'u, but something always went wrong. Finally, he accepted a post as chief magistrate in the city of Lan-Ling.

## The Philosophy of Hsün Tzu

Hsün Tzu considered himself to be an orthodox Confucian, but this perception was not widely shared. Other people thought he was too mean to be a Confucian. They preferred the rosier outlook of Mencius. One group of people who did like Hsün Tzu were the Han rulers. This is because his dim view of human nature played right into their hands. If people were incapable of virtue on their own and needed to be controlled, the Han just happened to be around to do it.

Hsün Tzu demonstrated the truth of his own principles by being pretty hateful himself. His favorite targets were Taoists, who he said were threats to human civilization. (This didn't bother the Taoists much, who weren't that crazy about human civilization to begin with.)

According to Hsün Tzu, the only way to control people is through strict laws. Like the Buddha, he believed that desire caused a lot of trouble and that ritual was the way to control desire, although he was more concerned with its social consequences than its personal ones. "People desire and hate the same things. Their desires are many, but things are few. Since they are few, there will inevitably be strife." There does appear to be an inexorable logic here.

If people were so good, Hsün Tzu wanted to know, then why did they require teachers, laws, and philosophy? "You've got to heat wood in order to straighten it out," he remarked dryly. He complained that Mencius knew nothing whatever about human nature. Surely if people were naturally good, they wouldn't need any of these things. It seems as if Hsün Tzu made a telling point here, but because Mencius was dead at the time, he couldn't be expected to respond to it. At any rate, Hsün Tzu provided the foundation for the later development of Chinese legalism.

To be fair, Hsün Tzu placed a high value on education, because he felt that it was an important way to counteract people's bad tendencies. So we see that both the orthodox Confucians and Hsün Tzu valued learning, although from opposed views about mankind. "Therefore, the sage improves original nature and gives rise to acquired training," he said. He believed that the inevitable differences in people's virtues came from their exposure to different teachers. Virtue had to be *taught,* and even though we are born evil, we are also born with enough intelligence to understand that virtue is the only way to produce a happy society.

Hsün Tzu did seem to believe that music was a great help in producing a tranquil spirit and in establishing harmony among people. "Music, when performed in the ancestral temples, inspires reverence among the emperor and his ministers; when performed at home, affection between spouses; when performed in the village square, amity among the people."

As for the universe, Hsün Tzu maintained that it was not guided by a benevolent spirit, as Confucius seemed to believe. On the contrary, it was cold, inanimate, and didn't give a rip about human beings. It has its own job, which has nothing to do with us. (This viewpoint is rather similar to that of the Taoists.)

## THE LEGALISTS

Legalism is a logical development from the teachings of Hsün Tzu, but the Legalists (400–200 B.C.E.) really cut the last thread connecting them with any true Confucian ideas. Some Legalists advocated the position that central power should be absolute; others that the ruler should be able to control his subordinates with power and art; still others that laws should be strictly enforced.

One of the most influential of the Legalists was Han Fei Tzu (c. 281–233 B.C.E.). He was descended from a royal family in the state of Han, an area that suffered horribly during the endless wars of the period. Not only did it suffer invasion from without, it was also prey to internal wars. Han Fei Tzu, almost inevitably, gravitated toward the idea that a strong political structure was the only way to save society. He thought that the ruler must execute absolute authority, but only in accord with a strict body of laws.

Han Fei Tzu quotes approvingly a story about a ruler named Chao who had fallen asleep in the cold. A retainer put a coat over him to keep him from freezing. The ruler was furious, however, because it wasn't the retainer's job to cover him with a coat. Chao had the poor guy put to death. "People should mind their own business and do the duties assigned to them," announced Han Fei Tzu. "The world works better that way." It certainly would have worked better for the retainer.

> "The reason subjects don't deceive the king is not because they love him, but because they fear him."
>
> —*Shen Tao*

According to Han Fei Tzu, however, a "strict" system of law does not mean "mechanical." Skilled statesmen must learn to read and apply the law carefully. Thus, the three concepts of authority *(shih)*, artful manipulation *(shu)*, and strict administration *(fa)* all went hand in hand. Earlier thinkers had stated that while high-class people could be controlled with rites and ceremonies and noble expectations *(li)*, the common people responded only to punishment *(hsing)*. Han Fei Tzu tended to agree with Confucius that *li* was an adequate symbol of guidance for all people.

He also made a list of eight kinds of people rulers had to watch out for: people who shared the ruler's bed (male or female); syco-phantic attendants; relatives; brown-nosing assistants; administra-tors who pass money around to the people to weaken the position of the ruler and gain favor for themselves; smooth talkers who interpret and manipulate news for the king; strongmen who can turn against one; and outside powers. That about covers it.

Han Fei Tzu's teachings were actually incorporated as ruling pol-icy by the first emperor of the Ch'in dynasty, a rival to the state of Han. The emperor invited Han Fei Tzu to come to his court, but the man remained loyal to his own homeland of Han. Eventually, Han Fei Tzu was sent to the emperor as a sort of goodwill ambassador. He was thrown into jail instead, however, and was falsely accused of treachery. When the emperor learned the truth and tried to set Han Fei Tzu free, the man had already died in prison.

> "Force can always secure obedience; an appeal to morality, very seldom."
> —*Han Fei Tzu*

## HAN CONFUCIANISM

During the Han period (206 B.C.E.–220 C.E.), Confucianism was established as the state religion and official policy. The Emperor Wu, on the advice of the Confucian scholar Tung Chung-shu, made Confucian studies de rigueur in bureaucratic China. You couldn't get anywhere without successfully passing hard tests. This system remained in place until the twentieth century.

The Han scholars had a bit of a rough time of it, largely because in 213 C.E. many invaluable documents had been burned by the first Ch'in emperor, who went by the name Shih Huang Ti. Burning all those books was a major accomplishment, since paper wouldn't be invented for a hundred years or so. A film, directed by Chen Kaige,

**CONFUCIANISM
OUTSIDE CHINA**

*Confucianism came to
Japan in 405 by means of
a Korean scholar named
Wani.*

*The Emperor and the Assassin,* was recently made about his exploits. The movie did nothing to clean up Shih Huang Ti's reputation, by the way. It probably made it worse—although it didn't mention the book-burning part. Shih Huang Ti predicted that his empire would last for ten thousand generations, but it was gone in four years.

The most important Han scholar was Tung Chung-shu (179– 104 B.C.E.). Like most Confucians, he expended a good deal of effort persuading rulers to become benevolent. He used the ancient Chinese concept of yin and yang to explain his ideas. Tung Chung-shu also developed the Five Elements Theory.

## NEO-CONFUCIANISM

The Neo-Confucian *(Li–hsueh)* period in Chinese thought began in the Ming dynasty (1368–1644), largely in response to the growth of Buddhism in China and has lasted up to the present time. In China it's called "The Study of Nature and Propriety." The Neo-Confucians were getting a little sick of Buddhism themselves, but they had their own reasons. In the first place, they decided that Buddhism was an inferior foreign religion not worthy of serious Chinese attention. They thought its emphasis on meditation and salvation destroyed family values. (The Jesuit missionaries, however, preferred classical Confucianism, which they felt was no threat to Christian beliefs. Neo-Confucianism still smacked a little too much of Buddhism for their liking, and they opposed it vigorously.)

The Neo-Confucians were also very big on rites and ceremonies, reinstituting many ancient sacrifices. It got to be such a large and complicated affair that the government itself had to take charge of most of them. The emperor performed the most important ones. On the scholarly front, Neo-Confucians did a lot of work editing, clarifying, and interpreting Confucian texts.

One group really suffered under Neo-Confucianism—women. Even under classic Confucianism, women were expected to remain largely in the background, but they were considered fully human beings whose strength, wisdom, and common sense were greatly admired. The Neo-Confucians thought otherwise. Women were expected to be entirely subservient to men, and their greatest virtue was supposed to be self-sacrifice for the benefit of men. Widows, in particular, were to consider that their lives were essentially over. Although the Chinese never developed a concept comparable to the Hindu suttee, they might as well have.

One major Neo-Confucian, mentioned earlier, was Chu Hsi (1130–1200), who tried to synthesize all previous spiritual traditions, including Taoism and Buddhism. He also decided exactly who was orthodox and who was not. (Mencius was, Hsün Tzu wasn't.) He didn't like Mahayana metaphysics either, especially the doctrine of emptiness, which he thought was ridiculous. He did understand the changing nature of reality, but thought that the Taoist concept of natural flowing expressed it much better than Buddhist ideas. Another important Neo-Confucian was Wang Yangming (1473–1529). He believed that truth could be discovered by looking inward.

## CONFUCIANISM TODAY

Like everything else traditional, Confucianism has suffered under the Communist regime. During the cultural revolution of 1966–1976, Confucianism was given short shrift as one of the "Four Olds" (old culture, old customs, old habits, and old ideas). Part of this was personal animus on the part of Mao, who declared he had always hated Confucianism from childhood. In the early 1980s, major moves to preserve the Confucian heritage began in China and Confucius's ancestral home, which was destroyed during the cultural revolution, was rebuilt.

### THE ART OF CONFUCIANISM

*In the Confucian scheme, all art, including painting, poetry, and calligraphy, were considered marks of the superior scholar. Calligraphy, the art of "beautiful writing," was the visual expression of poetry, and both were used to illuminate the visual artistry of a painting. The great calligrapher expressed in his art his sensitivity, scholarship, and aesthetic sense.*

## CHAPTER RECAP

- Mencius, Confucius's great follower, believed that human nature was basically good.

- Later philosophers such as Hsun Tzu, and Confucianism's legalist school, thought that people were evil by nature.

- Confucianism became the state religion during the Han dynasty.

- The Neo-Confucians tried to purify Confucianism from Buddhist and other foreign influences.

- Confucian principles still thrive throughout east Asia, despite Chinese Communist attempts to wipe them out.

*Recommended Reading*

Fung, Y. I. *A History of Chinese Philosophy.* Trans. by Derk Bodde. Princeton, NJ: Princeton University Press, 1952.

Nivison, David S., and Arthur Wright, eds. *Confucianism in Action.* Palo Alto, CA: Stanford University Press, 1959.

Taylor, Rodney. *The Religious Dimensions of Confucianism.* Albany, NY: State University of New York Press, 1990.

Wright, Arthur F., ed. *The Confucian Persuasion.* Palo Alto, CA: Stanford University Press, 1960.

# *Taoism —*

# *The Transformation*

In most books about Eastern religions, Taoism is treated after Confucianism. This is because in many ways it seems as if Taoism is a reaction to the Confucian tradition. In reality, Taoism is much older than Confucianism and is representative of the "natural" rather than the "civilized" approach to life.

Like all Chinese traditions, Taoism has a positive attitude toward life. In contrast to Buddhism, say, which focuses on suffering, the chief text of Taoism, the Tao Te Ching, doesn't even mention the word. Even what most people think of as the greatest suffering, death, is no problem for the great Taoist philosophers. "If I think well of life," said the mystical Taoist philosopher Chuang Tzu, "I should also think well of death." (In another place, Chuang Tzu tells the story of Tzu Li, who goes to visit his dying friend. "Nature is wonderful," he tells his friend cheerfully. "I wonder what she'll make out of you? The liver of a rat? The leg of a cockroach?")

Still, despite this rather positive, if quirky, attitude about the end, the Taoists were in no great hurry to arrive there. Life on earth was good, and many wanted it to last as long as possible. That was their version of one kind of immortality: life on this earth, happily extended for as long as possible.

This view is sometimes called "religious" as opposed to "philosophical" Taoism. Philosophical Taoism may have had a more

*Taoist Immortal with Porcupine
Japan, eighteenth century (ivory)*

elevated and spiritual notion of immortality. But it's unclear. The two ideas, physical and spiritual immortality, may be related, as indeed they are in orthodox Christianity, which insists upon bodily resurrection as an article of faith.

Taoism began as a philosophy and later developed into a religion, which is just the opposite of what one might think, or what is true of many religions. Philosophical Taoism flourished about 300 B.C.E., while religious (or, to their enemies, "superstitious" Taoism) began about two hundred years later. The two traditions are not so different as one might think, however.

Currently there are about 20 million practicing Taoists. Nearly all of them are in Asia, although basic Taoist ideas are very popular in the U.S. as well.

# *Lao Tzu and*

# *the Tao Te Ching*

Lao Tzu is often touted as the founder of Taoism, but this isn't true at all. He was certainly one of Taoism's most famous and important philosophers, but Lao Tzu was drawing upon a very long and richly embroidered tradition when he wrote.

On the other hand, some spoilsports contend that Lao Tzu never really existed. This isn't true. He did exist, and he rode away from China to the West on the back of an ox. And he lived to be more than two hundred years old. Other than that, we can't say a lot about him with certainty. Undeterred by the uncertainty of Lao Tzu's existence, the T'ang dynasty (618–907 C.E.) claimed him as its ancestor.

His real name was Li Erh (or maybe Lai Tan). The name Erh means "ears" and the name Tan means "long" ears. Although we might be tempted to think these names refer to an anatomical curiosity of Lao Tzu's, the words are really symbolic. In Chinese lore, long ears represent long life. In contrast, the name Lao Tzu means either "old master" or "old boy." The latter term refers to the belief that Lao Tzu was born an old man.

## LAO TZU'S LIFE

What we know about Lao Tzu is contained in Shih Chi, the Historical Records of Ssu-ma Ch'ien (c. 100 B.C.E.). And even Ssu-ma Ch'ien

**SPELLING TEST**

*Taoism is pronounced "Daoism," and is sometimes now spelled that way. Because most people are familiar with the older orthography, I'll use that here.*

admits that considering all the conflicting historical evidence, he doesn't know what was true and what wasn't. That didn't stop him from writing Lao Tzu's biography, however.

According to Ssu-ma Ch'ien, Lao Tzu was born in the village of Chu Jen in the kingdom of Ch'u. (He may have been born sometime in the sixth century B.C.E. Traditionally, he is said to have lived at the same time as Confucius, but recent scholarship places him about two centuries later.) A twelve-foot statue of Lao Tzu as well as a couple of graves said to belong to him and his mother are located near Chu Jen. Since the official version is that Lao Tzu never died at all, or that he lived to be two hundred years old and left China on the back of an ox, most scholars simply assume the graves are phoney. Of course, it is just possible that Lao Tzu did actually die after all, and was buried near where he was born.

There is a famous, although probably apocryphal, story about a meeting between Lao Tzu and a half-century younger Confucius. Confucius reportedly said later that Lao Tzu was a dragon who could not be snared. In the famous discussion, Lao Tzu apparently told Confucius to give up his "proud airs, artificial manners, and sensual appetites." This story is told by Taoists, of course. They are also proud of the fact that their founder outlived Confucius by 129 years. In another version of the same tale, Lao Tzu sneered at Confucius's teachings about patriotism, education, and filial obedience. "The man who is a son no longer belongs to himself," said Lao Tzu, "and the man who is a subject no longer belongs to himself." For Confucius that was just the point, but Lao Tzu didn't get it.

Another Confucius/Lao Tzu encounter supposedly occurred while Lao Tzu was taking a bath in a stream. He stood up politely but stark naked to greet Confucius, whereupon Confucius practically went insane with indignation. "Is this a proper way to behave—going about naked outdoors? Without clothes, how are we different from birds and beasts?" I could answer that question myself, but Lao Tzu took the direct attack and responded: "Well, what's wrong with the birds and beasts anyway? They are strangers to covetousness, fame, stinginess, and wallowing around in luxury." You have to admit he had a point. Later on, Confucius caught Lao Tzu drinking in a wine shop and raved at him for that. "Honestly," Lao Tzu said, "I can't figure you out. First you complain because I act like an animal. Now here I am acting like a human being and getting drunk. Animals don't get drunk. You just can't please some people." And he went on drinking.

Lao Tzu spent most of his life as an archivist in the Chinese bureaucracy, a boring job that gave him lots of time to think. He quit when he saw things were getting corrupt, and then went into exile.

At any rate, Lao Tzu became disturbed by the corruption he saw everywhere around him and decided to take the easy way out—literally, and leave the country. Attempting to do so, he was stopped by a border guard who recognized him and wouldn't allow him to depart unless he left behind some of his words of wisdom. He was reportedly 160 years old at the time.

## LAO TZU BECOMES A GOD

By the second century B.C.E., some people considered Lao Tzu a god. An inscription from the Han dynasty tells us that when he died (if he did), his left eye became the sun, and his right the moon. His head became the Kunlun Mountains, and his beard turned into the planets. His flesh became the animals, his belly became the sea, his intestines snakes, his fingers the Five Peaks, his body hair the grass and trees. His heart became a constellation, and his kidneys united to become the Father and Mother of the Real. And what of his bones? Ah, they became dragons in the most impressive transformation of all.

Like the Buddha, Lao Tzu was supposed to have a series of avatars (81!), including in some people's minds, the Buddha himself.

In 667 C.E., the T'ang dynasty gave Lao Tzu a title surpassing that even of a god—at least to them: Very Noble Celestial and Primordial Emperor. Taoist classics were studied side by side with Confucian works.

## THE TAO

The Tao is the Way, which is the root meaning of the word *Tao*. As a verb, it means "to guide," and so it has a moral as well as a metaphysical component. Its symbol is the ancient Chinese yin/yang symbol, the *T'ai Ji Tu*, although this symbol is much older than Taoism.

THE *T'AI JI TU*

THE ENIGMATIC TAO

*The word* Tao *occurs in the sacred Tao Te Ching seventy-six times. Each time it is said, it means something different.*

The Tao is the ultimate Ground of Being, and the principle of order in the universe. These aren't exactly the same thing, for the ultimate Ground of Being is what gives rise to the order of things. It is best to think of two kinds of Tao (for starters). The first kind is the Unmanifest Tao.

The Unmanifest Tao is the source and creator of reality (the "ten thousand things") as we know it. Before the universe was, Tao is. This ultimate Tao can neither be seen nor heard nor touched, yet it shows itself everywhere. (Compare this idea to the atom, which has no sensible qualities, yet its simple structure underlies everything that exists.) The Tao can have no name, because names limit, categorize, and put things into hierarchy. The Tao is beyond all that.

This Tao that we can see and touch and feel is the Manifest Tao. The Manifest Tao is part of, rather than the cause of, time and space. The best symbol for the Tao is the river. Even the concept of Tao is fluid, which is why Taoists often compare it to a river, always flowing, always pure, always the same, always changing. You might think about the concept of river as the Unmanifest Tao, while the visible river is the Manifest Tao.

Other Taoists think of it differently. They say the very "changing-ness" of the world is indeed the Tao itself. It is visible, but cannot be grasped because it is so elusive. It is like the mist and the river. They say that the mist and river and clouds are just a symbol of the Tao in action. Of course the "action" here is a passive action *(wu-wei)*, because it flows along its natural path without effort. Mists, rivers, and clouds go with the currents of sky and air and water, not against it.

Some Taoists describe their own teachings as the absolute Unmanifest Tao, while the teachings of the rival Confucians are merely those of the Manifest Tao. The unstated implication is that the Confucians are too dim-witted to grasp the reality behind the appearances.

## Human Beings and the Tao

For humans to reach their true, natural potential, we should be like rivers—flowing, receptive, and powerful. Perhaps paradoxically (but everything about the Tao is paradoxical) an equally important word Taoists use is *stillness*. However, this makes more sense than it appears. A river flows differently in different places; sometimes it rushes fiercely through narrow channels, sometimes it skips and tumbles over rocks; sometimes it flows gently around wide curves. It even takes a break from time to time and meanders into still, deep ponds. Whatever it does, though, it follows the course of the Tao.

### The Tao and the Feminine

In Chinese thought, water is the emblem of the yin: the dark, feminine, flowing source of the universe. And although yang and yin need to be in balance, it is interesting that Taoists conceive of Tao itself as a basically yin force. Partly this is in honor of the Eternal Feminine, always perceived as the Mother of Existence. Partly it is a nod to the changing, apparent instability that flows through all phenomena; women have always been considered slightly unstable. In fact, one of the names for the Tao is the *T'ai Ji:* the Great Changer. Some Taoists, however, consider the Tao to be the parent of both yin and yang forces.

One way the yang and yin forces keep in balance is by the movement of energy through what the Taoists call "dragon veins," invisible channels from heaven (yang) to earth (yin). Now you know why we have lightning. Actually, the dragon veins cannot be perceived by ordinary people in their day-to-day lives, but that doesn't mean they don't exist. The whole notion of dragon veins is connected to the Chinese concept of feng shui, which may be defined as either geomancy or interior decorating, depending on your point of view.

Taoists cultivate a close relationship with nature, by which Taoists mean not only trees and rocks and water, but the way the entire universe works. "It is vast and active. It moves in great cycles," says the old master.

All things, says the Tao, come into existence from Being *(yu)*. *Yu* comes into existence from non-Being *(wu)*. This isn't an easy concept to grasp. How is it that Being can come into existence from non-Being? Through Tao, the energizing force. (You could think of it as a dynamo or generator or battery if you want to.) This impalpable energy takes form in the One, the Manifest Tao, which in turn generates the Two—the yin and yang, the primeval complementary forces.

"When the inferior man hears of the Tao, he bursts out laughing."

—*Lao Tzu*

"Man conforms to Earth

Earth conforms to

 Heaven

Heaven conforms to Tao

And Tao conforms to the

 way of Nature."

—*Lao Tzu*

### The Void

In other places, Lao Tzu characterizes the Tao as a "great void"; however, his meaning here seems more in accord with the Buddhist concept of *sunyata,* or emptiness: the emptiness that contains all. This is paradoxical, but that's the way it is. "The Valley Spirit never dies," says the Tao Te Ching.

This spirit not only does not die, but brings the entire universe to birth. "Mystery upon mystery," murmured Lao Tzu.

Perhaps it's not so mysterious after all. The emptiness of a bowl is what makes it useful. The Tao belongs to no one. Therefore it is all of ours.

### The Return

One important element of Tao teaching is the concept of "return," the idea of circularity or perfection. Here is another example of how Asian notions of time differ from those in the West. In the West, time runs forward in a straight line—that's where we get our ideas about progress and the glories of the future. In Taoism, everything returns at last to its starting point, as the river runs into the sea, which was its original source. The river may be compared to the Manifest Tao, and the sea to the Unmanifest Tao.

## THE TAO TE CHING

The Tao Te Ching *(Dao De Jing)* is the holy text of Taoism and represents the very heart of Taoist philosophy. (Only the Bible has been translated more often.) There are two main theories about its authorship.

- Lao Tzu wrote it.

- Somebody else wrote it.

One of these theories is bound to be correct, although there is a middle position that claims Lao Tzu wrote it and then somebody else edited it. In any case, it does appear that something was done to it between 350 and 275 B.C.E.

The story is that Lao Tzu was forced to write the book. Remember the border guard who wouldn't let Lao Tzu out of the country without some words of wisdom? Supposedly he became Lao Tzu's first disciple.

This famous but mysterious text is very short—only about five thousand Chinese characters, now usually arranged in eighty-one brief chapters. (The current chapter divisions were created by later editors.) The number eighty-one has a mystical value of nine times nine (and nine is composed of triple threes, a mystical number.) So the book has great mystical power.

Until the time of Emperor Ching (156–141 B.C.E.), it was split into only two parts: one section (1–37) on Tao or Way and one (38–81) on Te or Power. The Tao section is sometimes called the Upper Part and the Te section the Lower Part. Then the book was put together again. Then it was divided again into two parts. No one knows which part should come first; the most ancient texts have the parts in the reverse order of what is most common today. Since the book doesn't seem to be written in any order, perhaps it doesn't matter. It is true that the first chapter concerns the Tao and chapter thirty-eight concerns the Te, but that's about all you can say about it.

> "Your own mind is destined to become the universe."
>
> —*Master Tsêng*

### HOLY TAO

*Originally, the title of the Tao Te Ching was simply the Lao Tzu, after its supposed author. The present title was given to it after it had already become a classic. The Chinese word Ching is given to works that have received canonical status.*

The sentences are short, cryptic, and often rhymed, at least in Chinese, although radically different meters are employed. This convinces many scholars that the work had multiple authorship, although it certainly is possible for a writer to compose in more than one meter. In fact, it seems a rather Taoist thing to do, even as a river does not flow at the same speed everywhere along its course. Most scholars believe the work was composed during the Spring and Autumn period (770–476 B.C.E.).

Every chapter, and almost every line in the Tao Te Ching, is open to interpretation, and inevitably, argument. The very purpose of the text is disputed. For some, it's a guidebook for rulers. For others, it's a mystical celebration of the heart of life. For some it teaches pacifism, for others, the art of war. For all, it is enigmatic and mysterious. Although some like to think that the book's ambiguity lies in the complexity of its thought, it's at least equally likely that the confusion arises because of its varied authorship, with each writer trying to make a different point.

In any case, the ambivalence of this book only adds to its charm. By being fluid, it can resonate with the fluidity of the natural and political worlds it describes. By being mysterious, it remains open to visions and new interpretations. It is undoubtedly the very ambiguity of the Tao Te Ching that has led to its popularity.

"Emperor Wen was fond of the sayings of Lao Tzu, but there were many passages he could not understand—and he could not find anyone to explain them to him."

—*Ancient Chinese Legend*

## GOING WITH THE FLOW

"The Tao that can be spoken is not the Eternal Tao." These lines open the first chapter of the Tao Te Ching. They are curious words. If the Tao cannot be spoken, why is the poet trying to speak of it? But look again. The poet says that the Tao that can be spoken is not the Eternal Tao. This statement is merely in agreement with nearly every other religious tradition. The ultimate escapes words. Language can't hem it in, any more than a sieve can hold water, but if you dip the sieve quickly enough, a few glittering beads cling to the wire. The glittering beads are the Tao Te Ching.

> Darkness within darkness.
> The gate to all mystery.

These lines close the first chapter. And herein lies the complexity. The Tao is the Way. We might think of the Tao as a secret path through a forest, winding and narrow. It follows the natural contours of the earth and takes the traveler along with it. A broad, flat path is destructive: it cuts through landscape and destroys the very beauty it enters.

---

**A TAOIST ODDITY**

*One of the stranger things about the Tao Te Ching is its apparent disdain for commonly accepted virtues like "benevolence" and "kindness." In actual fact, it's likely that Lao Tzu had nothing against benevolence, but what he hated were the Confucians, who were always making a big deal about benevolence. It was just his way of getting back at them.*

---

Unlike the constructs of human beings, the Tao does not set itself up against the natural world. The Tao honors nature, and its narrow track takes us ever deeper into its mysteries.

The Tao is slight, hidden. It's easy to pass it by, the way we pass by, unseeing, the secret marvels of the earth. The Tao is also a flowing river, though, and water is one of its most sacred images. Flow is the absolutely essential component of Taoism. Water flows downward, into the most secret places of the earth. Other religions place their greatest triumphs upon mountains and put emphasis on struggle. In most faiths, there is always something to "conquer"— sin, ignorance, suffering, the self. In fact, struggle defines the very heart of many religious philosophies, from "Onward, Christian Soldier" to Islam's "holy war" (an idea borrowed from Judaism) to St. Paul's "I have fought the good fight." But Taoism turns away from this incessant battle. Struggle means going against the flow. Nothing could be further from the Tao. The Tao goes deep, and stresses *wu wei*—no action, no struggle. Paradoxically, the highest good is like water, which always seeks the low places. Yet water gives life to the Ten Thousand things and does not strive. It flows in places people reject, and so is like the Tao.

But the Tao is a living being, also—and contains all beings in its living heart. Of all the world's great spiritual traditions, Taoism and only Taoism understands that the way to salvation is not an escape from the natural world, or a triumph over it, but an ever-deepening meshing with it. Tao in the world is like a river flowing home to the sea.

> "No one in the world can say whether all this is true or not. Lao Tzu was a hidden sage."
>
> —*Ssu-ma Ch'ien*

## CHAPTER RECAP

- The traditional founder of Taoism is Lao Tzu, but almost nothing is known of his life—even if he ever existed.

- The Tao, or the Way, is regarded as the most important facet of the universe.

- The Tao is often compared to a secret river flowing through the landscape.

- The Tao Te Ching, Taoism's most important text, is a brief, but very complex and mysterious book.

*Recommended Reading*
Blackney, R.B. *The Way of Life: Lao Tzu.* Mentor, 1955.

Blofeld, John. *Taoism: The Road to Immortality.* Boston: Shambhala Publications, Inc. 1978.

Kaltenmark, Max. *Lao Tzu and Taoism.* Stanford, CA: Stanford University Press, 1969.

Kohn, Livia. *The Taoist Experience: An Anthology.* Albany, NY: State Univeristy of New York, 1993.

Liu I-Ming. *Awakening to the Tao.* trans. Thomas Cleary. Boston: Shambhala Publications, Inc., 1988.

*Tao Te Ching.* Numerous translations. Best to look at more than one!

Wong, Eva. *Taoism.* Boston: Shambhala Publications, Inc., 1997.

# *The Philosophy of Tao*

*T*aoist philosophy is often extremely difficult for Westerners to fully understand, as it flies in the face of our traditional linear thinking. Probably the most fundamental idea of Taoist thought is that of *wu wei.*

## WU WEI

"Tao does nothing, and yet there is nothing that is not done." This is the central tenet of Taoism and this concept exemplifies the Taoist philosophy of life. It doesn't mean nothingness; it means to be spontaneous, natural, and flowing. It means to move with the Tao. It is the original policy of nonintervention.

Although it seems simple to do nothing, to go with the flow, human beings persist in doing the exact opposite—fighting nature, creating our own structures, struggling upstream against the ceaseless Tao. This is what gets us into trouble, of course. Taoists thought that Confucians were sort of degenerated Taoists; they had lost the knack of following nature and had to cultivate virtues by relying on artificial structures. The great advantage of *wu wei* is that it enables one to adjust to change. When you make an effort, you are struggling against the flow, and that's bound to end in disaster.

In fact, sustaining and augmenting the ability to go with the flow is one way to achieve immortality. The early Chinese believed that people had only so much energy to expend; every time you used some up, there was that much less to live on. When all the energy was gone—you died. *Wu wei* is an excellent energy conserver.

**HOW LONG IS FOREVER?**

*Unfortunately for Westerners, the Chinese character for immortality can also mean simply longevity. Without further textual explanation, one cannot always be sure just what is intended.*

## POLITICAL PHILOSOPHY

It may seem odd in some ways that the Tao Te Ching, being such a mystical work in so many ways, spends a fair amount of time discussing political matters. But so it is. All Chinese religion and philosophy in some way concern government.

For the Chinese culture, government of a people was as important as liberation of the self, and both were functions of religion. The Tao Te Ching once again brings forth the analogy of water. If the ruler rules in accordance with the Tao, it says, then all his subjects will flow to him, and all will naturally be in accord with that great river. Lao Tzu had suggestions for political leaders, such as: "Govern a large country as you would cook a small fish." Apparently this means a lot to some people.

In describing his utopia, Lao Tzu thought it should be small, with a low population; however, he also suggested (rather disconcertingly, to my view) that one should be able to hear the neighbor's roosters crow and dogs bark. Lao Tzu also disliked all laws, because he was convinced that promulgating laws only tempted people to break them. Strangely enough, Lao Tzu did not always condemn war. He thought it had its place, as long as it was conducted using Taoist principles, not because he thought Taoist principles were more moral than other kinds; but because he thought they'd help you win.

## CHUANG TZU

Chuang Tzu (369–286 B.C.E.?) was Lao Tzu's most famous disciple. Very little is known of him, except that (maybe) he lived around 300 B.C.E. Rumor has it that he was a petty official at the Lacquer Garden.

Even more than Lao Tzu, Chuang Tzu exalted the simple life. One famous story tells about the time he was fishing in the P'u River.

Two messengers from a certain Prince Chu showed up to offer him a top job with the government. Chuang Tzu sent the messengers back, telling them he had no interest in being decked up like a ceremonial ox and led to the slaughter. Then he said he'd rather be a live tortoise wagging its tail in the mud than a dead one in a golden casket.

He also suggested that if a ruler really wanted to get rid of an annoying wise man, he should offer him the throne. The insult would be enough to make any self-respecting hermit plunge into the nearest river holding a rock. At another time, he remarked that it was the useless who survive. The good-for-nothing tree is the one that doesn't get chopped down. He mentioned that when sacrificing to the river god, certain victims were ineligible because they were not "good enough." He included in his list an ox with a white forehead, a pig with a turned-up snout, and a girl with hemorrhoids. There appear to be advantages to everything.

He also thought people were better off before they learned how to write. He thought the previous method of communication— knotting rope to create symbols—was far preferable. It's certainly easier to learn.

When Chuang Tzu's wife died, he was discovered singing cheerfully and beating time on a bowl. When his guest rebuked him, Chuang Tzu admitted, "I was upset at first. But then I remembered that death is just one more change—just as summer passes in fall, and fall into winter. She is asleep in the great resting place."

If this sounds a bit cold, Chuang Tzu was equally nonchalant about his own death. When he lay dying, his disciples asked for funeral instructions. Chuang Tzu responded, "Nothing fancy. The earth is my coffin and the sky my shroud. The moon and stars are my funerary gems. The ten thousand creatures can be my pall bearers." One of his disciples suggested diffidently that he was afraid his master's body would be consumed by vultures. "Vultures above the ground, or worms beneath it—what's the difference?" asked Chuang Tzu reasonably. "Why rob one to feed the other? What partiality!"

Among Chuang Tzu's followers was the highly skilled Lieh Tzu. Lieh Tzu took to heart the admonition to cut oneself off from the world, and managed to do so fairly completely—he could ride the wind. He wrote, "I felt as if my mind was solidifying, my body coming apart, and my bones and flesh dissolving. I no longer felt

"Let there be no seeing, no hearing; enfold the spirit in quietude and the body will right itself."

—*Chuang Tzu*

that body leaned against something, nor that my feet touched the ground, but let myself be borne east and west by the wind...until I could no longer tell whether I was carrying the wind along or whether the wind was carrying me."

Lieh Tzu confided all this to a student who had been bothering him for years about his secret of wind riding. Of course, Lieh Tzu had never answered him—most Tao masters teach in silence. The goal is to attain a mind as clear and deep and quiet as a still pond on a still day. The ever-present water imagery has transformed itself from a river to a pool. It should be said that some spoilsports claim Lieh Tzu never rode the wind at all—it's a spiritual metaphor. That could be, I suppose. At any rate, it's a sure bet that one who can ride the wind either figuratively or literally has achieved a high degree of holiness. The whole concept of spirit wandering became part of Chinese lore; the ability to do so successfully was a sign of spiritual attainment. King Mu of Chou got dizzy when he tried it and had to return home to his palace.

**THE BELOVED**

*Chuang Tzu had a favorite rival, Hui Shih. He loved debating Hui Shih and observed that he "had an answer for everything without even bothering to think."*

## The Chuang Tzu

Chuang Tzu's most famous work is simply named after him, the Chuang Tzu. Most scholars don't believe that Chuang Tzu wrote the entire work, although they have no better suggestions. Many theorists believe that the so-called "inner chapters" of the text (1–7) derive from Chuang Tzu himself via an authentic oral tradition. Our knowledge about Chuang Tzu is sparse, however, and scholars are unable to say anything about him with any certitude.

Unlike the Tao Te Ching, the Chuang Tzu is a nonpolitical work and addresses spiritual concerns only. Probably because of this, it manages to avoid some of the paradoxes that mark the Tao Te Ching, which sometimes seems to advocate action and sometimes nonaction. The Chuang Tzu never advocates action. In fact, it's hard to say what exactly it does advocate.

Like Confucianism, Taoism began as a formal tradition during the period of the Warring States (c. 475–222 B.C.E.). The pacifistic nature of the Tao Te Ching is probably a response to the chaotic state of affairs. In fact, as time went on, and the political situation got even worse, Taoist teachers gave up on the idea of a just government altogether. Although the early Tao Te Ching contains quite a bit of advice for rulers, by the time of Chuang Tzu, it was simply assumed that all government was evil by nature. Chuang Tzu did throw a couple of bones toward rulers, though. He said that they should look after their own souls.

Thus, Chuang Tzu's concern was almost solely for the spiritual life. He said that if you wanted to reach the heavens, you had to shut down the organs of sense. This is what Indian meditators had been saying for years, of course. The Taoists also believed that the sense organs were openings through which the vital fluids might escape if you didn't keep a close watch on them.

Like some Hindu philosophers, Chuang Tzu also apparently thought that the senses, rather than revealing reality, conceal it. He listed five causes for "impairment" of human nature: the five colors, which prevent us from seeing clearly; the five notes, which prevent us from hearing distinctly; the five odors, which clog up our olfactory senses; the five flavors, which destroy the taste buds; the fifth is our likes and dislikes, which make it impossible to discern correctly. Chuang Tzu called these the "five evils of life."

The second chapter of his book, "The Equality of All Things," is concerned with taking generally accepted truths and turning them upside down. Petty truths give rise to their own opposites—only the Tao can hold all complexities without conflict.

You could even accuse Chuang Tzu of being faintly immoral. At one point he wrote of the spiritual person: "Life and death do not affect her. How much less will she be concerned with good and evil!" (Because Chinese doesn't distinguish gender in language, one could use either "he" or "she" here.) Good and evil are not absolutes, but relative concepts. Only the Tao, vast and nameless, rises behind and inside them all.

For Chuang Tzu, the Tao was the ultimate life force. He said that it could be "transmitted, but not possessed. It exists before heaven and earth, and it lasts forever." Don't get the idea, however, that just because the Tao existed before heaven and earth that it therefore produced heaven and earth. No, they produced themselves. It was the great "hollowness" of the Tao that allowed them to come into being. A lot of this sounds a great deal like the *sunyata* concept of Buddhism, and it does seem as if Mahayana Buddhists and Taoists have come up with somewhat the same idea, however,

"Great knowledge is all-encompassing; small knowledge is limiting."

*—Chuang Tzu*

modern physicists have come up with pretty much the same explanation for the Big Bang.

The moral relativity apparent in the Chuang Tzu arises from its author's new conception of the Tao. For Lao Tzu, the Tao was a benevolent and caring force. For Chuang Tzu, it was a neutral, indifferent power. It was worthy of respect, but Chuang Tzu felt it was an error to treat the Tao as if it really gave a heck what happened to you.

The Chuang Tzu is mostly prose, unlike the Tao Te Ching, but it is just as beautiful. It's also very funny, which is a refreshing change from most religious literature. To give you a feel for what some of it is like, here's a passage from chapter 2: "The Equality of All Things" [trans. Burton Watson, Columbia University Press, p. 38].

> There is a beginning. There is a not yet beginning to be a beginning. There is a not yet beginning to be a not yet beginning to be a beginning. There is being. There is nonbeing. There is a not yet beginning to be nonbeing. There is a not yet beginning to be a not yet beginning to be nonbeing.

After going on like this a bit longer, Chuang Tzu confesses, "Now I don't know whether I've said anything here or not."

## Tales from the Chuang Tzu

In one famous story, Chuang Tzu recounts the predicament of some monkeys who receive seven acorns a day, three in the morning and four at night. The animals complain bitterly about this arrangement, so the trainer gives them four acorns in the morning and three at night. Then they're happy. Everyone laughs at this story, thinking it shows the absurdity of the monkeys, but I'm not so sure. Some of us prefer having a larger meal in the morning, and some don't.

Chuang Tzu's best-known remarks, however, concerned a butterfly.

> Last night I dreamed I was a butterfly. I flew about and enjoyed life without knowing who I was. Then I woke up and discovered I was Chuang Tzu. Now, did Chuang Tzu dream he was a butterfly? Or did the butterfly dream he was Chuang Tzu? There must be some difference between me and a butterfly. This is a case of transformation.

"Suppose you and I argue? If you win and I lose, are you indeed right and I wrong?"

—*Chuang Tzu*

With this conclusion, the chapter ends.

The most notable tale in the Chuang Tzu, however, is the story of Cook Ting, a master butcher. The story goes that Lord Wen-hui was watching the cook work. His knife seemed to fly through the meat. "Goodness," marveled the lord. "You work fast. How often do you need to sharpen your knife?"

"Well," responded the cook. "When I started in this business I had to do it pretty often. But now—well, I haven't sharpened this here blade for nineteen years now."

"How can that be?" asked the lord.

"Because," explained Ting, "I cut up the ox by spirit. My knife glides along through the natural interstices in the meat, between the bone and ligament, between the muscles and tendons. Because it never actually touches any tissue—only the space between them, the meat just falls apart and the knife stays sharp." This instructional tale, although highly improbable, teaches a valuable lesson. The first is obvious, that one should work by following the Tao— the natural "flow" of the work. In that way, one encounters no obstacles along the path. It also teaches us that following the Tao is a path for everyone—even a butcher. It is not a way limited to mystics, gurus, and adepts. The way of the Tao is the natural way for all people.

> "The Tao is an ant, a blade of grass, a tile, a manure heap."
>
> —*Chuang Tzu*

### Chuang Tzu's Epistemology

Chuang had an epistemology also, which means a theory of knowledge. According to him, there are two levels of knowledge, a lower level and a higher level. We acquire our lower level of knowledge from our senses, and the higher level from our mind. The lower level of knowledge is subject to change and argument; the higher level is not. "The knowledge of the ancients," he said, was "perfect." This was because they didn't know that there were any "things" in the universe. As soon as they found out about "things" and made "distinctions" and then "judgments," everything got all messed up. The understanding of the Tao was destroyed.

### Chuang Tzu and the Philosophy of Death

According to Chuang Tzu, the fear of death is the primary source of unhappiness in life, but Chuang Tzu said that death was nothing to fear. In fact, he tells a story wherein he happened upon a skull lying by the side of the road. Chuang Tzu gave it a good smack with his riding crop and demanded to know how it had come to its present state. "Perhaps," he suggested, "you were ambitious or greedy? Did you lead an evil life? Die in battle? Or just get old?" The skull kept mum, so Chuang Tzu picked it up, took it home, and used it as a pillow. During the night the skull appeared to him in a dream and appeared to have plenty to say. It spoke of the joys of death and claimed that it wouldn't go back to living in this evil old world for a million bucks. So Chuang Tzu concluded we have nothing to fear from death. As we have seen, Chuang Tzu put a lot of stock in dreams.

In Taoist thought, the yin and yang, which have temporarily combined in the human body during life, separate. The yang goes to heaven, and the yin goes back into earth. Then everything is ready for recycling.

> "And death is different from what anyone supposed, and luckier."
> —*Walt Whitman*

## CHAPTER RECAP

- The heart of Taoism is the concept of *wu wei*, the art of inaction, or going with the flow.

- Although Lao Tzu gave political advice, later Taoists believed that politics was a waste of time.

- Chuang Tzu was Lao Tzu's most mystical and important disciple.

*Recommended Reading*

Watson, Burton. *Chuang Tzu: Basic Writings.* New York: Columbia University Press, 1964.

Welch, Homes H. ed. *Facets of Taoism.* New Haven: Yale University Press, 1979.

# *Religious Taoism*

*I*t used to be said that religious Taoism *(Tao chiao)* and philosophical Taoism *(Tao chia)* were two entirely different things, the first dealing with control over the physical world by magic, and the second dealing with the spirit. This isn't really accurate, however, because for Taoists of all beliefs, the physical and spiritual worlds are not sharply divided. Still, the emphasis of each is different. Philosophical Taoism, for example, does not concern itself with gods at all, while religious Taoism is full of them. These differences make it worth considering them separately.

Religious Taoism reached its peak in China during the T'ang dynasty; these are the same people who claimed that Lao Tzu was their ancestor. These and later emperors became enamored of Taoist concepts (probably longing for immortality had something to do with it) and as a result, in the mid-800s, Emperor Wu-Tsung even persecuted Buddhists.

## THE EIGHT IMMORTALS

This colorful Taoist octet consists of the following members, who are largely recognizable by their gear:

**MAGIC CHARMS**

*Taoism even has its own version of the universal "magic charm." The charms are only available, however, to those who have already achieved the Tao. They are called Spontaneous Inscriptions of Jade Clarity and they will appear in your mind upon red and coral clouds.*

- Chung-li Ch'uan carries a fan and has a big gut bared to the breeze. In life he was a Han dynasty general who was sent to fight the Tibetans.

- Lu Tung-pin has a sword, but it's not a weapon (he wears it on his back). Lu uses it to make himself invisible and to cut off his desires.

- Chang Kuo-lao is an elderly man whose emblem is a drum. He is famous for his assortment of weird headgear and also for his mount, a white mule that can be folded up and stuck in one's pocket when not needed for traveling.

- Ts'ao Kuo-chiu carries a pair of wooden castanets, sort of like a Spanish dancer. He wears a winged hat, which marks him as a member of royalty, and in fact, he's the brother-in-law of some emperor. Ts'ao, when asked where heaven was, pointed at his own heart.

- Li Hsuan carries an iron staff and a bottle made from a gourd. He needs the staff because one of his legs is shorter than the other. (It's a long story.)

- Han Hsiang-Tzu carries a flute and is often depicted as a child. He lives upon midnight dew.

- Lan Ts'ai Ho carries a flower basket and is so sweet looking that he's often mistaken for a woman. When on earth he walked around with only one shoe, and he wore thin clothes in the winter and thick ones in the summer...

- Ho Hsien-ku carries a lotus. She is the only female among the lot, and she became immortal to flee an unwanted marriage arranged by her wicked stepmother.

Besides these eight, there are three other immortals who crop up from time to time: Fu, Lu, and Shou. These three stand for wealth, rank, and longevity.

The goal of the so-called Taoist immortals was the attainment of physical immortality, which they attempted by many means, including medicine and magic as well as alchemy. One method worked about as well as another.

You can always recognize the immortals because of their shining eyes and their smooth, unwrinkled skin. They are also said to move about with uncommon grace and freedom. The Taoist immortal has achieved a weightless body, composed of a magical jadelike substance. It is impervious to both fire and ice. The Taoist immortal can live upon wind and dew, and his body endures forever.

Many times Taoist immortals are depicted having a high old time drinking and playing games. Of course, they are drinking out of thimbles and playing chess, but when one has achieved a great age immortal-wise, that may be sufficient. More excitingly, some also ride dragons and unicorns.

Taoist literature is filled with the marvelous abilities of sages. Apart from the fact that they retained their youthful looks into old age, sages were also immune to poisons and could talk to the animals.

It's really rather hard to say who becomes an immortal and who doesn't. Even those who seem to die ordinary deaths may be just being discreet. Sure enough, sometimes their coffins have been opened after their deaths, and there is nothing left but a staff, sword, and sandals. The Immortal One himself has gone to one of the many Taoist heavens, or perhaps to one of the Islands of the Blessed that slide around on the ocean on the backs of giant turtles. Inhabitants of the isles can fly around and visit each other. The Queen of the Immortals is Hsi Wang Mu, Fairy Mother of the West. From the front, and when she wasn't smiling, she looked like an ordinary woman, but closer inspection revealed a leopard tail and tiger teeth. Later on, the Taoists got rid of the leopard tail and tiger teeth as being somewhat unladylike.

## THE TAOIST SOUL

Like the Confucians, and indeed like all traditional Chinese, Taoists believed that one has two souls: the yin-like *P'o* soul that is connected with the blood and hangs around the rotting corpse, and the yang-like *Hun* soul that governs the breath and soars about in heavenly realms. The *Hun* doesn't last forever, though. Immortality is a gift to be granted only through rigorous effort.

**SOUL SACRIFICE**

*If proper sacrifices are not performed for the P'o soul, it might become a kuei, or evil demon.*

## TAOIST ALCHEMY

Alchemy was already an ancient science in China by the time religious Taoism developed. "The ancient masters were profound and subtle," writes Lao Tzu. "Their wisdom was unfathomable..." (It's rumored that immortal ancient Taoist masters still live in the hinterlands of China and Korea. Others dwell in the more mythical land P'eng Lai Shan, and still more in the even more mythical abodes of cloud-coral. Others live on the moon.)

The Chinese name for alchemy is Green Dragon White Tiger, a fabulously evocative phrase that neatly sums up both the procedure and the philosophy behind it. (The dragon is the yang force and the tiger is the yin.)

In Taoism alchemy, the universal energy, or *ch'i,* is created in the body and purified by proper nutrition and life habits. *Ch'i* circulates up and down twelve psychic channels in the body and goes through many circulations before it is distilled and rarefied.

In 320 C.E. the first Chinese alchemical text, the *Nei P'ien,* was written, but it was based on an oral tradition already very old. The author was Ko Hung (253–333? C.E.).

### Ko Hung

Altogether Ko Hung wrote 116 works, quite a feat, especially considering he had to paint everything with a delicate brush rather than use a word processor. Ko Hung was reputed to be the greatest Tao master who ever lived, even though he started life off as a Confucian. Then he went into the army, but like so many others was disgusted by life there. He retired to the mountains and devoted himself to mystical studies. Ko Hung resembled the Hindu adepts in that he believed one could not achieve full realization without the help of a teacher. What is written down in words can never explain everything. Of course, this is also right in line with classic Taoist thought. "The Tao that can be spoken is not the Eternal Tao."

He died at the age of eighty-one, sitting in a yogic position, his body as supple as a young man's.

It should be pointed out, I suppose, that Ko Hung never actually did any alchemy himself. He said it was too expensive, and he was too poor. But he did own a lot of books about it. Ko Hung left

"A mind fed on words such as heaven, earth, dew, essence, cinnabar, moonlight, stillness, jade, pearl, cedar, and winter-plum is likely to have a serenity not to be found in minds ringing with the vocabulary of the present age—computer, tractor, jumbo jet, speedball, pop, dollar, liquidation, napalm, overkill!"

—*John Blofeld*

behind 149 secret recipes of various kinds, effective against wolves, demons, spiders, tigers, or whatever you might happen to come upon. He said he got the recipes from Lao Tzu, but he probably made them up himself.

Ko Hung's greatest disciple was T'ao Hung-chin, who began studying Ko Hung's works when he himself was still a child. He was especially interested in cultivating immortality, and although he didn't live forever, it is said that even at the age of eighty-five, he resembled a youth of twenty. (There seems to be a trend going on here.) He was so admired that some sources say that the emperor of China went to visit him in his mountain retreat!

### The Immortality Formula

It appears that the worldwide quest for the elusive elixir to attain immortality actually began in China; certainly that is our earliest reference to it. Ssu-ma Chi'ien's history of China, written in the second century B.C.E., provides several methods for attaining immortality—or at least staving off the inevitable for a very long time. (Ten thousand years is a commonly quoted figure.) These methods include avoiding the consumption of grain, worshiping the Stove (kitchen gods), and drinking out of vessels made from cinnabar (mercury ore) turned into gold. Turning mercury into gold isn't as easy as it sounds, however, because you need the Philosopher's Stone, which isn't all that easy to come by. Then you have to undertake the Niefold Transmutation. This isn't easy either.

In my mind, one of the great paradoxes about the whole Chinese tradition is the apparent contradiction between the calm acceptance of Heaven's Mandate (Confucianism) or of the Tao (Taoism) and the mad search for immortality. The Mandate and the Tao both celebrate death as part of the natural cycle of things. Despite these assurances, people just didn't want to die. They kept running about like mad searching for the secret to immortal life. (The alchemists in medieval Europe never did anything like this. They were too busy trying to turn lead into gold and never aimed for anything higher.)

Unfortunately, Taoist experiments to obtain immortality by ingesting poisonous substances had rather the reverse effect. Several emperors met their end this way. Safer methods, employing

**THE FANG SHIH**

*Apparently there were some very early alchemists around called the Fang Shih (the "masters of the formula") who were more than just druggists and doctors. Some of these men specialized in divination and healing, while others searched out, and reportedly found, the secret to immortality.*

jade and pearl, were also tried. At least they didn't kill anybody, so far as I know.

Eventually, Taoist practitioners became convinced that the ingredients for immortality were spiritual rather than physical substances. Instead of using real mercury or lead or arsenic, Taoist alchemists began talking about the "souls" of these various substances. This became known as *nei-tan* or secret alchemy. In another development, the alchemical metals were each identified with a particular animal and with various parts of the human body. In one system, mercury is represented by the dragon (yang) and is associated with semen and blood. Lead is the tiger (yin), who represents breath and physical power. Each element is also associated with a particular trigram of the I Ching.

The basic procedure is this: you have to turn your *ching* into *ch'i*, then you turn the *ch'i* into *shên*. (Not regular *shên*. Pure cosmic *shên*.) Simple as that.

Before plunging into alchemy, certain preparations are required. Among these are fasting for a week and bathing in scented water during the day. Purification rituals were often called "fasting of the heart" *(hsin chai)*.

---

### THE UNION OF THE THREE

*Wei Po-Yang, a Taoist master of the second century C.E., combined studies of the five elements with a Taoist interpretation of the I Ching. He wrote a book called Ts'an T'ung Ch'i, a title that is apparently untranslatable, as is most of the rest of the book. (It may mean something like "the union of three.") The "three" are presumably essence (ching), energy (ch'i), and spirit (shên), which constantly interact and form a "spirit body." Part of the Ts'an T'ung Ch'i is standard alchemical fare—turning base metals into gold and so on, but the rest has to do with golden elixirs, immortal fetuses, military strategy, or yoga.*

---

### ALCHEMY ACCESSORIES

*The top items in the Taoist pharmacopoeia are cinnabar, gold, silver, the five mushrooms, jade, mica, pearl, and arsenic. It's also important to gather the materials at exactly the right time.*

---

## TAOIST YOGA

Like the Hindu yoga of Patanjali, there exists a Taoist yoga, which has been described as internal alchemy. It too has eight steps, although they differ from the eight steps of Patanjali. The eight steps of Taoist yoga are:

1. Conservation of the *ching*

2. Restoration or reparation of the *ching*

3. Transmutation of the *ching*

4. Nourishing the *ch'i*

5. Transmutation of the *ch'i*

6. Nourishing the *shên*

7. Transmutation of the *shên*

8. Transmutation of the voided *shên* to make it one with the void

The eight steps may appear somewhat abstruse, but Taoist yoga is deliberately mystical. Practitioners undergo a long, very secretive initiation process.

To accomplish their objective, Taoists place great emphasis on proper breathing techniques. (These exercises must be done between midnight and noon, when the air is "alive.") Good breathing, by the way, involves not just the nose and lungs, but the whole body, starting at the heels, according to Chuang Tzu. The final goal is "fetal breathing." Here the practitioner breathes without either inhaling or exhaling. Taoists believe that a person is allotted a certain number of breaths at birth; when the breaths are all used up—the person dies. So the object of meditation is to breathe as little as possible. Another technique is to adjust the breathing rate to the heartbeat, gradually taking fewer and fewer breaths.

This is really hard and takes years of practice, although we can all do it easily before we're born. There's a lesson to be learned here. Anyway, once you perfect this technique, your pulse ceases (I can well believe it) and, according to Taoists, you enter the Great Quietude. I believe this too, although my version of the Great Quietude might be different from that of the Taoist masters.

Taoists also try to eat as little as possible. They feel that food simply clogs up the system and keeps the *shên* stuck in the gross body.

Taoist masters composed some of the earliest formal treatises on the art of meditation. As I noted before, the purpose of Taoist meditation (or yoga) was to free the yang spirit, the *shên,* from the yin body. The great thing was that you didn't have to actually die to free the spirit, either; you could do it while still in this very life.

Technically, there are three forms of Taoist meditation: concentrative meditation, insight meditation, and "ecstatic journeys." The ecstatic journeys allow one to leave the body and visit other spheres, a very handy trick.

## HUANG TI—THE YELLOW EMPEROR

Taoists are sometimes known in China as Huang Lao. This title incorporates two important names in Taoist history. One, of course, is Lao Tzu. The other is Huang Ti, the Yellow Emperor. A Taoist is one who follows the path of Lao Tzu and the Yellow Emperor. And who is the Yellow Emperor? I wish I knew. He was one of the so-called five Emperor Sages who reputedly existed during China's Golden Age (2852–2255 B.C.E.). The Emperor Sages invented all sorts of useful things: fire, plows, looms, and the like. The Yellow Emperor himself discovered the secret of personal immortality by experimenting with the "essences" of male and female couples.

The spiritually minded Chuang Tzu and his nonpolitical followers such as Lieh Tzu, I have to say, had no use for the Yellow Emperor. They said he was a meddler. To be fair, they said the same about all rulers.

## THE INSTITUTION OF TAOISM

Curiously, Taoism may owe its survival to Buddhism, its religious "competitor." Devout Taoists soon realized the advantages of temples, priests, and ceremony in capturing people's attention. Without these elements, Taoism would probably have shrunk to a tradition practiced by a few hermits in the middle of nowhere. (Even if that was what Lao Tzu had in mind, it's no way to become a world religion.)

While the earliest Taoists were wanderers, hermits, and recluses, later devotees became priests and community leaders. Taoist sages became renowned for their ability to control demons, heal the sick, and perhaps even give some good advice. Soon they took on the role of priests. It is commonly said that "religious Taoism" is somehow inferior to pure, or philosophical Taoism, but I see no need to "grade" them.

### Chang Tao Ling and the Celestial Masters

Chang Tao Ling (25–219 c.e.), the so-called Heavenly Master, is largely responsible for the development of Taoism as an organized religion. (Some people insist he is a mythical figure. The dates *are* a little suspicious; however, a slight mistake in dating doesn't prove one never existed.)

Chang Tao Ling hailed from south China, an area where traditional folk beliefs and magical practices remained strong. He began his career in the army, but had a life-changing experience when a plague hit his whole division. Chang was one of the few who escaped death, a fact he attributed to a lucky charm he happened to keep around for dealing with demons. After this scare, he moved to Snow Goose Mountain in far-west Szechuan province (Shu), another area of mystic beliefs and shamanistic practices. Here he lived a retired life and learned the secret of immortality.

Chang's religious calling began when he had a vision of Lao Tzu as a god. He said Lao Tzu had taught him how to heal sick people and how to dispose of evil spirits. He was apparently very good at it and won a large following. The religion was known unofficially as the Way of the Five Bushels of Rice, because that's what it cost to join up. The more official name of this Taoist branch is the Celestial Masters, which officially existed right up until 1949, when the Communists threw out the last of them. Followers of Chang still (quietly) exist today; their main focus is the attainment of immortality. This is in contradistinction to "philosophical Taoism," which aims at tranquility and enlightenment.

> **TAOISM OVER TIME**
>
> *Many secret and mystical Taoist societies sprang up, especially in the early part of the common era, when the Red Eyebrows overthrew Wang Ming. During the third century of the common era, Neo-Taoism, also referred to as the Dark Learning, developed.*

> **THE TAOIST LIBRARY**
>
> *The Tao Te Ching and Chuang Tzu are not the only books in the Taoist collection. Later Taoists began to write their own canon of holy texts (Tao Tsang). The present Taoist canon was compiled in 1445 c.e., and contains 1,464 titles. They are divided into three parts called the Three Caverns, an idea they got from the Buddhists.*

Soon Chang began writing works on various topics including health, hygiene, and demonology. (His experience in the army had made him an expert on all three.) For a while Chang meddled in political affairs, but he found the work unrewarding as he wasn't really able to effect much change in the way things were being run.

**TREASURE AND
JEWELS**

*Don't get the Three Treasures
of Taoism (Ling Pao, Yu
Huang, and Lao Chun, or
ching, ch'i, and shên) confused with the Three Jewels
of Buddhism (refuge in the
Buddha, the dharma, and the
sangha).*

After he discovered the secret of immortality (he used a "nine-times
refined" elixir), he mounted a dragon and entered the Immortal
Kingdom. He was 123 years old.

As chief of a community of priests, Chang Tao Ling's title was
T'ien Shih. His office became a hereditary one, passed on from
Chang to Chang through the centuries. Each successive spiritual
master was a reincarnation of the previous one, sort of like the Dalai
Lama. In this case, however, the reincarnation took place in the person of one's own offspring. Chang's descendants have been called
the "Taoist Popes," because Chang's teachings became authoritative
in Taoism.

The official text of the Celestial Masters was The Book of
Peace and Balance *(T'ai-p'ing ching)*. It is a revealed text rather
than a philosophical treatise like the Tao Te Ching and Chuang
Tzu. A revealed text is one written by the gods themselves and
revealed to human beings.

Most Celestial Masters remained in society and acted as priests
for layfolk, but a few, known as the Sect of Total Perfection *(Ch'uan-
chen Chiao)* forsook society and lived as hermit monks. This sect
united Taoist spiritual alchemy with Buddhist meditation practices
and Confucian social ethics.

In the fourth century C.E., many northern capitals were sacked and
the whole coterie of Celestial Masters and other aristocrats escaped
to southeast China. They founded another community on Dragon
Mountain in Kiangsi Province.

Later still, the Celestial Masters advocated a rather romantic
approach to nature, and still later, began to synthesize elements of
many other religions, including the native shamanism.

## THE TAOIST TRINITY OF TREASURE

Taoists eventually came up with their own trinity of gods: Ling
Pao (the marvelously responsive jewel), who was the embodiment
of yin and yang, and the lord of the past; Yu Huang (the Jade
Emperor), in charge of the First Cause and the present; and Lao
Chun, the deified name for Lao Tzu. Others say this is nonsense
and that the real Taoist trinity is *ching, ch'i,* and *shên*.

These elements are present in all of nature, and in the human body as well. In Taoist thought, the body is a microcosm of the universe. Within us are the three treasures. The *ching* is analogous to (and may even be) the sexual fluid of both sexes. It rises from a "cauldron" below the navel in a steamlike vapor up the spine until it reaches another "cauldron" in the head. Then it falls back through the "heart center" and back into the lower cauldron. There it becomes an Immortal Fetus, as they say. The Immortal Fetus is able to rise through the head and leave the body. (One way to create an Immortal Fetus is through sex, but it has to be a special kind of sex with which I am not familiar.)

Although Taoists maintained that the body contains the Three Treasures, they also thought it was composed of three areas known as the Three Fields of Cinnabar. The Higher Field of Cinnabar was the brain; the Middle was the heart area; the Lower was beneath the navel. In the Fields of Cinnabar dwell the guardian spirits *(shên)* but also the evil body demons called the Three Worms. The worms live on the ordinary food we eat. They want us to die quickly because that sets them free. To avoid this, Taoist spiritual masters do not eat regular food such as meat, wine, grains, or anything with a strong smell. The bulk of their diet is herbs and minerals. Very healthy. Once one has achieved immortality, one can live off dew or emanations from the universe.

> "The Perfect Man is pure spirit."
>
> —*Chuang Tzu*

## TAOIST COMMUNITIES

Taoists masters, although solitary by nature, sometimes formed isolated communities in spots of surpassing natural beauty. Favored locations included mountaintops or near streams of running water. They also prized stands of blossoming trees. Each Taoist hut contained one perfect object of art—an elegant vase, lovely painting, or fine bookshelf. Otherwise the masters lived in complete austerity, living on simple fare like bean curds and vegetables. They wore special clothing of antique design that marked them as Taoists— loose trousers, short jacket, a robe and white socks, heavy-soled cloth shoes. A brimless hat completed the outfit. An elaborate topknot secured with a hair peg protruded through the hat.

RETAINING
THE LIFE FORCE

*Taoists felt that having an
ejaculation used up the life
force. If a man refrained
from ejaculating, the life-
giving semen would freely
circulate around his body,
nourishing all his organs
and extending his life.*

Unlike Buddhist or Christian monasteries, Taoist ones had no rules, no set times to meditate or perform yoga. Because Taoist monasteries had no clocks, each person set his own schedule. They made most of their income by preparing charms for wandering pilgrims. The chief Taoist master was addressed as "Your Immortality."

## TAOIST PRIESTS

Taoist priests have two main functions in society: they exorcise demons and perform various rites on behalf of the public. Many wear ornate, even outlandish costumes and make use of rich incense, flute and lute music, and other impressive devices.

Exorcisms are very important, especially to clean the demons out of houses. For this purpose, the priest may use a willow branch, which he dips into water and sprinkles in the corners of the house. Then he may spit some of the water onto each wall of the home, adjuring the cursed demons to remove themselves and go back to the direction they came from. You can figure out the origin of a demon by its color. Blue demons, for example, live in the east, while white ones live in the west.

The most important rite of passage for a Taoist priest is the Chaio *(Jaio),* a sacrificial ceremony that may last for more than three days. Behind this public ritual, however, lie many years of study, hard work, and apprenticeship under a master. One group of priests is the so-called Red Heads, the other the Black Heads.

## TAOISTS AND CONFUCIANS

During the Han dynasty period (206 B.C.E.–220 C.E.), when Confucianism became the state religion, Taoism developed in its own quiet way. And when the Han dynasty eventually fell, Taoism took over the entire southern part of the country, while Buddhism became more influential in the north. One eastern Han emperor actually set up a shrine to Lao Tzu to honor him.

Tao exerted a great influence on Confucianism during the Ming dynasty (1368–1644). Not only were many Taoist terms such as *wu* incorporated into the Confucian lexicon, but many Confucians even took up meditating and other apparently strange or at least un-Confucian customs.

The Taoists and the Confucians have usually coexisted peacefully, but sometimes not. In the nineteenth century, hundreds of Tantric Taoists burned themselves to death rather than surrender to Confucian authorities. The Confucians had heard rumors about the sexual yoga of the Taoists and were intent upon stamping it out.

## CHAPTER RECAP

- Religious Taoism developed a kind of spiritual alchemy aimed at attaining immortality.

- Chang Tao Ling was an early priest and leader who was largely responsible for the creation of the Taoist religion.

- Tao has also developed its own yoga system.

*Recommended Reading*
Nan, Huai-Chin. *Tao and Longevity: Mind-Body Transformation.* Trans. Web Kuan Chu. York Beach, ME: Samuel Weiser, Inc., 1984.

# *Taoism Today*

*T*aoism became much stronger in Taiwan than on the Chinese mainland. During the Communist takeover of China, the thirty-seventh Heavenly Master moved to the island to avoid persecution. In Taiwan, there are two levels of Taoist priests, the Fa-shih, who perform most simple public rituals, and the Tao-shih, the masters who perform the most sacred and mystical rites, including the ceremonies to win favors from heaven and those to free souls from hell.

A few Taoist temples remain on the mainland, however.

## MARTIAL ARTS

One of the most famous of the martial arts is t'ai chi chuan *(tai ji)*. Technically, it's a soft form of kung fu, but it also inherited a lot from Taoist traditions. The original version appeared around the tenth century, but was perfected in the thirteenth century by one Chang San-feng, a Taoist monk. He got the idea by watching a snake fight with a crane. Tai chi chuan is a slow, dancelike set of movements, in which "the various parts of the body should be connected like pearls on a thread."

A quite remarkable martial art is seen in the Chinese film *Crouching Tiger, Hidden Dragon*. It is based, according to the story, on the secret knowledge of another Taoist monk, Jiu Hua. This particular art features soaring through the air and incomprehensibly quick movements. You might be surprised to learn that the name of the young male lover, Luo Xiao Hu, means small tiger, while the name of the young female, Yu Jiao Long, means delicate dragon.

**PAINTING IN FLOW**

*The ink used in Taoist painting is "watered," which, in and of itself, is quite Taoist.*

## TAOISM AND PAINTING

Taoism has had a strong influence on Chinese art, especially on landscape painting. In classical Taoist painting, nature is shown as overshadowing the human figure. It exemplifies the Taoist idea that it is nature that surrounds us, not we who control nature.

In honor of the changefulness and mobility of nature, Taoist artists always leave their works of art unfinished. This practice also invites the viewer to become co-creator of the piece, in effect "finishing" it himself. Even the most elaborate piece of Taoist art consists merely of brush strokes in varying shades of watered black on white paper. Empty space is critically important, because emptiness has its own kind of fullness. Buddhists agree with these precepts.

## POETRY

Taoist poetry is a fragile and beautiful thing. It is also richly compressed, with most lines being no more than five or seven syllables.

Taoist poetry in the original usually rhymed, with the rhyme falling on the first, second, and fourth lines. Here are a few examples, translated by John Blofeld:

> Dismounting from my horse
> Dusk falling on the wild
> I hear amidst the silence
> The splash of a mountain rill
> Birds sing and petals fall,
> Of men there is not a trace.
> The window of my hut
> Is curtained with a white cloud.

The idea of a cloud for a curtain is a very nice one, I think.

More in the philosophical vein, however:

Cool as ice
His Taoist heart
No vain strife
Toward the goal
The Tao arises
Of itself
So still his mind
A shining moon-disc
Glistening, immaculate.

And my favorite:

Under the cliff lives an ancient recluse
Pine and bamboo encompass his dwelling
Birds sing at dawn, and at evening is heard
The companionable roar of a cliff dwelling tiger.

The idea of a companionable tiger roar is irresistible, at least to me.

**THE GREAT LI PO**

*The most important Taoist poet was Li Po, who died while trying to embrace the moon's reflection in the water. He was drunk at the time, so I suppose that's some excuse.*

## CHAPTER RECAP

- Taoism is practiced more widely in Taiwan and other places than it is in China itself.

- Taoism has left a powerful legacy on Chinese martial arts, painting, and poetry.

*Recommended Audiotapes*

Capra, Fritjof. *The Tao of Physics.* Los Angeles, CA: Renaissance Media, Inc., 1990.

Heider, John. *The Tao of Leadership.* Los Angeles, CA: Renaissance Media, Inc., 1990.

Messing, Bob. *The Tao of Management.* Los Angeles, CA: Renaissance Media, Inc., 1990.

# Roads Less Traveled

Although Westerners are familiar with the East's major religious traditions such as Hinduism and Buddhism, some of the more esoteric paths are obscured from our view. Perhaps that only makes them all the more tantalizing. Many of the traditions in this section have remained rooted to a single culture, while others have comparatively few adherents, but all have something rare to offer the dedicated seeker.

*Jain "Goddess" Ambika*
*(derived from the Hindu goddess Parvati)*
*India, sixth century (sandstone)*

# 21

# Jainism — The Cult
# of Non - Violence

There are five million Jains in India today, most of them living in or near Bombay. The word *Jina,* which means "conqueror," may seem like a strange word to apply to such a nonviolent tradition, but the word is to be understood in its spiritual, not military, sense. The Jains have conquered the world in a spiritual, although uncompromising way.

Jainism, along with Buddhism, began as a rebellion against Brahmin-centered, Vedic Hinduism. Like Buddhism, it rejects the notion of sacrifice and denies authority to the Vedas. Like Buddhism it is atheistic. Tolerant as the Hindus are religiously, this was too much, and from very early days, Jainism has been a religion apart.

Much recent scholarship indicates that Jainism may be very close to the primal religion of the Indian subcontinent. It is certainly non-Vedic, and many of its most notable practices, such as kindness to animals and extreme asceticism, were not Aryan practices.

And although Jainist practices may seem extremist, their very inflexibility has served as inspiration to leaders like Mahatma Gandhi and Martin Luther King Jr.

### IN THIS CHAPTER

- *The peaceful conquerors*

- *The Tirthankaras*

- *Religious Jainism*

- *Jain asceticism*

- *The naked Jains*

- *The Jain way of death*

## THE TIRTHANKARAS

According to Jain belief, the first Jains were the *Tirthankaras,* the "ford-finders." Three of them, Rishabhadeva, Ajitanatha, and

Aristanemi are even mentioned in the Yajur Veda. This is interesting because the Jains deny the validity of the Vedas, saying that the truth of their philosophy is grounded in reality itself.

The *Tirthankaras* are the ones who show the rest of us how to cross the river into the realm of perfection and they provide inspiring models for the Jains. Still, they are only leaders, and every person has to cross the river himself.

The first *Tirthankara* of the modern era was Lord Rishabhadeva. Rishabhadeva instituted social customs such as marriage, laws, and government. He also taught agriculture, handcrafts, literacy, and mathematics. He even built the first towns and cities.

The eighth *Tirthankara* is Chandraprabha. In an interesting amalgam of Buddhism and Jainism, it is said that Chandraprabha accompanies the Bodhisattva Manjushri wherever he goes. When he's not doing that, Chandraprabha is the Lord of the Moon. In consequence he has five faces: the new moon, the first-quarter moon, the full moon, the last-quarter, and the waning crescent.

The twenty-second *Tirthankara* was supposed to be a cousin of Krishna. He was about to marry when he heard the groans of the poor animals due to be slaughtered in honor of the event. He thought the simplest solution was not to get married, and his bride made the same decision. One wonders why they just didn't decide to forget the animal-sacrifice part and get married without it, but perhaps they just didn't think of that. They both became ascetics. Thus the ideal of compassion to all animals entered the Jain consciousness.

The twenty-third *Tirthanakara*, Parshava (877–777 B.C.E.), was known for his extreme asceticism.

All together there have been twenty-four *Tirthankaras*, living in different centuries. They are not divine entities, but simply extraordinary human beings and role models.

The *Tirthankaras* are venerated through their images, a practice called *devapuja*.

## MAHAVIRA—THE GREAT HERO

Mahavira was the last of the *Tirthankaras*, at least of the present era. His dates are very uncertain, but Jain tradition gives them as 599–527 B.C.E. (Later scholarship places him from 540–468 B.C.E.) At any rate,

PERFECT JAINS

*Jains believe that human beings, by diligent practice and by emulating their saints, can achieve perfection in this life, which includes a perfect death.*

he was roughly contemporary with Buddha. His real name was Nataputta Vardhamana, which means "he who grows." The later title, Mahavira, is an honorific and means "Great Hero." The best source for facts about Mahavira's life comes from the Shvetambara scriptures, but as these were written more than nine hundred years after Mahavira lived, their accuracy is suspect.

He was born in Bihar, northeastern India, and his life story is in some way similar to that of Gautama Buddha, his contemporary, also from that neck of the woods. Mahavira started out resting peacefully in heaven, when he decided to save humanity by coming to earth via the birth canal of an unsuspecting lady, Devananda. While Mahavira was still a fetus in her womb, she received signs of her son's future greatness. She dreamed fourteen auspicious omens: an elephant (again, very Buddhalike), a bull, a lion, the goddess Sri, a garland of flowers, the moon, the sun, a banner, a vase, a lotus-filled lake, the ocean, a palace, gems, and an eternal flame. Whether fortunately for Devananda or not, the gods decided the future savior of man needed a higher caste birth and transferred the fetus to the womb of another woman, Trishala, who also observed the fourteen auspicious omens. Weirdly, the new "father" was Siddhartha, Buddha's given name.

Like the Buddha, Mahavira came (eventually) from the kshatriya, or warrior class. He was not the heir to a throne, however. Mahariva was only a second son with few responsibilities, and so had more opportunities for finding out the meaning of life and so forth. Like the Buddha, he had an easy childhood, with at least five servants: one to nurse him, one to bathe him, one to dress him, one to carry him, and one to play with him.

Jain sects disagree about whether Mahariva ever married. One sect says no, but the other insists he not only married but had a daughter as well. According to this group, his wife was named Yasoda, again creepily similar to Siddhartha's wife, Yasodhara.

Both groups agree that, like Buddha, he left his home at about the age of thirty to become a wanderer. This was right after both his parents starved themselves to death by mutual agreement, a rite known as *sallakhana*. This was (and is) an honorable way of death in pre-Jain and Jain religion.

Mahariva became an extreme ascetic for more than twelve years, wandering about naked and barefoot. He never stayed more than five nights in any one place. He took the ascetic's vow: "I will neglect my body and abandon its care. I will bear all calamities that befall me." He pulled out all his hair (Buddha just cut his off) in five handfuls and was tormented by village dogs and village idiots. The latter amused themselves by sticking pins into his bare skin, covering him with dirt, and repeatedly picking him up and dropping him. They called him "Khukkhu" and tried to set him on fire while he was meditating.

Mahavira ignored them. He refrained from injuring any living creature (including insects). He strained his water with a cloth to avoid killing them, which caused amazement among the townsfolk. Apparently everyone else gobbled the bugs right down. He also was careful about where he walked, and considering he walked barefoot, this was a pretty good idea as well. He begged for all his food, but would only accept items that had been prepared for someone else and was left over.

He allowed vermin to crawl all over him and refused even to scratch, for fear of hurting them. He also refused to take baths or brush his teeth.

---

### THE MOMENT (PRECISELY) OF ENLIGHTENMENT

*If you're looking for the exact place and time of Mahavira's great event, here it is. In the thirteenth year of his wandering, in the second month of summer, in the fourth fortnight, when the shadow has turned from east…outside the town of Grimbhikagrama, on the north bank of the Rigupalika River, in the field of the householder Samaga, in a northeastern direction from an old temple, under a teak tree, in a squatting position, with knees high and head low.*

---

## Enlightenment

Eventually Mahavira achieved enlightenment. Like Buddha, this occurred while he was sitting under a tree (a teak tree this time). At the same time that he received enlightenment, he became *kevalin,* or omniscient. At the magic moment, the sky became a richer blue, heavenly music played, and the neighboring lake suddenly filled with blue lotuses.

All this sounds very peaceful, but in actual fact, Mahavira was supposed to be watching some cows for a local farmer. While he was meditating, they had wandered off. The farmer returned and beat Mahavira about half to death, until he was saved by Indra.

### Mahavira's Death

Mahavira began teaching at age forty-two and kept it up for thirty years. At that point, he had reached not only enlightenment, but also the further stages of *moksha* (liberation) and *siddha* (perfection). He was ready to die, and to do so in style. He had himself transported to a diamond throne and began to preach until his listeners got bored and fell asleep. Then he died. The date of his death, 527 B.C.E., is the beginning of the Jain calendar.

Mahavira's teachings were not written down at first, because his disciples were ascetics and didn't own any pens or paper.

## JAIN ATHEISM

Jainism is an explicitly atheistic religion. To Westerners (and to many Easterners also), this seems like a contradiction in terms. What is religion if not about our relationship with God? (Some kinds of Buddhism and Taoism and Confucianism have little to say about God also, but only Jainism flatly rejects his existence.) Jainism doesn't bother to designate itself as a religion; it merely asserts what it believes to be true. To prove its point, Jainism resorts to several arguments. One such argument goes under the label of *theodicy*, the question of God's justice. Any God, say the Jains, to be worth the name of God, must be all-loving, all-just, and all-powerful. Why would such a being create a world full of suffering, injustice, and pain? God must not be all-loving. Or he must not be all-powerful. Or he must not exist.

Even if one could somehow prove that God was all-loving and that there was reason for the suffering of beings on earth, the Jains have another problem with God. This problem is not situated in ethics, but in logic. If one posits that the earth must have a creator, because everything has a cause, it must follow that God himself has a cause or a creator. One is then stuck with an infinite regress, unless one makes the bold move of assuming that perhaps the universe didn't have a creator after all. Maybe the universe is all that ever was. Maybe the universe is eternal. This seemed like the simplest explanation to Jain philosophers, and so for Jains, the universe has no beginning and no end.

**A TWIST ON ATHEISM**

*Just to confuse the issue further, some Jains worship "nondivine" gods. These gods are considered embodiments of the Tirthankaras.*

## THE SOUL

Just because there is no creator, however, doesn't mean that there is no soul. Quite the contrary. In the Jain universe, the entire cosmos is populated with immortal souls. In fact, almost everything in the universe is in some sense alive. This gets a little complicated. Even though there is a sort of "nonconscious" quality *(ajiva)* about some aspects of the universe, even things like rocks and fire have a living principle *(jiva)*. Everything has a living core. Humans are also composed of *jiva* and *ajiva*. Unlike other beings, however, we are aware of both sides of our nature.

Nonconscious things are either "formless," like motion, rest, space, and time—or "formed" like matter. The word *jiva* can also refer specifically to the soul itself, and each sentient creature has a *jiva*. There is an infinite number of *jivas*, each of which is both an agent and something acted upon.

Each *jiva* is similar to every other one, but they will never be merged together in some all-encompassing unity. There is no ultimate *jiva*, unlike the Hindu concept of Brahman. The two components of *jiva* are consciousness and bliss. Its pure state is one of infinite intelligence, power, peace, and faith, although these qualities are obscured when the *jiva* is united with the body.

The soul can save itself. It is in bondage to the world and karma, however, and the only way it can ever be freed is to reduce or eliminate the activities that make up the ensnaring karma. For Jains, karma is physical; it's matter (although very subtle matter). By clinging like fine dust to the soul, it keeps it from obtaining liberation. In the Jain view, all deeds leave a physical residue upon the soul. Even good deeds do so. The best thing is to do nothing at all.

Jains put souls into five classes, depending upon how many "senses" they have. Human beings, most animals, gods, and demons have five senses, so we are all together in the highest class. Big insects like wasps and butterflies have, according to Jains, only four senses, so they're in a lower tier. Moths and small insects are further down the ladder. Then come worms, shellfish, leeches, and itsy bitsy things. They have only two senses—touch and taste. At the bottom, with only the touch sense are trees, vegetables, earth bodies, fire bodies, water bodies, and wind bodies.

## REINCARNATION AND KARMA

Like Hindus and Buddhists, Jains believe in the cycle of birth, death, and rebirth, all governed by the laws of karma. It takes many cycles of rebirth for the soul to realize its true and perfect nature, which is shining, omniscient, blissful, and completely self-contained. The way to find the soul is to uncover it from its karmic accumulations. (In the Jain way of looking at things, *all* karma is bad.)

## HELL, HEAVEN, AND BEYOND

The Jains have lots of hells. Depending upon where you are, special torture gods will: scrape your nerves, slice the flesh from your bones, beat you with sticks, tear out bits of flesh with hot pincers (the old stand-by), mince your flesh in grinders, roast you, cut you, shoot you, stab you, bury you in hot sand, dash you against rocks, or stick you naked into rosebushes.

Luckily hell doesn't last forever. It doesn't need to, because it seems as though you'd learn your lesson after a very short time in the place.

There are several heavens as well, where the gods live. Each class of god enjoys its own sort of heaven. The gods themselves are not immortal, though, although they live a long time. Sooner or later they must return to an earthly existence.

There is also a place beyond heaven. This is the abode of the enlightened beings who have shaken off karma forever. This is the top of the universe—*lokakasa*.

> "Liberation is the freedom from all karmic matter, owing to the nonexistence of the cause of bondage and to the shedding of the karmas."
>
> —*Tattvarthadhigama Sutra*

## THE JAIN VIEW OF REALITY

The universe does, however, have cycles. At the beginning of each cycle, human beings are happy and are long-lived. They are so ethical that they have no need for religion. Religion develops only when things begin to decline: then people look to prophets and authorities. According to the Jains, things will be taking a turn for the better in another thousand years or so.

In Jain cosmology, space is not infinite, although it is pretty large. It is also empty. In the center of space rises the great Mount Meru.

### The Meaning of Matter

Matter is eternal in the Jain view. Atoms clump together to form visible objects. The fact that the Jains came up with this concept before modern physicists, and even possibly before the ancient Greeks, is intriguing.

Reality itself is a kind of indeterminate state, having the qualities of birth, death, and persistence. The world can be looked at from many points of view, each of which renders a different aspect. The Jains developed something they called the *sapta-bhangi* or seven-fold formula for discussing reality. It is a typically Indian way of looking at things. Here are the seven steps:

1. Maybe, is *(syat asti)*

2. Maybe, is not *(syate nasti)*

3. Maybe, is and is not *(syat asti nasti)*

4. Maybe, is inexpressible *(syat avaktavyah)*

5. Maybe, is and is inexpressible *(syat asti ca avaktavyah)*

6. Maybe, is not and is inexpressible *(syat nasti ce avaktavyah)*

7. Maybe, is, is not, and is inexpressible *(syat asti ca nasti ca avaktavyah)*

Well, maybe, that's all I can say.

No one view can be completely true or false. This brings us to Jain epistemology, or theory of knowledge.

## JAIN EPISTEMOLOGY

According to the basic Jain principle of relativity *(Anekantwad),* no one person has a lock on truth. The Jains invented the famous story of the blind men and the elephant. Each got hold of a different part of the beast, and each thus "saw" the elephant in a different way: one as a snake, one as a wall, another as a tree trunk. No one was completely wrong, no one altogether right. Nothing is completely true or totally false. Jains believe this parable is true for everyone every day, and thus cultivate the virtues of tolerance and open-mindedness.

---

**JAIN WORSHIP**

*Strictly speaking, Jains do not believe that acts of devotion and worship are of any use. There are Jains, however, who worship the Tirthankaras, although they are cautioned not to ask for or expect to get a personal response from any of them. Pilgrimage is also important, especially to Patna, the place where Mahavira died.*

In Jain philosophy there are five kinds of knowledge *(jnana)*:

- *Mati-jnana:* knowledge obtained through the senses

- *Shruta-jnana:* knowledge obtained through study and contemplation

- *Avadhi-jnana:* knowledge of the future, a knowledge mostly restricted to the gods and demons

- *Manaparyana-jnana:* mind reading, limited to the gifted

- *Kevala-jnana:* absolute, perfect knowledge or omniscience, achieved only by the spiritual adept

The first three kinds of knowledge are liable to error, but the last two are not. For Jains, consciousness is the very essence of the self. When one "knows" any object, one also "knows" oneself at the same time. When in perfect condition, the soul is pure knowledge *(jnana)* and also perfect intuition *(darshana)*. The passions that attend the imperfect state of the soul (and which allow the influx of polluting matter) are gone. Perfect souls are characterized by wisdom, not emotion.

"Right belief, right knowledge, right conduct— these together constitute the path to liberation."
—*Tattvarthadhigama Sutra*

## JAIN LIFESTYLES AND VALUES

Although monks and nuns live a much more austere life than do the laity, make no mistake about it—a life of absolute asceticism is the most prized of all. The way to final release from this life is through the Three Jewels (not the same Three Jewels as those of Buddhism): right faith, right knowledge, and right conduct. The Jain devotee begins his path by declaring his faith in the Jain scriptures and their teaching. Right knowledge naturally follows from this, with resultant enlightenment. Then one has to put into practice what one knows to be true.

### Asceticism

At least twelve years of life should be devoted to asceticism, according to the best Jain principles. This, of course, is in imitation of Mahavira. Monks and nuns sleep on the bare ground—or at most on wooden slabs. At initiation, they may pull out their hair by the roots, rather than simply shave their heads.

**DEGREES OF
NONVIOLENCE**

*Hindus and Buddhists also
practice the virtue of
*ahimsa, *but none carry it so
far as do the Jains.*

They believe that because one can achieve salvation only in the human body, there is no time to be lost. According to Jain belief, one passes through fourteen states of ascent. These stages involve removing false mental impressions and purifying oneself of the oppressive "shadow self." Then one can relinquish passion. Once one reaches perfection *(kevala),* one experiences perfect bliss and boundless vision. At this point, it is even possible to lead an active and productive life, because the individual is freed of the passion that binds him to earthly things.

## The Five Great Vows (Vrata)

Jain renunciates take the following five vows and live their lives by them. Jain laypeople do the best they can and make periodic special efforts.

### No-harm (Ahimsa)

One key concept in Jainism is *ahimsa,* which means literally "no injury, no harm." It is called the highest *dharma* and is key to understanding Jain philosophy and practice. All other Jain values are contained within it. Although it is phrased negatively, *ahimsa* has a strongly positive connotation. Jains rejected the ancient practice of animal sacrifices; for a Jain, one's whole life should be a sacrifice on the altar of truthfulness and righteousness. When *ahimsa* becomes active in one's life, it is said to be *caritra,* or good conduct.

Remember that in the Jain way of looking at things, the entire universe, every inch, is packed with living "beings," even though most of them are very tiny. Each one of them has as much right to live as a person does. Even kicking a stone is to do injury to the living principle.

For people outside the Jain tradition, the Jainist *ahimsa* practices are generally viewed as unbelievably extreme. Animals (including bugs), of course, may not be killed, and Jains were among the first people to establish animal hospitals. They also buy caged birds at the marketplace whenever possible to set them free or raise them at home. They have established a special hospital for wounded birds in Delhi, where the creatures live in air-conditioned comfort.

Jains are strict vegetarians and may not engage in agriculture or the manufacture of farm implements. Any harm caused to a living being results in the accumulation of karma. It doesn't matter that the deed may have been done by mistake or without such intention. Killing a being carries karma, no matter why it was done. This is one reason why Jains may be seen in India walking about with a soft brush to move small insects out of the path. They are expected to walk slowly, with their eyes downcast. In fact, it's even better if they don't walk at all—less chance of hurting something.

They may not extinguish or light fires, walk in the rain, fan themselves, walk on vegetation, or swim.

In fact, religious Jains, particularly monks and nuns, wear mouth-cloths to prevent the inhalation and death of some hapless insect. They also carry begging bowls and fly whisks wherever they go.

### Telling the Truth

Jains are expected to tell the strict truth under all circumstances. This includes refraining from exaggeration, even in jest. Jains are particularly conscious of the way words can hurt, regardless of the speaker's intent. They are to speak only after great deliberation, and never speak while greedy, angry, or anxious, since these states could force one into lying. No jokes or kidding around are allowed either.

### Non-Stealing

The Jains are strict about non-stealing, but their strictness has earned them a great reputation for honesty in India, where they are a highly trusted people. As a consequence, the Jains have paradoxically become rather wealthy.

### Sexual Purity

Jain monks vow to abstain from all sexual conduct. They are not even supposed to be interested.

### Non-Attachment (Apaigraha)

As Thoreau noted, we're more likely to be owned by our possessions than the other way around. Jain monks carry this virtue to an extreme. They wear little or nothing, eat little or nothing, and use little or nothing. Jains point out that this is a community service—the less they consume the more is available for impoverished people. They also point out that their lifestyle is environmentally friendly.

**THE JAIN SYMBOL**

*The circle in the open palm contains the word* ahimsa. *The swastika symbolizes* samsara, *and the three dots mean insight, knowledge, and conduct.*

*Rules for Layfolk*

The laity make twelve vows—more than the monks, but less strict. These are:

1. No killing

2. No lying

3. No stealing

4. No unfaithfulness

5. No greed

6. Avoid temptation to sin

7. Limit number of objects one owns

8. Take precautions against avoidable evil

9. Meditate regularly

10. Observe certain periods of asceticism

11. Spend a few days as a monk once in a while

12. Give alms to the poor

As can be observed from the similarity in rules and life patterns, there are no sharp divisions between laity and monks, but for the layperson, the Jain way of life is less austere. One is required to practice meditation, praise the *Tirthankaras,* respect the wandering teachers, and practice various forms of ascetic practice.

*Eating Practices*

Jain eating practices are strongly connected to the doctrine of *ahimsa.* For instance, Jains do not eat after sunset. Partly this is an ascetic practice, but it also is done to avoid inadvertently swallowing some unseen insect, which are both more abundant at night and harder to see. This is a good idea, in my opinion.

As I mentioned, Jains are also strict vegetarians, but it goes further than that. Certain fruits and vegetables may not be eaten. (It's best to choose those that have already fallen from the tree.)

Although everybody needs to eat to live, Jain monks aren't supposed to enjoy it. In fact, Jain sutras counsel begging monks not to smell the scent of cooking food if they can help it. While on a begging tour, Jain monks aren't allowed to eat any food in earthenware containers. The reasoning is that the earthenware container might shatter and break. Nor may they accept food that has been left on a high place. (The person who put it there might have fallen and hurt himself in the effort, or he might have fallen down on and crushed small creatures.)

### Approved Occupations

Jains may not enter any occupation that is considered harmful to other living beings. Of course, this includes butchering, the military, and agriculture (you might cut up worms). It also includes law. Everyone knows that lawyers are harmful, but the Jains are the first to actually forbid the job to its practitioners. Also forbidden is work in education or publishing. Brewing is also out.

## SECTS

There are several particularly interesting sects of Jainism. Monks of one sect, the *Digambaras,* or "sky-clad" monks, have renounced all their possessions—including their clothes. The origins of the split go back to the third century B.C.E., when the saintly Jain Bhadrabahu predicted there would be a major famine in northeast India (Mahavira's original stomping grounds). This did indeed come to pass, and Bhadrabahu led 12,000 followers to safety in south India. They stayed there for twelve years.

According to legend, these southern Jains retained many extremely conservative customs, including the naked monks, and were disgusted to find upon the return of some of them to the north, that the northern Jains had begun to wear clothes. (This would seem a necessity in the more northern climes. I myself am inclined to think that the nakedness was a southern Jain innovation, but that's only my opinion.) Not only that, but the northern Jains had also begun to collect Jain teachings into a canon of forty-five works. The southern Jains refused to accept the changes, and the split became permanent.

**THE NEED FOR NUDITY**

*Only sky-clad monks are required to go naked all the time. Layfolk only need be naked when on pilgrimages or during religious rites.*

**JAIN IMAGERY**

*In Jain art, the Tirthankaras
are always depicted either in
a lotus posture, or a standing meditation, which implies
even deeper connection.*

*Digambara* monks walk around buck-naked. (This is also how the *Tirthankaras* are depicted.) They have no possessions except a gourd for drinking water and a broom made of peacock feathers they use for brushing away insects that may cross their path. Of course, the feathers are picked up from those that have dropped naturally. Jains don't permit yanking attached feathers from their owners.

Sky-clad Jains do not permit nuns. They think women aren't strong enough to handle the rigors of the ascetic life. Nor do they have the willpower. The theory is that when one is ready to adopt a monk's lifestyle, one will be born a man. Not surprisingly, there are comparatively few *Digambaras* around nowadays.

The other major group, the white-clad Jains *(Svetamabara)*, permit women as well as men to live a monastic lifestyle. In their lineage, the thirteenth *Tirthankara* was even a woman. All members wear simple garments of white.

A third group, Reform Jains *(Sthanakavasi),* diverged from the white-clad branch in the eighteenth century. This sect does not use temples or images in their religious practice.

## THE IDEAL JAIN WAY OF DEATH

Unlike Western practice, suicide is not only permitted in Jainism, it's seen as a virtue. (To a lesser extent, this can also be true in Hinduism.) It is to be undertaken, however, only by those who are elderly and virtuous.

According to Jain tradition, both Mahavira and his parents died by voluntarily starving themselves to death. Violent means of suicide are not encouraged because that would violate the principle of *ahimsa*. So, the best way to die is to follow Mahavira's example and starve oneself to death. The dying person is expected to gradually eat less and less, finally giving up solid food altogether. In general, it takes about a month to complete. This prized method is called *sallekhana* (holy death) and is free from the cycle of rebirth. Walking into the ocean and drowning is fine also. Unbelievably, there are those who accuse Jainism of being a pessimistic religion.

## CHAPTER RECAP

- Jainism is a reaction and response to Hinduism.

- Jains honor all their founders, the *Tirthankaras*, but the greatest was the last, Mahavira.

- Jainism is an atheistic religion, but believes that the soul is eternal.

- For Jains, all karma is bad.

- Jains are totally nonviolent, even to the most obscure living creatures.

### *Recommended Reading*

Caillat, Colette. *The Jain Cosmology.* Trans. by K. R. Norman. Basel, 1981.

Chitrabhanu, Gurudev Shree. *Twelve Facets of Reality: The Jain Path to Freedom.* New York: Jain Meditation International Center/Dodd, Mead and Company, 1980.

Dundas, Paul. *The Jains.* London: Routledge, 1993.

Jaini, P. S. *The Jaina Path of Purification.* Berkeley: University of California Press, 1979.

Pal, P. *The Peaceful Liberators: Jain Art from India.* London: Thames & Hudson and the Los Angeles Museum of Art, 1994.

Samgave, Vilas A. *Jaina Community.* Second rev. ed. Bombay, 1980.

# *Tantra — The*
# *Forbidden Treasure*

$T$here lies a curious treasure chest just outside the gated walls of Hinduism and Buddhism. It is a treasure that has been plundered by both, yet claimed by neither. Its name is Tantra.

Tantra is a mysterious combination of exotic sexual practices, strange lore, and secret wisdom. But Tantra is also more than these, and in some ways, other than these.

As a religious practice, Tantra is both older and newer than Hinduism or Buddhism. It is distilled from the ancient pre-Vedic matrix that gave birth to the other great Indian religions. Yet it has been shaped, refined, and colored through the alembic of Hinduism and Buddhism, and it has taken on the flavors of each of them. Thus there is both a Hindu Tantra and a Buddhist Tantra. In the final analysis, though, Tantra is neither fully Buddhist nor completely Hindu. Buddhism and Hinduism renounce the world. Tantra embraces it, often literally.

## THE EARLY HISTORY OF TANTRA

Although no one knows precisely how old Tantra is, it certainly predates any written records. Its roots are deeply buried in the past. In fact, archaeologists have discovered Tantric elements in the 20,000-year-old cave art of France. Because Tantra is older than

Buddhism, older than Jainism, and older than any variety of Hinduism, each of these religions has absorbed Tantra into its own stream of tradition and thus transformed it. (Jaina Tantra is so different from the other forms that it can barely be identified with any recognized Tantra tradition, but it's still there.)

Scholars have noted that Tantra long flourished in areas that were least touched by the Aryan invasions, because it is so opposite to Aryan patriarchal ideas about the universe. However far back the roots of Tantra go, though, the modern and formalized movement probably started around 800 C.E. Today it survives, although officially discouraged, in places such as Bengal, Assam, Kashmir, and parts of southern India.

### THE ORIGINS OF TANTRA

*Tantra is a Sanskrit word meaning "to expand beyond."*

## THE TWO TANTRAS

Tantra has historically been divided into two branches: Tantra of the Right Hand *(daksinacara)* and Tantra of the Left Hand *(vama-marga)*. Right-Handed Tantra is a mainly symbolic enterprise that uses mantras, yantras, and mandalas. The Left-Handed Tantra is for a special few; this is the Tantra that explores what is forbidden by orthodox tradition. In simpler terms, Right-Handed Tantra is imaginary Tantra. Many Brahmins will accept Tantra of the Right Hand as orthodox practice, but consider Tantra of the Left Hand as impure and impermissible. This may be an unjust distinction, however. Some Tantrists of the Left Hand assert that so-called "Right-Handed Tantra" is not really Tantra at all. To them, the Tantra of the Left Hand is the only true Tantra. It is also, from the Hindu and Buddhist point of view, extremely unorthodox.

---

### THE TRAVELS OF TANTRA

*Tantric beliefs traveled to China in the eighth century C.E., and thence to Japan. Real Tantra has since been expunged from both places, largely because of a strong Confucian influence; however, a kind of symbolic, psychologically based Tantra still exists. Hindu Tantra was also exported to Cambodia and Java by about 800 C.E.*

---

Technically, Tantra is a form of yoga, but traditional believers have always looked upon it with fear or loathing, even though it fascinates them. And there's good reason for this attitude: Tantra is a wild animal. It refuses to confine itself to doctrine. It submits only to its own perverse laws. It embodies what is dreaded by Hindus and despised by Buddhists. And it has teeth.

The master word of Tantra is *paravritti:* to turn back around, turn upside down, and turn inside out. It celebrates what people most fear and embraces what people most hate. It slams life against death, shoves eternity into the present, turns virtue into cowardice, and throws conventional wisdom into the trash. It's liberating, and it's dangerous.

Pure Tantra has always been outside the Vedic tradition in India, partly because it has opened its doors to women and to persons of low caste. It has even welcomed them as gurus—while Brahmins are not acceptable. In fact, some experts claim that one of the original purposes of Tantra was to break down the whole class system.

Tantra is also clandestine. It celebrates sexuality and claims that one of its central tenets is *bhoga,* or pleasure. All these factors help account both for its popularity among the masses and the opprobrium in which it is held by puritanical Brahmins.

Most religions encourage people to suppress pleasure. Tantra practitioners believe that it can be harnessed for higher ends. And of course, pleasure is an end in itself as well, and is one of the four acceptable goals of life in Hinduism. Instead of suppressing pleasure, Tantra encourages people to use pleasure to attain the highest goal of all—to attain unity with the divine and to realize that all apparent differentiation is just that—apparent. We are all one, and we are all divine. Hinduism accepts this same premise but uses different methods to attain the goal.

Tantra also includes features officially discouraged by the more religiously orthodox. For example, it supports deity worship for "selfish" ends—to attain wealth or merit, for example. It has its own body of holy scripture, which doesn't always accord with traditional positions. Different schools of Tantra revere different texts, and there are hundreds of them. Still, many Tantrists downplay the importance of any scripture at all in their religious practice. For them, studying under a skillful guru is of much greater merit, and much more likely to help them achieve *moksha.* For Tantrists, action is more vital than words, and experience more important than knowledge. Every Tantrist will tell you that the most sacred knowledge is not written down anywhere.

"Exuberance is beauty."

—*William Blake*

As far as their extreme practices go, some Tantrists believe that in this modern corrupt age, their path is the only means to liberation. They believe most people are not spiritual enough to undergo severe ascetic discipline or learned enough to take the path of esoteric knowledge. And people are certainly not inclined to go about performing complex rituals in which the slightest error could invalidate the entire enterprise. This is one reason why Tantra is called the Short Path to Enlightenment.

## TANTRIC SCRIPTURES

Although Tantra does not rely on scripture to the same extent that Hinduism or even Buddhism does, many such collections exist and are used throughout India, especially in Kashmir and Bengal, where they are more highly regarded than even the Vedas by Tantric Hindus.

Tantric texts are not out of line with Vedic literature (although their tone, emphasis, and focus are quite different), but they do take a strong stand against Brahmin elitism. In fact, the first complete surviving Tantric literature is Buddhist rather than Hindu. The two earliest extant Tantric works, composed some time between 300 and 600 C.E., are the Buddhist works titled the Radical Institutions of Manjusri and the Tantra of Secret Organization. The first Hindu texts appeared much later: the Tantra of the Great Liberation in the eleventh century and the Description of the Garland of Adepts in the fourteenth. As I previously mentioned, however, the practice itself undoubtedly predates both religions, reaching back to the Indus Valley Civilization of 2500 B.C.E. and earlier. Some later writings even identify Tantra with the Atharva Veda.

Most Tantric texts take the form of a dialogue between Shiva and Sakti (God and Power), and each considers the following five

---

### A TYPE OF TANTRA

*One branch of Indian Tantra, called Srividya Tantra, is open to both men and women of all castes. It has been historically limited, however, to those who have a sufficient literacy in Sanskrit to perform its rituals. This Tantra is found today mainly in south India, although it once flourished in Kashmir, also. Srividya claims to be both Vedic and Tantric.*

topics: creation, destruction of the world, worship, attainment of superhuman powers, and achieving union with the divine.

## TANTRIC PHILOSOPHY

Many orthodox Hindus summarily dismiss Tantra as "witchcraft," "sorcery," or shamanism. They relegate it to the realm of "women's religion," which in the patriarchal Brahmin tradition, is meant as a distinct insult. It's important, however, to understand that Tantric philosophical teachings are fairly mainstream Hinduism; it's the sensual Tantric yogic practices, deeply distasteful to normative Hindus and Buddhists, which have earned them censure.

This attitude makes many people overlook the interesting philosophy that underlies Tantra. In brief, this is that the human person is a microcosm of the whole universe; in a spiritual sense, he is the whole universe, especially in the union of the sexes.

Like Advaita Vendantists, Hindu Tantrists are ultimately non-dualists. They posit the existence of the One, the Brahman, who encompasses all and whose nature is *satchitananda*—complete being, total knowledge, perfect bliss. The Brahman is conceptualized, however, as an amalgam of two principles: the male principle is sometimes pictured as Shiva in the form of Mahakala, meaning "greatest time" and Shakti, or energy, depicted as female, often in the form of the dangerous goddess Kali, who also represents time. In this form, the Brahman is known as *parasamvit:* the supreme truth.

In this formulation also, the male is considered as representative of knowledge, and the female as emblematic of action. Their sexual union gives birth to the entire universe, and this universe is the result of a cosmic pleasure-game between the two primary forces. (Most Tantrists believe that the male generated the female for his own pleasure.) In this sense, the universe is not ultimately "real" at all. It could be compared to the creation of an artist. The characters in a play are not real in the sense that human beings are real, but they are the result of human creation and have a powerful impact while they are "playing the part."

The goal of the Tantric adept is to practice *paravritti,* to turn things back around and to re-create the original unity of being,

"There are truths which are not for all men, nor for all time."

—*Voltaire*

from which the universe, rather unhappily, descended. In the process, the male adept identifies with Shiva, and the female with Shakti, thus becoming godlike themselves in their efforts to reach the absolute and to dissolve their own separate egos or concept of self.

Transmitted orally from teacher to pupil, often in family groups, Tantra reached its peak in India between the ninth and fourteenth centuries. A combination of factors, including the destruction of two of the primary Tantric Buddhist spiritual centers in the eleventh century and the growth of Bhakti Hinduism, drove Tantra deeper underground in most of India.

## TIBETAN TANTRA

In the rarefied, more egalitarian atmosphere of Tibetan Buddhism, Tantra is still accepted as fully orthodox. It also denies any connection with Hindu Tantra. In Tibet, the practice is called Vajrayana, the Diamond Vehicle, the Path of the Thunderbolt. The two words *diamond* and *thunderbolt* are instructive. *Diamond* signifies the enduring, indestructible truth of Tantra, while *thunderbolt* suggests the lightning quick dawning of enlightenment. (See chapter 11 for a full discussion of Tibetan Buddhism.) In Tantra, liberation comes like a thunderbolt, but once it strikes, it endures forever.

Buddhist Tantrists also envision the formation of the universe as a result of a divine coupling. In their view, however, the male principle is the active one and is also called Buddhahood. The male principle thus represents the means *(upaya)* to liberation. The female principle represents wisdom and quietude *(prajna)*. The male is symbolized as a small diamond or thunderbolt *(dorje)*. The connection may not seem obvious at first, and it's highly symbolic. In ancient cultures, lightning was considered a fertilizing agent, and the gems found in the earth were beautifully conceived to be solidified pieces

---

### KUNDALINI RISING

*During Tantra's most popular era, a rather frightening Tantra sect known as the Kapalika, a group fiercely devoted to Shiva in his most destructive form, practiced both human and animal sacrifice. They preferred to sacrifice Brahmins, when they could get them. Afterward, however, the sacrificer took a "great vow" of penitence. He followed a life of extreme abstinence for twelve years, carrying the victim's skull around with him the whole time.*

of lightning. The concept of the diamond, additionally, was an emblem of the divinity experienced through orgasm. The female is symbolized by a bell in Tibetan Tantra.

As mentioned in chapter 11, Tantra came to Tibet in the eighth century c.e., brought by Padma-Sambhava. For a relatively brief period, the Tibetan lamas advocated the real-life enactment of the sexual excesses described by Tantra; later on, however, these practices became mental and symbolic exercises only. Tibetan Tantric meditation always begins and ends with a mental dissolving into emptiness. The point is to use physical energy to liberate the mind.

### The Tibetan Chöd Ritual

The forbidden Chöd rite is very old, and only men were allowed to participate. It took place in a cemetery or other creepy location— some spot where the occult powers were already somewhat stirred up. Most scholars assume that some of these practices were left over from the native Bön religion.

The Tantra leader performed a yantra by dancing it out on the ground, meanwhile ringing a bell or playing a drum. He may also have used a trumpet made of human bone, usually the femur. The whole point of the ritual is that the practitioner is offering himself as sacrifice to the dark powers. His sacrifice eventually causes them to dissolve into the nothingness that they really are. A true Tibetan adept would perform the Chöd ritual at 108 lakes plus 108 cemeteries. Because Tibet doesn't even have that many lakes (or cemeteries), the lamas wandered all over their known world in search of likely spots.

## THE SRI YANTRA

Tantric philosophy is beautifully diagrammed in its master image, the Sri Yantra. The Sri Yantra, which means the Auspicious Yantra, is a universal tantric symbol, but it is especially sacred to Hindu Tantrists. A yantra is an abstract, linear "shortcut" mandala used as a meditation aid. (The word *yantra* comes from Sanskrit and means "machine" or "engine," thus characterizing both the diagrammatic nature of the mandala and its dynamism and energy.)

THE SRI YANTRA

Although this and other yantras are commonly used as objects of worship, they are more properly thought of as focusing devices that enable the devotee to concentrate his mental powers.

The Sri Yantra, often depicted in brilliant and symbolic colors, features nine interlocking triangles within a circle. The circle represents the universe, which rests atop outlying circles of eight and sixteen lotus petals. (The pink lotus is specifically a feminine symbol. Circles also signify completion and are emblems of the feminine force.)

Within the central circle, the five downward oriented triangles (*yoni* yantra) represent the feminine energy; the four upward thrusting figures (*lingam* yantra) represent the male force. Many other triangles are formed at the intersections of the main triangles. These smaller figures represent both continuing generation and the multiplicity and interdependence of entities in the cosmos.

At the very center of the diagram is a small white dot within the primal red down-pointing triangle. This is the *bindu*, the tiny spark of new life. (In some cases, the dot is not shown and must be imagined by the practitioner.) This is the seed of the cosmos, and from the central seed and primary feminine triangle the entire universe evolves. The same color symbolism applies to sex. The semen is represented as white, and the vagina red. In fact, in Tantra of the Left Hand, intercourse during a woman's menstrual cycle was considered the most powerful.

## RAISING THE KUNDALINI

A Tantric disciple begins his studies in a fairly regular way: He learns the correct breathing techniques and physical postures of *hatha* yoga. This is just a prelude, however, to the next step: the raising of the kundalini, the sleeping serpent within. (*Kundalini* is a Sanskrit term that literally means "the coiled one.")

Far from being a symbol of evil, serpents connote both wisdom and power in India. In Tantra, the kundalini is considered a female symbol, in contradistinction to the way the serpents are viewed in the Freudian West—as phallic symbols. The kundalini is part of what is called "the subtle body," and in most people lies sleeping, coiled three and one-half times around.

Tantric yoga awakens the kundalini, and it rises from its base in the perineum. This is the *muladhara,* or root support, the first "chakra," located at the base of the spine. The word *chakra* literally means "circle" or "wheel," and although chakras are invisible to ordinary sight, practitioners believe these "mystic lotus centers" may be perceived clairvoyantly. The lotus is generally regarded as a feminine symbol, but the chakra may originally have been a sun-symbol, which is traditionally regarded as masculine. The Hindu god Shiva gave his fellow god Vishnu a chakra as a weapon to destroy demons. It is said that if anyone is born with a chakra in his hand, or the sign of a chakra on his forehead or chest, he will rule the earth. It hasn't happened yet.

The function of the *muladhara* is preservation of the body. In Hindu Tantra, the elephant god Ganesha is seated on this chakra, where he wields a stabilizing effect.

The chakras are connected to each other by *nadis,* channels that carry the subtle energy. Each chakra has its distinctive color,

**TANTRA TIDBIT**

*Not all practitioners of kundalini yoga are Tantrists, and vice versa. But there is strong overlap.*

mantra sounds, symbolic shape, and number of petals or spokes. Practitioners can "read" the color and condition of their chakras and thus determine the state of their mental and physical health.

The kundalini gradually moves upward. As it climbs, it winds around the *merudanda,* the mystical spine of the practitioner. It moves along between two special *nadis:* the solar *(pingala)* channel and the lunar *(ida)* channel, which together form a kind of double helix. They end at the left and right nostrils. Ideally, the kundalini, awakened through yoga, moves up the normally closed central *nadi,* the hairlike *sushumna,* that takes in energy from the ether field around the body. (If the kundalini moves up the *ida* or *pingala,* the practitioner can be in a world of trouble.) The channels do not go through the chakras; they wind around them, and their job is the release of energy.

The second, or sacral, chakra is located in the sex organs, the *svadhisthana,* "her particular residence." Its province is sexual energy. Just above the solar plexus is the *manipura,* or the City of the Shining Jewel, located at the navel. (Navel gem–wear has always been popular.) The Hindu god of this chakra is *Karttikeya,* a scarlet-colored god who seems to be in charge of the kundalini. He carries a lance symbolizing deep insight.

The next important chakra is located at the heart, the *anahata;* it governs resistance to disease. These lower chakras represent the material universe. During the rising of the kundalini through these lower stages, the body feels pleasantly warm and comfortable, but that soon stops.

The three higher chakras take the kundalini into the region beyond the material plane. Now the body becomes freezing cold and blazing hot by turns. The yogin hears strange sounds and experiences weird visions. Some yogins feel pain or a tickling sensation; some undergo twitching or paralysis.

At the larynx is the *vishuddha* or purification chakra, also called the Gateway of Liberation. It handles expanded consciousness. Then comes *ajna,* the "command" chakra, found between the eyebrows. It is often called the Third Eye and governs psychic powers.

Eventually, the kundalini unites with the *sahasrara* chakra, the Thousand-Petalled Center of the Mind/Light. (According to some versions, it has only 972 petals. Either somebody miscounted

## A CHOICE OF CHAKRAS

*The number of major chakras differs from tradition to tradition. In Buddhist Tantra, the number of chakras is given as four, and some versions of Hindu Tantra list more or fewer chakras than I have given here. In addition to the chakras mentioned, there are hundreds of less importance.*

or perhaps the 1,000 figure is just the result of a natural tendency to round off.) It springs from the crown of the head and is a brilliant glowing purple, the color of the spirit. At this point, the practitioner achieves the deepest state of concentration, *samadhi.* Total liberation follows forthwith, as the serpent power joins her mate Shiva. The fully awakened kundalini, according to those who have experienced it, is like liquid fire and liquid light. It gives one almost superhuman powers, transcendental bliss, and some odd physical sensations as well.

**CHAKRA SYMBOLISM**

*The* merudanda *is an individual representation of the* axis mundi, *the center pole of the earth.*

Many adepts consider the raising of the kundalini an extremely dangerous proposition, however. Not only is the process one of extreme difficulty, but if the kundalini is only partially awakened, the yogin is in great peril, physically and spiritually. An interesting book, *Kundalini: The Evolutionary Energy in Man* by Gopi Krishna (1903–1984), gives an autobiographical account of the spiritual and psychological terrors that can result from partially awakened kundalini. Poor Gopi Krishna underwent twelve years of complete misery trying to deal with his unruly kundalini before he finally achieved full awakening, a state in which he said he saw everything bathed in a sil-

---

**RAISING THE INNER GIRL**

*Buddhist Tantra puts very little emphasis on the lower, more "earthy" chakras. Nor does it use the image of the kundalini. Instead it pictures an "inner girl" climbing the spinal cord. The inner girl is often depicted as the Red Dakini or dancing girl of Hindu Tantra.*

---

very glow. (Before that time, he had some problems with his halo.) He also heard an inner music he called the "unstruck melody," apparently a common phenomenon for kundalini adepts.

On the other hand, Gopi reports that as far as lotuses go, "I did not come across any in the course of my long adventure, not even a vestige of one in any part of the cerebro-spinal system." On the other hand, he never practiced Tantra either, and Gopi Krishna hypothesizes, "The idea of chakras and lotuses must have been suggested to the mind of the ancient teachers by the singular resemblance which, in the awakened state, the lustrous nerve centers bear to a luminous revolving disc, studded with lights, or to a lotus flower in full bloom, glistening in the rays of the sun."

Once the kundalini is fully awakened, however, the practitioner is free from hatred and fear. He has attained cosmic love and understands the unity of all things. As a special bonus, he acquires the occult powers of Siddhi. The kundalini is then allowed to recede to the lower chakras, but the adept never allows it to go below the heart chakra, for to do so would be to re-enter the world of the selfish ego.

## *THE* CHAKRAPUJA

The most celebrated Tantric rite is the *chakrapuja*. It takes place at night, with the participants forming a circle (chakra). The woman *(shakti)* sits to the left of the man *(sadhaka)*, a custom which gave rise to the name "Left-Handed Tantra." There are generally an equal number of men and women, although the master leading the rite is usually male. He also has his partner, or *shakti*, and they both remain in the center of the chakra.

---

### CHAKRA ENERGY

*Although chakras are generally considered imaginary by Westerners, Eastern scientists are not so ready to dismiss them. One Japanese scientist, Hiroshi Motoyama, did some experimental work with "enlightened" subjects whose bodies produced significantly more energy at chakra points than did those of normal subjects.*

---

Both partners have bathed, and the *shakti* is anointed with perfume of musk, sandalwood, or patchouli. Hymns are sung and mantras recited.

Incense is lit. The participants then indulge themselves in an interesting mixture of marijuana, milk, and sherbet. This concoction is called *vijaya*, meaning "victory."

### The Five Ms

The critical part of the ritual comes next—the partaking of the Five Ms—the five Forbidden Things. (This is another anti-Brahmin rite. The forbidden things are "more forbidden" in high-caste society than in low.) The first two are meat, usually pork *(mamsa)*, and fish *(matsya)*, both prohibited by Hindu dietary laws. Next alcohol *(mada)* is drunk. (This is apparently an informal practice even among the comparatively austere Tibetan Tantrists.) Then a dried grain or kidney bean *(mudra)* is devoured as an aphrodisiac. Nowadays, substitutes are often used instead: ginger, lemon, rice, and marijuana.

Last comes sexual intercourse *(maithuna)*, the woman astride the man, in imitation of Shakti/Kali and Shiva. The male is not supposed to ejaculate during this procedure; retention of the semen aids the kundalini in its journey toward the Thousand-Petalled Lotus. (This is in contrast to typical Hindu Tantra of the Left Hand; in that case, the semen is ejaculated as a kind of sacrifice to the god.) The whole business is supposed to resemble a sacrificial rite, wherein the woman's lap is a sacrificial altar, her hair the sacrificial grass, her skin a press for making soma, and her vulva is fire.

In Tibetan Buddhism, semen is mystically referred to as *bodhicitta,* a term that literally means "knowledge/mind." The obvious correlation is that by retaining the semen, one is also retaining knowledge/mind. In ancient times, it was also believed that ejaculation weakened the body.

> "Those who restrain desire, do so because theirs is weak enough to be restrained."
>
> —*William Blake*

## SYMBOLIC SEX

Just what is it about sex, anyway, that gets everybody so interested? Well, I'm not sure, but Tantrists have always claimed that it's what sex represents that's important, and not merely the fact that sex is pleasurable. As if to prove their point, some Tantrists have gone out of their way to practice sex with dead and decaying bodies in midnight cemetery rites. These midnight rituals were performed under the aegis of a *dakini,* a Tantra priestess, who was a human emanation of Kali. The most important of the *dakini* was the Red Dakini, a death goddess who must be realized for a Tantra yogin to reach liberation. The *dakinis* are famous for feasting upon human blood.

Some say that Tantrists practice taboo sex not because they find it pleasurable, but precisely because it isn't. Another reason given for the necrophilia is religious. One of the master images in Tantric art and literature is that of the great goddess Kali in sexual congress with the corpse of Shiva, her consort. (She is shown astride him, in case you're wondering.) It's the female who represents energy; she is the one who must initiate and control the sexual act. The male is only a body to be worked upon. The Tantrists who perform the taboo sex are merely embodying the cosmic myth in an extremely literal way.

In some of these paintings and sculptures, Kali doesn't look too good herself, with her fanglike teeth, necklace of skulls, and swollen body. Her four arms may make her more or less attractive, depending on your viewpoint. Shiva, on the other hand, looks fairly normal, aside from the fact that he does seem a little pale, in keeping with his corpselike status. Often the goddess is holding a severed head or two in her hands. Sometimes she wields a knife, as well, as if to further violate the corpse of her late husband. In one painting, however, the dead god appears to be winking at the viewer and repressing a conspiratorial smile. The whole thing seems to be a divine fantasy of the kinkier sort. More typically, the divine couple is depicted as seated, both displaying a real mastery of classical *hatha* yoga postures. In these works, Shiva and Kali appear quite calm, as if meditating. As indeed they are.

## TANTRA TODAY

Tantra today is in sharp decline in India, largely because of official pressure against the sect. The spread of the less excessive, mostly nonphysical Buddhist Tantra, however, has grown wildly in popularity, partly due to the expansion of Tibetan Buddhism in the West. In Tibet itself, Tantra no longer exists at all, as it has been outlawed by the Chinese who run the country. Knowledge of Tantra came to the West largely through the efforts of Sir John Woodroffe, an Englishman serving as Justice of the High Court of India during the 1890s. Using the rather incredible name of Arthur Avalon, he translated, wrote about, and spoke about many of the most important Tantric texts. Woodroffe tried his best to play down the sexual elements of the practice and may in fact not have known about many of them. The texts he was able to find had probably already been extensively censured.

## CHAPTER RECAP

- Tantra is an ancient religious practice, believed to predate both Hinduism and Buddhism.

- Tantrists seek to celebrate the senses.

- Tantric disciples practice raising the kundalini, through which one achieves complete liberation.

- Today, Tantra is rejected by orthodox Hindus. Tibetan Buddhists have transformed Tantra into a meditative practice using the body to liberate the mind.

*Recommended Reading*

Gyatso, Geshe Kelsang. *Tantric Grounds and Paths.* London: Tharpa Publications, 1994.

Rawsin, Philip. *The Art of Tantra.* London: Thames and Hudson, 1973, 1978.

*Recommended Audiotape*

Osho. *Meditations on Tantra by Osho.* Los Angeles, CA: Renaissance Media. Inc., 1997.

# *Zoroastrianism—*
# *The Religion of Joy*

*A*nd there were Wise Men in the East..." Yes indeed, the Magi of New Testament fame were Zoroastrians, a faith native to Persia (Iran, as it is known today). It is the first world religion to promote a universal monotheism, the belief that only one God rules the universe. (Early Judaism postulated that there was one God for the Jews and other gods for other people.)

Sadly, Zoroastrianism is persecuted in the land of its birth, where its numbers have shrunk to less than 30,000, most of them in Tehran. Muslims call them *gabors* which means "unbelievers." This isn't very fair, since the Zoroastrians believe in plenty of things; they just don't believe in the same things as Muslims.

The reason I am including Zoroastrians in a book on Eastern religions and philosophy is that most Zoroastrians now live in India. Besides, their ancestors and the Aryans undoubtedly rubbed elbows and exchanged ideas.

## THE LIFE OF ZARATHUSTRA

Scholars place Zarathustra anywhere from the twelfth to the sixth century B.C.E., and it's obvious they are just guessing. (The best guess, however, is probably about 630 B.C.E., or even a little earlier.)

Although it's not at all unusual to be uncertain about the dates of an early historical figure, we usually know where he lived. Not so with Zarathustra. So many stories and legends have accrued around the famous name that his actual origins are shrouded in historical mists. Still, based on various kinds of evidence, most scholars believe that he was born in Rhages, a town not far from modern Tehran.

At any rate, whenever he lived, legend tells us that he was the third of five sons, in a poor family. The religion of the time and area was a form of Vedism, the same polytheistic religion that gave birth to Hinduism in India (with the names of the gods somewhat altered).

---

### DEVAS AND ASURAS

Both Hinduism and Zoroastrianism use the terms deva and asura to refer to gods and demons. Unfortunately for the purposes of clarity, in Hinduism the devas are the gods and the asuras are the demons, while in Zoroastrianism the terms are reversed. To confuse things even more, the meanings of each term changed (or even flip-flopped) over time.

---

Zarathustra may have been trained as a Persian priest, but later rejected the priesthood. He was famed for his kindness to others. He left his family home at the age of twenty to meditate in the mountains and experienced a great vision ten years later, when he had a direct vision of the great God Ahura Mazda himself. He was actually released from his material body and transported directly to heaven for the meeting.

The experience gave birth to an inspired series of hymns to the god. These are called the Gathas.

Despite his enlightenment, Zarathustra just couldn't seem to convince anyone how right he was about everything. He had to leave his own homeland and travel to foreign climes before he could get someone to listen to him. But he struck gold with the king Vishtaspa, who was so impressed with Zarathustra's teachings that he declared them the basis of the state religion.

One important reform to Vedism that Zarathustra made was the abolishment of blood sacrifices, as well as the sacrificial drink *haoma*, undoubtedly identical to the mysterious soma of Vedic fame. He thought God should be honored with praise alone. (Zoroastrianism had its ups and downs on this issue. During the late Avestan period, sacrifices were brought back, but now they are gone again.) He did, however, advocate continuing the fire ritual, and it remains a powerful rite of the faith.

**YOU SAY ZOROASTER, I SAY ZARATHUSTRA**

*Zarathustra is also called Zoroaster. It's all a matter of preference. Zoroaster is a Greek transliteration of the Persian word. Obviously, I prefer Zarathustra, even though it's probably a little harder to pronounce.*

Many conflicting accounts exist of Zarathustra's death. According to one story, the prophet was murdered by a rival priest. Others insist that he lived a full and peaceful life, finally dying at the age of seventy-seven.

## SACRED TEXTS

The Zoroastrian scriptures are called the Avesta, which means "teaching." It is written in a very ancient Iranian language, known, reasonably enough, as Avestan, probably because the Avesta is just about the only thing left written in it. Its various elements include the following.

### The Yasna

The Yasna is a collection of liturgical writings. The most important of them are the Gathas. Of all Zarathustra's teachings, only these seventeen short, metrical hymns have been left to us (five of which are believed to be from Zarathustra himself). They are quite old, dating from the second millennium B.C.E. When inspired to sing these hymns, Zarathustra asked Ahura Mazda to speak to him friend to friend, and indeed the god does just that.

The Gathas were passed on orally for many generations and were finally committed to writing by priests who used them as part of their worship. Like the Vedas, the Gathas are so sacred that their very sounds convey the power of the eternal, whether the reciter understands the words or not. Contemporary Zoroastrian priests still recite the words of the Gathas every day. The reciting of the words must be exact in order for the ritual to be effective.

The Gathas are largely written in the form of a discourse between Zarathustra and the great god Ahura Mazda.

Mostly Zarathustra asks for the guidance of Ahura Mazda, although sometimes he complains about the state of religiosity in his world. One popular character in the Gathas is one called "Ox-soul," who complains about the ill treatment of cattle on earth.

### Later Writings

The rest of the Avesta was penned later than the Gathas, a few portions dating to just before 600 C.E. Interestingly, Zoroastrianism

**THEM AND US**

*In Nietzsche's work,* Thus Spake Zarathustra, *the words of Zarathustra are made up. Whatever Nietzsche's talents as a philosopher may have been, he was slightly shaky on his Zoroastrianism.*

became more polytheistic over time, and the later writings reflect this trend. The rest of the Avesta includes the Visparad, which is a series of invocations to the gods to use at festivals, the Yashts (hymns to various gods) and the Venidad, which contains many purification formulas. It also contains imprecations against demons. Unfortunately, much of the original Avesta was destroyed when the Arabs invaded Persia in 641 C.E.

### WEDDING SONG

*The last of the hymns, the Vahishtoishti Gatha, is a hymn Zarathustra wrote for his daughter on the occasion of her wedding. In it, he told her that if she wanted to please Ahura Mazda, she ought to please her earthly lord, namely her husband.*

## THE GOD(S)

The good god of Zoroastrianism is the aforementioned Ahura Mazda, the Lord of Wisdom. Ahura Mazda is a supreme god whose symbol is a winged disc. The name Ahura Mazda means "Great God" or "Wise Lord" and he is the creator, or good god, whom all people are expected to worship.

Originally, Ahura Mazda was considered only one member of a trinity that also included the Indo-Iranian gods Mitra and Varuna. (The Aryans brought these two with them to India.) Zarathustra rejected another important Vedic god, Indra, as a warrior god who spent too much time drinking soma.

It used to be common to say that Zarathustra denied the existence of all other gods and demons, but this doesn't seem exactly true. He did believe that Ahura Mazda reigned supreme, but he also acknowledged the power of the evil deity Ahriman, also called Angra Mainyu. The belief that there are two equal (or nearly equal) forces in the universe, one good and one evil, is called dualism. And using this definition, Zoroastrianism is certainly

---

#### MORE BOVINE BITS

*Like the related faith of the Aryans and later the Hindus, cows were important to early Zoroastrians. They were considered a sign of abundance and prosperity, and the Gathas urge shepherds to take darned good care of them. In another Gatha, Zarathustra roundly condemns some people who got drunk and were engaging in cattle-killing.*

---

a dualistic faith. Many Christians, following Augustine, define evil as a mere absence of good, but for Zarathustra, evil was a powerful and concrete force in the world, not just the absence of goodness. (The source of Zoroastrian dualism may be found in Babylonian myth, in which Tiamat (the nasty female god) battled Marduk (the good-boy god) for control over creation. Marduk won.)

Obviously, then, the question arises as to whether Zoroastrianism can be considered a truly monotheistic faith. Zoroastrians themselves and most scholars agree that it is, especially when compared with Christianity, which, with its doctrine of the trinity and belief in the great power of the devil, is considered monotheistic.

Ahriman is the uncreated spirit of deceit and evil. Neither Ahura Mazda nor Ahriman compels worship; human beings have complete freedom to follow either the good path of Ahura Mazda or the evil path of Ahriman. It's nice to know that in the Zoroastrian view, good will eventually prevail over evil, but it will be a long haul.

The philosophic value of a dualistic faith is that if there is a god of evil, then the good god is not held responsible for all the bad things that happen in the world. (The weak point, of course, is that the good god loses some omnipotence thereby—not a good thing in the divine world.

It is uncertain whether King Cyrus, who liberated the Jews from their Babylonian captivity, was a Zoroastrian, but it is known that the son of King Vishtaspa, Darius the Great (522–486 B.C.E.), was an enthusiastic practitioner. Under his Persian empire, Zoroastrianism expanded enormously, and its influence spread far and wide.

> "As long as I am able I shall look out for truth."
>
> —*Zarathustra*

---

### THE CULT OF MITHRA

*A god related to early Zoroastrian gods was Mithra, who, although a fairly minor figure in Zoroastrianism, became the focus of a powerful cult in Roman times, particularly among the soldiers. At one time, Mithraism posed a serious threat to Christianity.*

---

## The Six Spirits

Not precisely gods and not precisely creatures, Zoroastrians believe in the power of the six spirits, the Amesha Spentas. The spirits have their origin in Ahura Mazda, although scholars say that many of them hark back to ancient Vedic beliefs.

- Vohu Manah: Vohu Manah takes the souls of the righteous dead to paradise. He is sometimes called Good Mind or Good Vision, and he imparts two kinds of wisdom upon those who heed him: intuitive wisdom and acquired wisdom. In ancient days, when Zoroastrians sacrificed animals,

**SONS OF TIME**

*A group of unorthodox Zoroastrians, the Zurvanites claimed that Ahriman and Ahura Mazda were both sons of Zurvan, or time.*

Vohu Manah was supposed to be resident in the sacrificed animal. Today, however, he is said to be present in the milk and butter used in the ritual.

- Kshathra: Kshathra is a sublime and royal warrior who defends the poor. He is probably derived from the old Vedic god Indra, though certainly Zarathustra would have denied this. He is sometimes called the Good Dominion of Ahura Mazda. (If you notice in the word *Kshatra* a similarity to the Hindu word *Kshatriya* for the warrior class, you are very astute.)

- Asha Vahista: This god protects the order of the world and fights demons. He is the spirit of truth and righteousness, whose goal is to fight *druj,* or the Lie, which is the major principle of evil in Zoroastrianism. Zarathustra would not believe than any evil could emanate from God, but obviously it came from somewhere.

- Armati: Armati is the wise patroness of the earth, the feminine spirit of holy devotion and right-mindedness. In contemporary Zoroastrian rituals, Armati is represented by the sacred ground *(pawi)* where the ritual is held. Although all creation is considered good in Zoroastrianism, and all is under the care of Armati, some places have special holiness. Only these places are suitable for Zoroastrian rites.

- Haurvatat: Haurvatat brings prosperity, wholeness, and health. She is also in charge of water and is represented by water in the Yasna ceremony.

- Ameretat: Ameretat grants immortality, or at least long life, or long life leading to immortality. She is represented by *haoma* in the Yasna ceremony. Ameretat and Haurvatat are almost always considered as a pair.

## The Holy Spirit

Spenta Mainyu, the Holy Spirit of god, is a related concept. He is not considered one of the Amesha Spentas, because his qualities are almost identical with those of Ahura Mazda, and for practical purposes, they are one and the same. It is said that Ahura Mazda created the world through his Holy Spirit.

Spenta Mainyu has no independent existence from Ahura Mazda, but has been called the "augmenting spirit," because his presence helps distribute the divine Ahura Mazda throughout creation. He also seems to help accomplish Ahura Mazda's divine self-realization. It should be remembered, however, that Spenta Mainyu is almost indistinguishable from Ahura Mazda himself, not a separate being in the sense that the six spirits might be considered separate beings.

At any rate, Zoroastrians are greatly comforted in that each individual of the holy heptad is available for praise, guidance, and worship as he progresses through life.

> "These are two spirits existing from the beginning... the better and the evil."
>
> —*Zarathustra*

## ZOROASTRIAN PHILOSOPHY

Although Zoroastrian philosophy does not have a strong metaphysical component (unlike Buddhism and Hinduism), it makes up for it in the ethics and eschatology departments.

### Zoroastrian Ethics

For Zoroastrians, the ideal life can be summed up rather simply: good thoughts, good words, and good deeds. However, it is easier to sum these things up than actually practice any of them.

According to Zoroastrian thought, the universe is continually evolving, inexorably moving toward "renovation of the world," when the Right will conquer the Lie. Especially in its earliest form, this religion strongly emphasizes the freedom of each person to choose good or evil for himself, to move with the current of the universe or against it. Those who follow Ahriman do so freely— they choose their own evilness. "Sin" in Zoroastrianism is the refusal to align one's will with the "good thought" aspect of Ahura Mazda.

Nothing is predetermined; nothing is predestined. Everything you choose in this life will affect your fate after death. Those choices include not just the things you do, either, but what you say and think as well.

## Eschatology

At death, one stands before Sraoha (obedience to God), Rashnu (justice), and Mithra (truth). If one can prove that one's good deeds outweighed the bad ones, one is saved. If good and bad deeds balance exactly, one goes to an intermediate state called Hamestakan and waits there until the Last Judgment. I'm not sure what happens then, except that a flood of hot metal will be poured over everything and the wicked will be consumed. Apparently the molten metal won't hurt the rest of us. The historical importance of this whole concept is that Zarathustra was apparently the first person in history to invent or reveal a coherent end-of-history scenario, one that was later largely copied by Jews, Christians, and Muslims.

### THE OPPOSITE OF ASCETICISM

*Because Zoroastrians regard creation as good, there is no room in their philosophy for self-denial and stern asceticism. To reject the world is to reject creation. To reject creation is to reject the Wise Lord who made it.*

## LIFE AFTER DEATH

This is my favorite part to write about in Zoroastrianism, because I get to talk about the Chinvat Bridge, which is one of the greatest imaginative concepts in religious literature. Once you find yourself dead, you are on a long bridge. So you start across. *If* you are destined for the heavenly abode, the bridge very gradually becomes wider, more level, and pleasanter. Soon flowers appear, and you walk right into heaven. That's if you've been good. If you've been bad, a different experience awaits you. The Chinvat Bridge becomes slowly narrower, more rugged, and uphill. You won't even notice at first. Eventually it narrows to the width of a razor blade and you just fall off into hell. One may wonder why the discerning sinner doesn't simply retreat after noticing things aren't looking too good. Well, the answer is that he can't because the minute he realizes something is up, demons appear and chase him along.

It is true that the story of the Chinvat Bridge is somewhat at odds with the Last Judgment myth, but Zoroastrianism is not alone in having apparently contradictory doctrines. Zoroastrian theory has evolved over time and this explains, at least in part, the disparity.

## LATER ZOROASTRIANISM

Later Zoroastrianism is divided into two main eras: the Achaemenid period and the Sassanian period. During the Achaemenid period, the trend toward polytheism gained strength, and the six spirits were considered more like persons and less like ideas. Also, the concept of guardian angels became important. In this regard, the Achaemenid Zoroastrians simply appropriated the figures of the ancestral spirits. The practice of ritual took on greater importance.

In the Sassanian period, doctrine and dogma developed, including the religion's theories of the universe, time, and the problem of evil. The Sassanians didn't solve any of these problems, but at least they considered them. For all Zoroastrians, time is linear, not cyclical: it tends toward a particular end of days. The world was divided into four periods, each 3,000 years long. At the end of days, saviors will appear to make ready for the resurrection of the dead, and the universe will be restored to a pure state. The final savior may be Zarathustra himself. Evil will disappear.

### SINS OF ZOROASTRIANISM

*Among the ritual sins that can get Zoroastrians into trouble are improperly disposing of nail parings, killing otters and land-frogs, and feeding your dog food that is too hot.*

## ZOROASTRIANS TODAY

Most Zororastrians today live not in the land of their origin, but in India. A good number reside in the Bombay area, but overall they are a small part of the Indian population.

They fled from their native country when the Muslims came for fear of persecution. Those living in India are called Parsis (for Persians) of whom they are the direct descendants. Actually the word *Parsi* is an ethnic rather than a religious designation, and those who have converted to another religion are still called Parsis. In India, Zoroastrians live peaceably with members of other religions. They are well respected and generally well-to-do. Zoroastrians are not a part of India's caste system.

Modern Parsis are initiated into their faith by receiving the *kusti,* a cord made of lambswool that the individual will wear around his waist for his entire life. The fire temple, in which a fire is kept constantly burning inside, is the central symbol of Zoroastrianism. In fact, the fire ceremony is the most important ritual in Zoroastrianism. The fire is not a symbol of God as such, but merely a representation of his purity. In fact, the devotees wear masks over their mouths and noses during the ceremony so as not to pollute the sacred flame. Zoroastrians do not "worship" fire and offer only bread and milk at their services.

The most notable thing about the Parsis is their method of disposing of their dead. Burial in the earth is not permitted because the earth is sacred. Cremation is not permitted, either, because fire is too pure for dead bodies. The solution is to place the body on a *dakhma,* or a tower of silence, a round stone column surrounding a dry well, with separate sections for men, women, and children. The body is stripped of its clothing and placed on the top level, where the vultures pick off the flesh. A few hours later, the bones are placed in the well.

## CHAPTER RECAP

- The founder of Zoroastrianism was Zarathustra, a Persian prophet and priest.

- Zarathustra taught the existence of two ultimate forces, Ahura Mazda, the good god, and Ahriman, the spirit of evil.

- A driving tenet of Zoroastrianism is the free will of the individual to follow a path of good deeds and thought, or to follow a path of evil.

- Most Zoroastrians today live in India and are called Parsis.

*Recommended Reading*

Boyce, Mary. *Textual Sources for the Study of Zoroastrianism.* Manchester, UK: Manchester University Press, 1984.

Choksy, Jamsheed K. *Purity and Pollution in Zoroastrianism: Triumph over Evil.* Austin: University of Texas Press, 1989.

Clark, Peter. *Zoroastrianism: An Introduction to an Ancient Faith.* Brighton, UK: Sussex Academy Press, 1998.

Duchesne-Guillemin, Jacques. *Symbols and Values in Zoroastrianism.* New York: Harper and Row, 1966.

Hinnells, John R. *Zoroastrianism and the Parsis.* London: Ward Lock International, 1981.

Masani, Rustom. *Zoroastrianism: The Religion of the Good Life.* New York: Macmillan Publishing, Inc., 1968.

Mehr, Farhang. *The Zoroastrian Tradition: An Introduction to the Ancient Wisdom of the Zarathustra.* New York: Amity House, 1989.

Taraporewala, Irach J. S., ed., *Gathas of Zarathrusta.* New York: AMS Press, Inc., 1947.

Zaehner, R. C. *The Dawn and Twilight of Zoroastrianism.* New York: Putnam Berkeley Group, Inc., 1961.

# Sikhism—The Lion and the Sword

Sikhism is India's youngest religion. The word *Sikh* derives from Sikha, which means "disciple." The Sikhs are indeed disciples, in this case of Guru Nanak (1469–1539), who lived in Lahore. Today there are about 17 million Sikhs. Significant numbers of Sikhs live in Canada, the United Kingdom, Malaysia, Singapore, East Africa, and the United States. On the subcontinent, Sikhs are a majority in the Punjab, and strong minority in Kashmir, Uttar Pradesh, Rajasthan, and Gujarat.

Sikhism is an eclectic faith, drawing upon the elements of many others, including Bhakti Hinduism and the mystical Sufi cult of Islam.

## GURU NANAK

Nanak was born about forty miles from today's Lahore, Pakistan, in the village of Talwandi. This is part of the area known as the Punjab, which also includes part of northwestern India. The Punjab has long been known as the "gateway to India," as its peculiar geographical location makes it open to new influences from the West. (Most invaders had their eye on Delhi, which is in the southeast corner of the Punjab.)

**TALES OF
GURU NANAK**

*Stories of Guru Nanak's life
are collected in traditional
narratives known as the
janam-sakhis. Most non-Sikh
scholars believe they contain
much mythological material.*

As with so many other founders of great religious traditions, it is hard to separate the historical Guru Nanak from the religious construct. Legends tell us that he could discourse learnedly about divine subjects when he was only five years old. He so impressed the village astrologers with his wisdom that they began immediately to worship him.

Born into the Hindu Kshatriya caste, Nanak had a Muslim tutor while growing up. (The whole area was well supplied with both Hindus and Muslims, and Nanak knew children of both religions.)

He lived in a time of political upheaval. His secular education was slight, although it's apparent that he did learn some Persian. According to the story, Nanak wanted to study only divine subjects. He was invested with the sacred thread (initiated into the "twice-born") at the age of nine. Nanak reportedly told the officiating Brahmin that (in so many words) the ceremony was bunk.

When he was sixteen years old, he married the daughter of a pious Hindu merchant. Nanak said he didn't mind, if it didn't take too much time away from his spiritual studies. The marriage turned out to be a happy one, and the couple had two sons, Siri Chand and Lakshmi Das. Worried about his attachment to the life of the spirit, his family tried to keep him busy keeping shop, tending water buffalo, and dealing in horses, to no avail.

One day, after a bath, Nanak disappeared. Everyone thought he had drowned in the river but that wasn't the case. Nanak had simply gone for a walk in the forest and met God. When he reappeared three days later, he was transfigured, with a divine light in his eyes.

God imparted a lot of good advice and gave him some hymns. After the experience, Nanak gave away all his possessions but a loincloth. He began to preach at age thirty. No one is positive as to whether his original aim was to reform the Hinduism of his time, to unify Islam and Hinduism, to simply draw them closer together, or to start a new religion of his own. His most characteristic words were, "There is no Hindu, there is no Muslim."

Although he eventually traded in his loincloth for more ample attire, Nanak's garb was part Hindu and part Muslim. Sometimes he wore a hat suggestive of Islam, but a Hindu style necklace of bones, as well as saffron marks on this forehead. He carried a prayer carpet and a cup for ablutions. He also underwent severe asceticism—living first on just milk, then on just water, and finally just air. Later, however, he was heard to remark, "Asceticism doesn't lie in ascetic robes...nor in ashes. Asceticism lies in remaining pure amidst impurities."

Later in life, Nanak undertook a pilgrimage to Mecca, to see if God could be found more abundantly in holy places. He was distinctly unimpressed and actually fell asleep with his feet pointing toward the *kaaba,* which houses the sacred Black Stone of Islam. He was kicked awake by a watchman. "How dare you fall asleep with your feet toward the house of God?" he shouted.

"Okay," said Nanak agreeably. "Then please turn my feet where God is not." The watchman was stumped.

Guru Nanak is credited with many miracles. Two men offered him bread; Nanak took the bread and squeezed it. From one piece came milk and from another came blood. These events, said Nanak, meant that the first man had earned his bread honestly, while the second had stolen and swindled to get it. Squeezing milk and blood from flour, however, was just a warm-up for Nanak's next miracle—bringing an elephant back from the dead.

For Nanak, the ultimate underlying reality of existence was "true name." Guru Nanak believed in reincarnation and in karma, however, he strongly disliked Hindu rituals and the Hindu worship of many gods. He believed that God had many personal qualities, such as love and compassion. Nanak organized religious groups to help the poor and worship God. He freely allowed both men and women to join, without any restrictions on the latter whatever. Nanak felt that the word of God was equally true for all, a rather revolutionary concept.

Guru Nanak died peacefully in bed after naming his successor, Angad, a Hindu convert, who had been previously devoted to Durga. When his followers removed the sheet that had covered his corpse, they found only fresh flowers. The former Hindus took their share of the flowers and burned them, as was their custom for the treatment of dead bodies. The former Muslims took their share and buried them, as was their own funerary custom.

"This age is like a drawn sword, the Kings are butchers. Goodness has taken wings and flown."

—*Guru Nanak*

## NANAK'S FOLLOWERS

Sikhism was developed through the teachings of nine great gurus, masters who followed the steps of Guru Nanak. The teachings of this group are considered fully authoritative.

### The Second Guru—Angad Dev

Guru Angad (1504–1552) was known for his great humility. A great Indian yogi approached Angad and tried to convert him. Angad didn't argue with him, but merely stated that he was interested only in living a pure life. The yogi was impressed and asked him how he could help Angad. Angad merely told him that he would like to receive the famous adept's blessing.

Angad was responsible for instituting the *langar,* a kind of soup-kitchen open to people of every faith. He also encouraged his devotees to go out and play sports after prayers, so as to keep in good physical condition.

### The Third Guru—Amar Das

Amar Das (1479–1574) was a former Vaishnavite Hindu who became enchanted with the beautiful hymns of Guru Nanak. He had sought a guru all his life, until that moment. After years of devoted service, Angad appointed him as his successor, much to the displeasure of his own two sons, who thought one of them should have received the honor, but Angad found Amar Das more worthy.

One of the sons was so furious as the choice that he literally kicked the man, knocking him off his guru seat. Amar Das was seventy-three years old at the time. Instead of crying out, he merely rubbed the other man's foot, saying, "I am so old and bones are so hard, I am afraid I may have hurt you." (This is exactly the same trick the god Vishnu had performed once, so apparently Amar Das's days as a Vaishnavite were not in vain.)

Under Amar Das, the beginnings of a real religious community began to develop. Amar Das, although not abandoning the search for salvation that was Nanak's goal, added important life ceremonies to help make his co-religionists into a more cohesive unit. He also established three festival days.

Amar Das strongly believed in the equality of women, and of his 146 major disciples, fifty-two were female. The disciples were sent all

> "Me, the bard out of work, the Lord has applied me to his service."
>
> —*Guru Nanak*

over India to gain converts to Sikhism. Amar Das also believed that the wearing of veils was demeaning to women and actually refused to meet the Queen of Haripur because she was wearing one. He thought that widows should not only *not* throw themselves on a funeral pyre, but should remarry as soon as they liked.

He named his son-in-law, Ram Das, as his disciple. His own two sons weren't happy about it, but not engaging in nepotism was becoming a Sikh tradition.

### The Fourth Guru—Ram Das

Ram Das (1479–1581) created the city of Amritsar, site of the Golden Temple. This was his major contribution to the development of Sikhism. He is also known for composing the hymn now used as a wedding song in Sikh marriages. The hymn has four stanzas and is called the Lawan. The couple marches around a copy of the Adi Granth, the Sikhs' sacred scripture, one circumlocution for every stanza of the hymn. During the first circle, divine consent is prayed for. During the second, the consent is announced; during the third, the couple is described as blessed; during the fourth, the couple is congratulated for obtaining their heart's desire.

He chose his younger son, Arjun, to follow him. The older son, Prithi Chand, should have expected something like this, but apparently he didn't, raised a fuss, and was publicly condemned.

### The Fifth Guru—Arjun

This great Fifth Guru of Sikhism, Arjun (1563–1606), compiled the Sikh sacred scripture, the Adi Granth, and built its great temple in his father's city, Amritsar. He became quite rich by opening up trade with Persia, Turkey, and Afghanistan. He came to a bad end, though, being arrested on orders of Emperor Jahangir, and finally tortured and drowned.

### The Sixth Guru—Hargobind

Hargobind (1595–1644) respectfully declined to wear the headgear that had been passed on from the former gurus. He asked for a sword instead, but his faithful companion, Babe Buddha, not knowing anything about swords, put it on the wrong side. "That's all right," said Hargobind. "From now on I shall wear two swords, one for power and

> "Search not for the True One afar off; He is in every heart, and is known by the Guru's instruction."
> —*Guru Nanak*

one for meditation." Shikhs take this statement as representing the two kinds of authority: religious and secular. It was Hargobind who taught his followers to fight against their oppression and persecution. In his honor, the Sikhs are sometimes known as "soldier-saints."

### The Seventh Guru—Har Rai

Contrary to established practice, Guru Har Rai (1630–1661) was the eldest son of Guru Hargobind. He was famed for his love of all creatures—and also his passion for hunting. He solved his dilemma to his own satisfaction by keeping the animals he caught as pets. Considering the tumultuous times, Har Rai's guruship was relatively peaceful, although he did keep a personal guard of 2,200 cavalry. He died uneventfully.

### The Eighth Guru—Harkrishnan

Harkrishnan (1656–1664) was the younger son of Hai Rai. He had an older brother who proved something of a disappointment to his father by trying to make too many concessions to the Muslim Emperor Aurangzeb. In fact, he was only five years old when he received the guruship. The child contracted smallpox, however, and died at the age of eight.

### The Ninth Guru—Tegh Bahadur

This Guru (1621–1675) fought hard for the rights of all people to worship as they pleased. Muslim authorities tried to get Bahadur to convert to Islam, perform some miracles, and denounce Hinduism. He refused to do any of these. "Hinduism may not be my faith," he proclaimed, "and I may not believe in the supremacy of the Vedas or the Brahmins, not in idol worship or castes or pilgrimages or other rituals, but I would fight for the right of all Hindus to live with honor and practice their faith according to their own rites." As for miracles, he said, "This is the work of charlatans and mountebanks to hoodwink the people. Men of God submit to the will of God." He wouldn't turn Muslim, either.

The Muslim Emperor Aurangzeb had him jailed in an iron cage, starved, and finally decapitated. In the meantime, he had to watch some faithful followers be sawed in two, boiled, and set on fire. Bahadur's body and head were smuggled out of the area and later cremated separately. The noble death of Bahadur marks something extraordinary in the history of religion: the first time a religious leader was killed largely for proclaiming the rights of other people to follow their own faith.

### The Tenth Guru—Gobind Singh

The last (by his own decree) of the Sikh Gurus, Gobind Singh (1666–1708) was proclaimed Guru when he was only nine years old. He wished all to follow one faith, Sikhism, and enjoined Hindus to cease caste distinctions, stop their holy pilgrimages, and forgo the worship of their gods.

It is the rather militant Gobind Singh who created the *Khalsa,* a military fraternity, in 1699. The first *Khalsa* members were five disciples, the *panj piare,* or the "Cherished Five." They underwent an initiation ("baptism of the double-edged dagger") and were given the new name Singh, which means "lion." Ever since, initiation ceremonies are conducted by groups of *panj piare.* The initiates are then entitled to use the *Khalsa* greeting formula: *Wahi guru ji ka Khalsa. Wahi guru ji ki fateh.* This means: "The Khalsa are the chosen of the God. Victory be to God." Those who did not wish to join were called *sahajdhari:* ones who take time to join."

Gobind Singh struck a special blow for women's rights when he opened the sacred *Khalsa* initiation to both men and women. Both were permitted to wear the Five Ks, the special items that mark a Sikh as a Sikh. (I'll tell you all about the Five Ks later in this chapter.)

Gobind Singh lost all four of his sons during the war with the Moguls; he himself was assassinated on October 7, 1708. He always said the Adi Granth was his true successor, and today Sikhs declare that to be doctrine, thus the Adi Granth is also known as the Guru Granth Sahib. In Sikhism today, they say, there is no place for a living guru.

**SACRED SONGS**

*The Adi Granth contains more than 6,000 hymns; Guru Arjun wrote 2,000 of them himself.*

## THE ADI GRANTH

The Adi Granth is written in a special thirty-five-letter alphabet of uncertain origin. The work is divided into three parts. The first, most critical part is the Japji, a poem by Guru Nanak himself. Another Granth, the Dasan Granth, or Tenth Granth, compiled by the Tenth

Guru, is also revered, although it is not held sacred. It was placed in the Golden Temple at Amritsar, under a jeweled canopy.

Today the Adi Granth is kept in a special room in every Sikh place of worship *(gurdwara)*. It sits on a cushion and is wrapped in cloths that resemble vestments. Like a god, it is put to bed at night and awakened in the morning. Offerings are made to it. Treated as if it were a king, worshippers are careful not to turn their backs on it. The Adi Granth is always located in the most elevated spot in the room, and when it is carried, it's always placed upon the bearer's head. All this, of course, goes back to the Hindu roots of Sikhism, where the statues of the gods are treated in just this manner.

The Adi Granth plays a critical part in Sikh worship, a procedure called *Vak Lao*—taking the advice of the word. During the service, the officiating priest opens the Adi Granth at random and begins reading. Worshippers understand that the words read will have a special meaning for each of them and will be just the words they needed to hear. Sikhs also practice *Vak Lao* individually in their private morning worship *(jap ji)* and also at special ceremonies. Although the Adi Granth is their only holy book, Sikhs are permitted to study other religious books for the sake of acquiring knowledge.

## SIKH RELIGIOUS PHILOSOPHY

It's commonly said that the Sikhs mix Hindu and Muslim religious ideas, and although undoubtedly an oversimplification, there is truth to the statement. Guru Nanak combined the stern monotheism of Islam with a basically Hindu worldview, including ideas about reincarnation and karma. He despised image veneration and the sacrifice system, however, and even today the emphasis of Sikhism is not ritual or even prophecy, but on the consciousness of God within each person.

Sikhs are strong monotheists and have no idols or statues in their worship service. Some Sikh temples *(gurdwaras)* display paintings of the ten gurus, but these are for inspirational purposes only. Sikhs do not believe that God can ever take human form.

Sikh teaching emphasizes *seva*, which means selfless service. It has no priests or caste system and emphasizes equality between men and women. Sikhs believe in reincarnation; they also believe

"A Sikh is any person who believes in God (Akal Purakh); in the ten Gurus; in the Adi Granth, other writings of the ten Gurus and their teachings; in the *Khalsa* initiation ceremony instituted by the tenth Guru; and who does not believe in any other system of religious doctrine."

—*Sikh Rahit Maryada*

that the goal to human life is to escape the birth-death-rebirth cycle and achieve unity with God. Sikhs attempt to reach liberation through prayer, faith, and righteous living. The religion emphasizes a daily devotion to God. Community service and frequent prayers are expected, and a regular family life is encouraged. Some Sikhs say the ideal Sikh is a solider-scholar-saint.

The main obstacles to salvation are the five cardinal sins:

- *Kam* (lust)

- *Krodh* (anger)

- *Lobh* (greed)

- *Moh* (earthly attachment)

- *Ahankar* (pride)

**THE GENEROUS SIKHS**

*Being of service is part of a Sikh's life. Not surprisingly, every gurdwara has a soup kitchen open to all.*

## SIKH PRACTICES

One interesting Sikh religious practice is the *nam simaran,* a discipline of inner meditation upon the Divine Name. In some cases, the devotee repeats a simple mantra over and over; in others, he sings devotional songs. The purpose is to bring the worshipper in concert with the holy rhythm of the universe.

Sikhs are forbidden to use intoxicants or to gamble. They denounce the caste system, sexism, racism, magical rites, pilgrimages, astrology, yoga, fasting, and religion-based vegetarianism. (Vegetarianism for health reasons or out of compassion is permitted.) Sikhs are not permitted to desecrate their bodies by piercing their ears or noses. (Notably, such piercings had been a mark of some Indian ascetics.)

Both men and women are expected to dress modestly, although there are no formal restrictions, other than the required turban for men. Interestingly, women are to honor their bodies by not covering their faces with a veil.

### The Khalsa Path

As I mentioned earlier, the *Khalsa* is the Sikh brother- and sisterhood. The word itself means "pure." *Khalsa* include those Sikhs who have undergone the sacred initiation ceremony. All Sikhs are expected to join eventually. In the ceremony, the candidate drinks *amrit* (sugar water stirred with a dagger) in the presence of five members of the order. He then vows:

- Not to remove any hair from his body

- Not to use tobacco, alcohol, or any other intoxicants

- Not to eat the meat of an animal slaughtered in the Muslim fashion

- Not to commit adultery

After the ceremony, men are expected to add "Singh" (lion) after their names and women "Kaur" (princess). Every *Khalsa* member is also required to wear the physical symbols of the *Khalsa* at all times. These are called the Five Ks.

### The Five Ks

Sikhs agree to abide by the Five Ks, a practice that identifies them to others and helps maintain group solidarity. When a Sikh grooms and dresses himself, he symbolically clothes himself in the word of God. The Five Ks are:

- *Kesh:* uncut hair and beard (like a lion). This is a symbol of spirituality.

- *Khanga:* combed hair. This is a symbol of hygiene and discipline. (The Hindu ascetic typically has knotted or matted hair.) Sikhs are also expected to wash their hair frequently. Male Sikhs cover their hair with a *dastar,* a turban that symbolizes dignity and royalty. It is optional for women.

- *Kach:* underwear in the form of short trousers. They represent chastity and self-control.

- *Kirpan:* defensive short sword. This is a ceremonial device only, and is a symbol of the Sikh struggle against injustice and oppression. It is not a weapon.

- *Kara:* steel bracelet. This is a symbol of restraint, reminding the wearer to be disciplined in action at all times.

"He who keeps alight the unquenchable torch of truth, and never swerves from the thought of the one God...he is to be recognized a pure member of the *Khalsa.*"

—*Guru Gobind Singh*

Grooming has a symbolic meaning for Sikhs. For example, the Adi Granth counsels that as people comb their hair in the morning and at night, removing dead hair, so also should they "remove negative thoughts, evil thoughts. So you have two types of combs: the one is a wooden comb, the other a comb of *Gurbani*—of sacred Scripture."

"Whatever I do becomes the worship of God."

—*Kabir*

### The Golden Temple

The Golden Temple is the most holy of all Sikh shrines. It is located at Amritsar. The Sikhs call their temple *Harimandir*, the Temple of God. It's a truly fabulous building, made of marble and topped with gilded copper. It is completely surrounded by a pond and must be approached via bridge. It is open on all sides, symbolizing the democratic nature of Sikhism.

Here resides the Adi Granth, the most sacred Sikh scripture, which was formally installed there in 1604. The Golden Temple also contains holy Sikh relics and a picture gallery detailing Sikh history. Sadly, the Golden Temple was attacked in June 1984 by the Indian army, after Sikh extremists had entrenched themselves in the building. Many people lost their lives, and the Sikh library was burned to the ground. The Temple treasury was destroyed, and for the first time in hundreds of years, the continuous reading of the Adi Granth was interrupted.

---

#### KABIR

*One of the most beloved figures in Sikhism is not a prophet, but a poet, the great Kabir (1440–1518). Kabir rejected the holy writings of both Hindus and Muslims and insisted that all are equal before God. His most famous metaphor is that God has discharged his true word like an arrow into the world. Those who are "slain" by the arrow live forever in mystical communion with God.*

---

## SIKHISM TODAY

Modern times have been turbulent for the Sikhs. When the British left India, the country's subsequent division into India and Pakistan spelled disaster for the Sikh practitioners. Half were in India and half in Pakistan, where violent riots broke out between the Muslims and Sikhs. About 2½ million eventually left Pakistan for India, at a great economic loss to themselves. Today nearly all Sikhs on the subcontinent live in India.

**SIKH MILITANCY**

*During their rule of India, the British often used Sikhs as bodyguards. It is true that the Skihs make excellent soldiers and honor a military tradition, but there is no evidence that they are any more belligerent than anyone else.*

Most Sikhs are politically moderate, and one of them, *Zail Singh,* served as president of India from 1982 to 1987. However, there does exist a strong separatist movement—the *Khalsa Dal* (Society of the Pure)—who demand a Sikh state, the Punjab. The *Khalsa Dal* is widely considered to be a terrorist movement.

Sikhism has expanded widely throughout the world. Sikhs accept converts, but as a rule they do not actively seek to spread their religion.

## CHAPTER RECAP

- Sikhism was founded in India in the early sixteenth century by the spiritual thinker Guru Nanak.

- Sikhism draws from many religions and is often viewed as a combination of Hinduism and Islam.

- The Sikhs are monotheistic and believe that the purpose of human life is to end the cycle of reincarnation and thereby achieve unity with God.

- The Adi Granth is the sacred text of the Sikhs; it is also considered Sikhism's last Guru.

*Recommended Reading*

Cole, W. O., and Piara Singh Sambhi. *The Sikhs, Their Religious Beliefs and Practices.* London: Routledge and Kegan Paul, 1978.

McLeod, W. H. *Guru Nanak and the Sikh Religion.* New York: Oxford University Press, 1969.

Singh, Khushwant. *A History of the Sikhs.* Princeton, NJ: Princeton University Press, 1963.

# *Shinto — The*

# *Sacred Ceremony*

Shinto, the national faith of Japan, is one of the oldest religious traditions in the world. The word *Shinto* derives from the Chinese term *Shen Tao*, the Way of the Gods. (The Japanese often preferred Chinese words to their own; they thought the Chinese were a very sophisticated people.) The word *Shinto* didn't appear in writing until the year 720; it was apparently coined to distinguish it from the new religion of Buddhism. The Japanese term for this tradition is *Kami no michi*. The word we translate as "god" is *kami* in Japanese. The translation is only approximate, however, because *kami* means something somewhat different from Western concepts of god or gods. In fact, some *kami* seem to be merely abstract concentrations of energy.

In any case, according to early Japanese belief, everything in nature, both animate and inanimate, is a manifestation of divinity. Shinto is the product of a completely agrarian culture, which lived so close to nature that its dependence upon it was critical. It is sometimes called "nature worship," but that term is inadequate to encompass the richness and diversity of Shinto beliefs. Still, honoring and respecting nature has remained a strong element even in modern Japan, where the cherry blossom festivals and the maple-leaf viewing in the fall are national holidays.

Like Hinduism, Shinto has no founder. It doesn't even have an official sacred text. It has no dogma, nor any specific system of

UNDERSTANDING
THE *KAMI*

*The Japanese character used
to represent* kami *means
"above," usually taken in the
sense of being superior.*

ethics. It has no congregational worship. There is no concept of "sin" as such, meaning a moral offense against the gods, but Shinto does combine reverence for nature with respect for Japan's national and historical heritage in a unique and vital way.

With Japan's many hallmarks of modernity—its high prices, crowded living, and technological advancements—it may be curious that the Japanese have chosen to adhere to a religion that seems to many so "cult-ridden" and even "backward." But this is a misreading of what Shinto means to Japan. Far more than a set of rituals and practices, Shinto is an expression of ancient power and beauty.

To practice Shinto is to enter a timeless world that underlies the fast-paced life we associate with Japan. In fact, the Association of Shinto Shrines stands today as one of the foremost proponents of environmental preservation in the country. This ancient tradition understands that in the final analysis, the land, the trees, the water, and the sacred sky are, as much as ever, our parents and the source of our spiritual strength.

## ANCIENT PRACTICES

The earliest Japanese religion included many shamanistic practices. A shaman is one who has a special communication or pathway to the divine. Sometimes, shamans inherited their positions; sometimes one simply was chosen—either by the old shaman or by the gods themselves.

Early practices also included orgiastic rituals associated with spring planting and fall harvest, puberty rites, and memorial services for the dead.

Another ancient practice was open-air worship. The very earliest Japanese probably did not worship at shrines at all. They paid their respects to the *kami* directly, worshipping the natural objects inhabited by the spirits. Later, two kinds of religious practices developed. One type, the *uji-gami,* was based on the family, and each family and each clan had its own shrine. These early shrines were simple structures covered with thatch and supported by plain pillars. Even today most important Shinto rites are intimately connected with the family.

The other type, the *hito-gami*, was the product of a special relationship between a *kami* and a religious professional such as a shaman. About 80 percent of Shinto shrines are related to *hito-gami*, but of course the two types are by no means mutually exclusive. In any case, whether the worship took place out in the open or within a shrine enclosure, ancient Shinto used no images.

## THE AINU

Although Shinto is often portrayed as the original Japanese religion, the aboriginal (and Caucasian) inhabitants of Japan, the Ainu people, had their own rites and ceremonies. (The Japanese always referred to them as "hairy," thus giving Westerners who had never seen them, the idea that the Ainu were hirsute, perhaps apelike creatures. As a matter of fact, Ainu have considerably less hair than most Caucasians.)

According to ancient Ainu belief, the whole cosmos is pervaded by *ramat* (spirit). *Ramat* inhabits not only animate things, but also objects. The amount of *ramat* present in any one object varies from particular to particular. The Ainu also worshipped many *kamui* (gods and godlings) of various forms and of diverse temperaments. Of these, Kamui Fichi, the Supreme Mother, was the most important. She guarded the hearth, the very center of Ainu life. The Ainu had no temples, and sacrifices were made to the gods by the butchering of a sacred animal, usually a bear specially raised for the purpose.

The most important sacred objects in Ainu worship were the *inau*. These were sacred sticks of wood, usually willow. The *inau* were seen as protection against evil spirits and were carefully arranged in rows outside the east window of a home.

Around the end of the first millennium B.C.E. and the first century C.E., invaders from China and Korea gradually took over the island. Japanese culture was forever changed. Elements of Taoism, Confucianism, the Chinese yin/yang system, and later Buddhism were all incorporated in Japanese thought. The Japanese also imported many elements of Chinese divination, especially astrology. Unfortunately for women, the Japanese took the Chinese yin/yang system very literally. Women were associated with pollution and

**SPIRIT POSSESSION**

*One ancient belief that has survived into recent times is the idea of spirit possession. The spirits of foxes and dogs seem particularly adept at this sort of thing.*

death, and were encouraged to lead very separate lives from those of men, so as not to taint them. The same sort of thing was happening in Neo-Confucian China. Still, women's association with the "dark powers" made their services in religious rituals essential, no matter how badly they were treated in their domestic life.

The tribe who called themselves the Yamoto eventually became the dominant group. These are the people who assimilated the legends, beliefs, and practices that are now called Shinto. Today the Ainu, though they still exist, have been largely assimilated into the dominant Japanese culture. The Yamoto claim to have been the original clan in Japan, but this is doubtful.

**GROUP GODS**

*Many of the same Japanese deities appear in both Shinto and Buddhism. In fact, the* kami *are popularly supposed to protect the bodhisattvas enshrined in Buddhist temples. They are considered to be persons, are given names, and have the power of speech.*

## JAPANESE KAMI

As I mentioned earlier, the easiest way for us to translate the Japanese word *kami* is by the word "god," but there are important differences. First of all, the word has a broad meaning, for it not only refers to a divine being, but also to the holy, numinous power inherent in many things (such as lightning, sacred trees or rocks, mountains, waterfalls, and even echoes).

One's ancestors also become *kami* and hover nearby. These spirits do have some influence over human lives, but their power is rather nebulous. It's not clear just what they can and cannot do. In the old days, the clan leader of each kinship group also became a powerful *kami*.

### Izanagi and Izanami

Izanagi (he-who-invites) and Isanami (she-who-invites) are the "first parents," largely responsible for the creation of the world. They managed this feat by standing on the Floating Rainbow Bridge of Heaven and stirring up the ocean with a jeweled spear. When they pulled the spear out of the ocean, the dripping foam coagulated into eight islands, which, curiously enough, turned out to be Japan.

### Amaterasu Omigami

The "heavenly shining" goddess Amaterasu Omigami is the chief deity in Shinto. She is the child of the divine pair, Izanagi and Izanami. Although originally a sun goddess, Amaterasu Omigami is now closely associated with other shining things, including the imperial sword, gems, and mirrors. Her sacred tree is the *sakaki*, an evergreen of fragrant wood.

The most famous story about her concerns the day she got into a temper tantrum and retired into a cave. Things got pretty dark and cold, but Ama no Uzume, the goddess of persuasion, managed to save the world by performing a lascivious dance. Everyone started laughing, and Amaterasu got so curious about the cause of the noise that she came out of the cave.

Not only does she rule the light, but also all heaven and earth. Amaterasu's shrine, the famed Ise Grand Shrine, is the most holy place in Japan. It is located on the island of Honshu, on the Isuzu River, in a place of great natural beauty. The shrine is supposed to be entirely rebuilt every twenty years, but lately there has been a lot of squabbling about who has to pay for it. Amaterasu's grandson, Ninigino-mikoto, was given authority to rule Japan, and his grandson, Jimmu Tenno, was the first Yamoto emperor. He reigned about 600 B.C.E.

### Hachiman

Hachiman is the Japanese war god, and he has both Shinto and (strangely) Buddhist followers. In Shinto, Hachiman is really a complex mixture of three separate deities: the Emperor Ojin, the Empress Jingu, and the deity Hime-gami. Because war has been rather unpopular in Japan lately, Hachiman has taken up duties as a fishing god and lord of agriculture.

### Other Popular Gods

Shintoists believe that the moon is subject to Tsuki-yomi. Takehaya-susanowo, whose name means Valiant Swift Impetuous Hero, controls the netherworld.

Minor deities who sometimes show up in Shinto include Doso-jin, the spirit of cross-roads; Kamado-no-kami, the kitchen stove god; Ryu-jin, the snake god who controls the wind and rain; and Daikokuten, a good luck god.

Shrines to these gods appear throughout the rural areas in Japan. The traveler is expected to pay obeisance by clapping his hands, bowing silently, and perhaps tossing a small stone for good luck.

**SHINTO HINT**

*The word kami is both singular and plural.*

### Shinto Religion and Folk Traditions

As I've mentioned, popular religion in Japan is a synthesis of Shinto, folk religion, and Buddhism. In modern, popular thought, there exist Seven Gods of Happiness, beginning with Hotei, the fat Buddha. The other six are: Bishamonten (the watchman); Fukurokuju (god of longevity); Jurojin (god of scholarship); Daikoku (god of nutrition); Ebisu (god of fishing), and Benzaiten (goddess of music).

Shinto does not formally contain a code of ethics like the Ten Commandments. Nor does it believe in a judgmental god or sin. The closest thing is the ancient idea of "pollution," found also in Greek culture. Cleanliness, both ritual and day-to-day, is extremely important in Japanese life. The Japanese are even more fanatic than Americans about bathing, hand washing, and rinsing the mouth. They discern a strong connection between physical and spiritual cleanliness; one had to be physically clean to be in the presence of the gods.

The relationship between Shintoism and Buddhism is historically complex. Sometimes one religion rose to the ascendancy, sometimes the other. Often they co-existed in an uneasy balance. Since Shinto is the national religion of Japan, ardent nationalists have always gravitated toward it, often at the expense of Buddhism. It infuriated some of them when certain Buddhists declared Shintoism to be merely another not very orthodox sect of Buddhism. Shintoists struggled to define themselves in opposition to the "upstart" religion.

Much of this defining came during the eighteenth century, when Motoori Norinaga (1730–1801) and Kamo Mabuchi (1697–1769) worked hard to develop a "pure" Shinto. The separation has never been complete. Although the earliest Shinto shrines were empty of images, today they often contain Buddhist images, while Buddhist temples reciprocated with Shinto symbols. There is also a strong Taoist influence on Shinto, although, intriguingly, Taoism itself has never been a component of Japanese religion. Most Shinto shrines contain a *jingu-ji*, a special Buddhist section dedicated to the *kami* of the shrine. On the opposite side, most Buddhist temples included a symbol of the *kami*.

Other enshrined objects may include mirrors, swords, clothing, stones, and large natural features such as mountains and waterfalls.

"A knight scorns to lie in order to avoid hurt or harm to himself."

—*The* Bushido *Code*

## TEMPLES AND WORSHIP

The earliest Shinto rites probably involved purification rituals, thanksgiving festivals, and petitionary prayers. All these still exist to some extent. The whole system of Shinto depends upon the concept of *ho-on,* the reciprocal exchange of gifts between greater and lesser beings. Over the centuries, Shinto has also developed an elaborate shrine system, although shrines are still enclosed by groves.

Shinto shrines are beautifully simple, composed of straight, pleasing lines and unpainted wood. The excessive ornamentation of some comes from outside influences. Many are bounded by pure running water, needed for purification of worshippers. Typically, water is a way of separating the sacred and profane realms. Shrines with no running water provide a special basin or pool for the purpose.

> ### THE ORIGINS OF ORIGAMI
>
> *The famous Japanese art form of origami means "paper of the spirits." It dates back to pre-literate times, when the devout would say their prayers over pieces of paper and then tie them to trees. When the wind blew, the prayers went directly to the gods. This is still a Shinto custom, and out of respect for the tree spirit from which paper comes, origami paper is never cut with scissors or any other sharp implement.*

More formal temples are entered through a gate *(torii)* to the oratory building *(haiden).* In fact, the *torii* has become the symbol of Shinto itself. Altogether, there are about 80,000 Shinto shrines in Japan. The main sanctuary is called a *honden.* Some shrines, those that have a mountain or other large natural object for its center of worship, have no sanctuary as such. One can stand on the pavilion and merely gaze.

After purification, the worshipper enters a public worship hall through which he passes to enter the offering hall where the priests pay homage to the gods. The *kami* are enshrined in a small cabinet. Worshippers bow, make a small donation, and ring a bell or clap three times to get the *kami*'s attention. Then they pray and toss a coin in the offering box. Unlike worshippers in many Western traditions, people do not pray to the *kami* for help or guidance. The act of worship is more like a reverent recognition of the *kami*'s great powers. Its purpose is to help heighten a worshipper's awareness of the great energies all about him, as well as to help him get in harmony with the natural forces of life. If a pilgrim has made a trip to a

THE SYMBOL OF SHINTOISM, THE *TORII.*

shrine of great importance, he takes home with him a symbolic reminder of the shrine in a brocade bag.

Priests are also present at Shinto shrines. They wear long robes of symbolic colors, shoes made of lacquered paper, and horsehair hats. Some temple ceremonies are so complex that Shinto priests must go through a ten-year apprenticeship to master them. Priests also perform ceremonies at weddings, which are held away from the shrine itself. As in Hindu and ancient Jewish tradition, the priesthood is hereditary, with some people able to trace their priestly ancestry back for a hundred generations. Women may also attain the priesthood, and both men and women priests are allowed to marry.

### Purification Rituals

Among the most important rites in Shinto are purification rituals. It is astonishingly easy to become defiled: menstruation, sexual intercourse, wounds, disease, and contact with dead bodies will all do it. It's important to remember, though, that the concepts of defilement and pollution are not the same thing as sin.

---

**CONCEPTS OF CLEANLINESS**

*Even in Western culture, people with terrible diseases are often regarded with horror, although it's plain they haven't committed any sins. And in some forms of Judaism, a menstruating woman is considered "unclean" and polluting to others. In Japan, it is also customary to purify the land before building on a site, because the earth might already have spirits inhabiting it.*

---

Even though one cannot commit an ethical sin against the *kami*, one can certainly make one angry. If one happens to earn the *kami*'s disfavor, a condition called *tsumi*, the only way out is through a purification ritual. My favorite such ritual is the *misogi*, or purification by waterfall. First you put on all white clothing. Then you "shake the soul" by moving your hands quickly up and down in front of your stomach. Then comes a physical vocal exercise called "bird rowing," which is designed to release your inner energy *(ki)*. After this, you are sprinkled with salt to completely purify you, and then you are given some sake. You don't get to drink the sake, instead you must spit three mouthfuls of the stuff into the waterfall. The leader (you must have a leader in the rite) counts from one to nine and then yells, "*Yei!*" Everyone then jumps into the waterfall yelling, "*Harae tamae*

*Kiyome tamae ro kon sho jo!"* Then (at last) you get to stand in the cooling spray of the waterfall, which washes away all your impurities. Till next time.

### Mountain Worship

Like many traditional peoples, the ancient Japanese had a special regard for mountains. They were regarded as a link between heaven and earth (axis mundi), between the profane world and the sacred one. Mountains are believed to be responsible for the birth of humans and animals, and they are usually considered female. Some mountains were esteemed as the source of rivers and streams—the waters of life. Still another class were the mountains that the Japanese believed to be the abode of the dead. Thus the mountains rule over birth, life, and death itself. Most sacred mountains in Japan have two shrines—one at the base and one at the peak.

The dormant volcano Mt. Fuji, correctly known as Fujisan (not Fujiyama), has long held a central place in Japanese religion. The earliest recorded ascents date back to the ninth century c.e. Today a Shinto shrine stands atop the peak, and pilgrims, garbed in white and wearing straw sandals, have traditionally made the climb in honor of the mountain goddess, Konohana-sakuyahime. (As is so depressingly often the case, women were not permitted to climb above a certain level until fairly recently.) It takes about two days to make the entire trip, and lodges are scattered on the mountain for overnight stays. The best time to arrive at the summit is at dawn, when the most auspicious rituals can be performed. Both Buddhist and Shinto Japanese are fond of climbing the mountain.

> "No matter how deeply one is moved, feelings should not be shown."
>
> —*The* Bushido *Code*

## SHINTO SCRIPTURES

Although Shinto does not have a sacred text the way Hinduism or Buddhism does, there are several writings that are important to Shinto. The two most famous texts are the Chronicle of Ancient Events (Kojiki), written in 712 c.e., and the Chronicle of Japan (Nihongi), written in 720 c.e. No one knows how much of the Nihongi is genuine historical fact and how much was made up to exaggerate the virtues of the ruling family.

## SHINTO HOLIDAYS

The most important holiday is the celebration of the New Year, which begins in December with a giant housecleaning (which doesn't really sound like that much fun). People place pine trees in their doorway and dress in traditional garments. All the other seasons are celebrated as well. In fact, the entire March-April period is a great spring festival.

Stations in life are also celebrated, beginning when you are a five-month-old fetus, the time when the soul enters the body. About thirty-three days after the birth of the child, he or she is brought to the family temple for initiation by the *kami*. Special ceremonies are also conducted for children of ages three, five, and seven. These ancient ceremonies date back more than one thousand years, when most children never lived to see adulthood. Other important life milestones include coming of age (thirteen), adult hair arrangement for women (sixteen); and certain special birthdays: sixty-one, seventy-seven, and eighty-eight.

**SHINTO'S OPEN ARMS**

*One of the most interesting facts about Shinto is its inclusivity. One can identify oneself as Shinto, and, at the same time, Buddhist, Confucian, or even Christian.*

## JAPAN, SHINTO, AND THE WEST

Japan's attitude toward the West seems to go in cycles. At some points in its history, Japan has "gone West" culturally. At other periods, it has attempted to preserve its own culture. Shinto was an important part of this effort. During the Meiji period, when the old feudal system was abolished and Japan became strongly united, the emperor actually created a governmental department of Shinto. This body oversaw festivals and ceremonies, and developed regulations for priests and shrines. A governmental "white paper" was issued to define Shinto and explain its relationship to the government. (It stated for the record that Shinto was a "sun goddess cult.") This attempt was short-lived, however (the Buddhists weren't having any of it), and the government eventually gave up, abolishing the Shinto Department in 1871. Instead a Ministry of Religion was established to oversee both Buddhism and Shinto. The hope was that Buddhism and Shinto would eventually combine into one national religion, a religion that would ascribe to the following principles:

- Veneration of the national deities of Japan

- Obedience to the dictates of heaven and the laws of humanity

- Reverence to the throne of the emperor

This didn't work either. The Japanese were very good about appropriating elements of both religions to fulfill their needs, but never got around to actually considering Buddhism and Shinto one religion. In 1877, the Ministry of Religion was disbanded.

### State Shinto

As its name suggests, State Shinto was supported by the Japanese government. Its whole purpose was to foster obedience and patriotism. Rather weirdly, State Shinto was declared to be nonreligious, but it was actually "above" religion, subsuming all other religions under it. Preaching was not even allowed in State Shinto temples. Varieties of State Shinto included Tennoism, Imperial Family Shinto, Household Shinto, and Shrine Shinto. Its proponents claimed that it was an eternal tradition that had no earthly founders.

#### Tennoism

The Japanese have always been famous for Tennoism, or emperor worship. Or if not always, at least since the third or fourth century of our era. Tennoism (named after Tenno, the first emperor) holds that the emperor is the incarnation of Amateraso, the sun goddess. A god, the emperor was therefore infallible. Ordinary people weren't even allowed to look at him. Although held most strongly by the Tenno sect of Shinto, emperor worship was an important element in all Japanese Shinto sects.

"Death is preferable to disgrace. A knight always carries two swords, a long one to fight his foes, a short one to turn upon his own body in the case of blunder or defeat."

—*The* Bushido *Code*

> **RELIGION AND POLITICS**
>
> *The Japanese are known to be politically minded, so it shouldn't be surprising to learn that there is a special class of kami called goryo, noble persons who have died in a political intrigue or uprising. They are bad news when they show up.*

#### Imperial Family Shinto

Imperial Family Shinto is exactly what it sounds like: a practice involving only the imperial family of Japan. The family has four shrines within the palace ground devoted to their exclusive use.

### Household Shinto

Practitioners of Household Shinto honor deceased relatives. The worship centers on a small shrine *(kamidana)* placed on a high shelf above a closet door. This shrine may contain a mirror. It may serve as a spot for daily devotions and for a few special occasions such as the naming of a child.

Offerings of rice, fruit, salt, or water are placed at the shrine at the start of every day. These offerings are symbolic: rice gives health and water cleanses. Fruit sweetens life, and salt seasons it. Some homes also have an outdoor shrine.

### Shrine Shinto

To establish Shrine Shinto, government authorities took over private shrines that had been under the control of certain families for centuries. The Meiji oligarchs basically tried to re-create traditional Shinto, which was diverse. They instituted worship of Amaterasu as the divine ancestor of the emperor. This was news to many Japanese, some of whom had never even heard of Amaterasu. The emperor himself was moved from his house of royal seclusion in Kyoto and taken to Tokyo, the new capital. Here he played a prominent part in focusing the worship and attention of the Japanese people. His portrait was worshipped as an icon, his words considered divine speech.

One priest was put in charge of several shrines. Priests were in the government's employ from 1868 to 1945. They were expected to support government policies and Japanese culture. At one point, the government of Japan had 200,000 shrines under its direct control. Most of the priests who served under Shrine Shinto had no special religious training; many of them were retired army officers who needed a job. Priests were paid about the same as schoolteachers, and it wasn't a bad way to make a living.

### State Shinto and the Military

After the Japanese victory in the Russo-Japanese War (a victory that surprised the Japanese almost as much as it did the Russians), State Shinto became a propaganda platform that eventually led to a military buildup and eventually to World War II.

**HOTOKU MOVEMENT**

*The Japanese genius for combining religions is shown in the work of Ninomiya Sontoku (1787–1856), who founded the Hotoku Movement, a combination of two parts Shinto and one part each Buddhism and Confucianism. The goal of the movement was to use ethical principles to solve agricultural and economic difficulties.*

State Shinto promoted a warrior code known as *Bushido*, which outlined a spiritual path for warriors. The culmination of this trend was the role that the kamikaze suicidal pilots played during World War II. Kamikaze pilots (notice the word *kami* hidden in kamikaze) gained notoriety for taking off from Japan with a one-way ticket to bomb Allied ships and so on. Although some people blame Shinto's "warlike" attitude for this development, it should be said that Japanese Buddhists also supported their country's war effort.

After the war, the Occupation forces abolished State Shinto (at least officially). Despite the fact that Shinto is once again a private faith, it still plays an important role in the Japanese consciousness.

**HONORABLE DEATH**

*Ritual suicide has always been treated respectfully and even honorably in Japan. One word, familiar to Westerners, for this practice is* hara-kiri.

### Sectarian Shinto

Sectarian Shinto was divided into thirteen major denominations, some based on ancient practices, others more modern. Three of these denominations, Tai-kyo, Shinri-kyo, and Taisha-kyo carry on very ancient Shinto traditions. Many emphasize the need for spiritual purification. Others focus on the importance of loyalty to the emperor. Another branch focuses on mountain worship, especially Mt. Fuji, which some Japanese consider the creative spirit of the world. Still other Shinto sects have strong Confucian elements.

The followers of Sectarian Shinto suffered disadvantages with the establishment of Shrine Shinto as the state religion. For one thing, they were forbidden, except in special instances, to use the *torii*.

## KONKO-KYO

Konko-kyo is one of the many "new religions" of Japan, although it began during the nineteenth century. The founder is Kawate Bunjiro (1814–1883), who officially registered himself as a Shinto priest. Practitioners of Konko-kyo can contact the divine by means of a mediator. The divine is considered a benevolent god, with many of the characteristics of the god of Christianity and Judaism. Quite unlike many of the traditional *kami*, he has no demonic qualities. The head of a Konko-kyo church, who can be male or female, must be a descendant of Kawate Bunjiro. Konko-kyo is extremely popular with Japanese women, possibly because of its doctrine of equality.

## SHINTOISM IN THE WEST

One form of Shinto has been exported, Johrei, a kind of eclectic religion that also incorporates Buddhist and Christian ideas. Johrei temples can be found in the United States and Brazil.

## CHAPTER RECAP

- Shinto has absorbed many ancient folk traditions.

- The *kami* are the ancient Japanese "gods."

- Unlike many other religions, Shinto tradition has no moral code or holy book.

- Shinto rites are primarily purification rituals.

- From the late 1800s to the end of World War II, the Japanese government oversaw the practice of Shinto.

*Recommended Reading*

Anesaki, Masaharu. *Religious Life of the Japanese People*. Tokyo: The Society for International Cultural Relations, 1961.

Hebert, Jean. *Shinto: At the Fountainhead of Japan*. New York: Stein and Day, 1973.

Hori, Ichiro. *Folk Religion in Japan*. Chicago: University of Chicago Press, 1968.

Picken, Stuart D. B. *Shinto: Japan's Spiritual Roots*. Stanford, CA: Stanford University Press, 1974.

Ross, Floyd. *Shinto, the Way of Japan*. Boston: Beacon Press, 1965.

Yamamoto, Yukitaka. *Way of the Kami*. Stockton, GA: Tsubaki American Publications, 1987.

# GLOSSARY

*Abhidhamma Pitaka* (Buddhism)—One of the three divisions of the Tripitaka, the sacred canon of Theravada Buddhism.

*Advaita Vedanta* (Hinduism)—Nondualism, a point of view espoused by Shankara.

*Adi-Buddha* (Buddhism)—The self-existent Buddha without a beginning.

*Adi Granth* (Sikhism)—Sacred Sikh scripture, compiled by Guru Arjan (1581–1606).

*Agni* (Hinduism)—Vedic God of fire and light.

*Ahimsa* (Buddhism, Hinduism, Jainism)—The principle of non-violence.

*Ahura Mazda* (Zoroastrianism)—God. Also known as Ormuzd.

*Ainu* (Shinto)—Original, Caucasian inhabitants of Japan.

*Ajiva* (Jainism)—Nonliving, nonsentient matter.

*Amaterasu* (Shinto)—Sun goddess.

*Amitabha* (Buddhism)—The Buddha who rules over the Western paradise.

*Analects* (Confucianism)—Collections of Confucius's sayings; one of the Four Books.

*Ananda* (Hinduism)—Bliss. (Buddhism)—Buddha's cousin and favorite disciple.

*Anatman* (Buddhism)—No self.

*Angra Mainyu* (Zoroastrianism)—The Dark Spirit of evil.

*Anicca* (Buddhism)—Impermanence. One of the Three Marks of Existence, along with *anatman* and *dukkha*.

*Aranyakas* (Hinduism)—"Forest treatises." Vedic instructions for hermits. Usually considered the second part of the Vedas and found between the Brahmansa and the Upanishads.

*Arhat* (Buddhism)—In Theravada Buddhism, an enlightened person, a "worthy one."

*Artha* (Hinduism)—Wealth or material success. One of the four permissible goals of life.

*Ashramas* (Hinduism)—Stages of life, including student, householder, hermit, and wanderer.

*Atharva Veda* (Hinduism)—Veda containing magic spells and formulas.

*Atman* (Hinduism)—The soul, the self, the spirit.

*Aum* (Hinduism)—The sacred syllable, symbol of the Brahman.

*Avatar* (Hinduism)—An incarnation assumed by a god.

*Avesta* (Zoroastrianism)—Sacred scripture.

*Avidya* (Hinduism)—A deep, powerful ignorance.

*Bhagavad Gita* (Hinduism)—"The Song of God." A section of the Mahabharata, in which Krishna instructs Arjuna.

*Bhakti* (Hinduism)—Devotional movement.

*Brahma* (Hinduism)—The creator god. He has four arms and four mouths.

*Brahman* (Hinduism)—Uncreated, absolute essence of the universe. The *one.*

*Brahmanas* (Hinduism)—Portion of the Vedas containing rites for various sacrifices.

*Brahmin* (Hinduism)—Priestly caste, the highest of the four castes.

*Buddha* (Buddhism)—The "awakened" one. Usually refers to Siddhartha Gautma.

*Buddha Nature* (Buddhism)—A fully enlightened consciousness.

*Celestial Masters* (Taoism)—A school (still in existence) whose masters trace their lineage back to Chang Tao-ling.

*Chan* (Buddhism)—Chinese meditational Buddhism.

*Chang Tao Ling* (Taoism)—Founder of the Celestial Masters School.

*Chit* (Hinduism)—Knowledge.

*Chuang Tzu* (Taoism)—Disciple of Lao Tzu, author of mystical book of the same title. Now often spelled Zhuangzi. Fourth century B.C.E.

*Chu Hsi* (Confucianism)—Twelfth-century scholar who established Neo-Confucian orthodoxy.

*Dakhma* (Zoroastrianism)—"Towers of Silence." Burial sites.

*Dalai Lama* (Buddhism)—Secular and religious leader of Yellow Hat Tibetan Buddhism.

*David-Neel, Alexandra* (Buddhism)—French explorer and mystic (1868–1969). First Western woman to enter Lhasa.

*Deva* (Hinduism)—A Vedic deity.

*Devi* (Hinduism)—Feminine form of Deva.

*Dharma* (Buddhism, Hinduism)—In Buddhism, Buddha's teachings. In Hinduism, the principle of order.

*Dravidians* (Hinduism)—Dark-skinned, non-Aryan peoples native to India.

*Druj* (Zoroastrianism)—The Lie, the major principle of evil.

*Dualism*—Belief that there exist two realities, spiritual and material; or belief that there exist two equal deities, one good and one evil.

*Dukkha* (Buddhism)—Suffering, discontent. The central fact of existence.

*Durga* (Hinduism)—The great destroyer goddess.

*Dyaus* (Hinduism)—The Aryan shining god of heaven.

*Four Noble Truths* (Buddhism)—Buddha's basic doctine: suffering, the cause of suffering, the cessation of suffering, and the path out of suffering (the Noble Eightfold Path).

*Gathas* (Zoroastrianism)—Hymns attributed to Zarathustra.

*Gautama* (Buddhism)—The clan name of Siddhartha, the Buddha.

*Gobind Singh* (Sikhism)—The tenth and last guru. Founder of the *Khalsa* order.

*Ground of Being* (Taoism)—The foundation of reality.

*Gurdwara* (Sikhism)—Place of worship; contains the Adi Granth.

*Guru* (Hinduism)—Teacher or spiritual guide.

*Guru Nanak* (Sikhism)—Founder of Sikhism.

*Haoma* (Zoroastrianism)—Soma, a sacrificial plant.

*Hara-Kiri* (Shinto)—Ritual suicide.

*Hinayana* (Buddhism)—The "smaller vehicle." A pejorative term for Theravada Buddhism, used primarily by Tibetans.

*I Ching* (Confucianism)—Chinese system of divination.

*Immortals* (Taoism)—Human beings who have become godlike. Some live on earth, others in heaven.

*Indus Valley Civilization* (Hinduism)—Pre-Vedic culture of northwestern India and Pakistan.

*Insight Meditation* (Buddhism)—*Vipassana*, meditation designed to bring insight to the practitioner.

*Izanagi and Izanami* (Shinto)—Original creative pair; authors of the world.

*Jap ji* (Sikhism)—First morning prayer.

*Jataka* (Buddhism)—Stories of the Buddha's previous lives.

*Jen* (Confucianism)—Confucian virtue of human-heartedness.

*Jina* (Jainism)—"Conqueror." A perfected soul who will not be reborn.

*Jiva* (Jainism)—The soul or spirit.

*Ju chia* (Confucianism)—The way of the scholar or gentleman.

*Kabir* (Sikhism)—Sikh/Hindu poet and saint (1440–1518).

*Kali* (Hinduism)—Violent goddess, consort of Shiva.

*Kalpa* (Hinduism, Jainism)—An era of time.

*Kama Sutra* (Hinduism)—Fifth-century text on the science of lovemaking.

*Kami* (Shinto)—Elemental spirits and deities.

*Kamikazi* (Shinto)—Spirit wind, applied to the Japanese suicide pilots of World War II.

*Karma* (Buddhism, Hinduism, Jainism)—Law of cause and effect.

*Karuna* (Buddhism)—Compassion or empathy.

*Koan* (Buddhism)—A word puzzle or riddle in Zen and Chan Buddhism.

*Kojiki* (Shinto)—The earliest chronicles of Japanese history.

*Kshatriya* (Hinduism)—The warrior, ruling caste, the second highest caste.

*Laws of Manu* (Hinduism)—Law book attributed to an ancient king. Contains rules for each caste.

*Legalists* (Confucianism)—Philosophic school that advocated strict laws and harsh punishments.

*Li* (Confucianism)—Ritual, appropriate ceremony, etiquette.

*Loka* (Hinduism)—The universe where sentient beings are reborn.

*Lotus Sutra* (Buddhism)—Scripture venerated by Nichiren sect.

*Mahabharata* (Hinduism)—Immensely long Indian epic. Story of the Bharat War.

*Mahavira* (Jainism)—Founder of Jainism, sixth century B.C.E. The twenty-fourth *Tirthankara*.

*Mahayana* (Buddhism)—The Great Vehicle of Buddhism, the liberal wing emphasizing compassion and salvation for all.

*Mandala* (Buddhism)—Sacred circle chart of the universe and path to salvation.

*Manifest Tao* (Taoism)—Being as it appears.

*Mantra* (Buddhism, Hinduism)—Short sacred phrase. The most famous mantra is *AUM*.

*Mara* (Buddhism)—The evil tempter of Buddha.

*Marga* (Hinduism)—A path or way. Another word for *yoga*.

*Maya* (Hinduism)—Illusion. The world as it appears to the senses.

*Mencius* (Confucianism)—Later disciple of Confucius who emphasized innate human goodness.

*Milarepa* (Buddhism)—Tibetan Buddhist saint, leader of Kagyupa sect, eleventh and twelfth centuries.

*Monotheism*—Belief in one god.

*Motoori Norinaga* (Shinto)—Eighteenth-century reformer and reviver of Shinto.

*Nadi* (Tantra)—Conduit, energy channel of the subtle (inner) body.

*Nagarjuna* (Buddhism)—Philosopher who established the Madhyamika school of philosophy.

*Nanak* (Sikhism)—Founder of Sikhism (1469–1538).

*Nihongi* (Shinto)—Chronicle of Japan, historical Shinto text.

*Nirvana* (Buddhism)—Literally "blowing out." The ultimate state of enlightenment.

*Noble Eightfold Path* (Buddhism)—Practical discipline to achieve Nirvana: right understanding, right thought, right speech, right action, right livelihood, right effort, right mindfulness, right concentration.

*Om* (Hinduism)—*See* Aum.

*P'eng Lai Shan* (Taoism)—The Blessed Isles, mythical land of immortal masters.

*P'o* (Confucianism)—The earthly soul.

*Pali* (Buddhism)—Indian language in which the sacred writings of Buddhism were first composed.

*Patanjali* (Hinduism)—Author of the Yoga Sutras.

*Prana* (Hinduism)—Breath.

*Pure Land Buddhism* (Buddhism)—Variety of Mahayana Buddhism popular in Japan.

*Ramanuja* (Hinduism)—Formulator of the school of Qualified Non-Dualism (1017–1137).

*Ram Das* (Sikhism)—The Fourth Guru, creator of the city of Amritsar, site of the Golden Temple.

*Ram Dass* (Hinduism)—Richard Alpert, American LSD researcher, philosopher, consciousness raiser.

*Rig Veda* (Hinduism)—Holy Scripture of Hinduism.

*Rita* (Hinduism)—Vedic principle of moral and cosmic order.

*Saicho* (Buddhism)—Monk who brought Tendai Buddhism to Japan.

*Samadhi* (Hinduism, Tantra)—Intense concentration, a super-conscious trance.

*Samsara* (Hinduism)—Cycle of birth, death, and rebirth.

*Sanatana* (Hinduism)—The eternal way of truth.

*Sangha* (Buddhism)—Monastic community founded by the Buddha.

*Sankhya* (Hinduism)—One of the six orthodox schools of Hindu philosophy. Asserts many souls and one undifferentiated matter.

*Sat* (Hinduism)—Being.

*Satori* (Buddhism)—Zen state of enlightened awareness.

*Shaman* (Shinto)—A Siberian word, referring to a spiritual leader who has direct communication with spirits.

*Shang Ti* (Confucianism)—Chinese supreme god.

*Shih* (Confucianism)—Power, authority.

*Shiva* (Hinduism)—Epic deity; god of destruction.

*Shruti* (Hinduism)—Sacred literature such as the Vedas. That which is "heard."

*Shu* (Confucianism)—The principle of reciprocity.

*Shudra* (Hinduism)—The laboring caste.

*Siddhartha* (Buddhism)—The "goal-attainer." The Buddha's first name before his enlightenment.

*Sita* (Hinduism)—Goddess and wife of Rama.

*Smriti* (Hinduism)—Scriptures that are "remembered;" considered secondary to *shruti* or "heard" scriptures.

*Soma* (Hinduism)—A god and a sacred intoxicating drink.

*Stupa* (Buddhism)—Bell-shaped mound containing holy relics.

*Tanha* (Buddhism)—Craving, grasping, desire that lies at the root of suffering.

*Tala* (Hinduism)—Plane or world. Root of the name of the seven realms of lower consciousness.

*Tao* (Taoism)—The Way, the eternal principle.

*Tao Te Ching* (Taoism)—"The Way and Its Power." Master Taoist text, attributed to Lao Tzu.

*Tara* (Buddhism)—Protective goddess.

*Tathagata* (Buddhism)—Title used for the Buddha, "the one who has gone before."

*Tathata* (Buddhism)—The state of "thusness."

*Theravada* (Buddhism)—The Way of the Elders, the "conservative" wing of Buddhism, emphasizing wisdom.

*Tirthankara* (Jainism)—A "ford-finder;" one of the twenty-four founders of Jainism.

*Torii* (Shinto)—Gate leading into Shinto shrine. Symbol of Shinto.

*Trikaya* (Buddhism)—The "three bodies" doctrine of Buddhism.

*Tripitaka* (Buddhism)—The "three baskets"; in Theravada Buddhism, the collection of sacred writings.

*Unmanifest Tao* (Taoism)—Being and non-being in their ultimate form.

*Ushas* (Hinduism)—White-clothed Vedic dawn goddess.

*Vaishya* (Hinduism)—Merchant caste.

*Vajra* (Buddhism)—The diamond scepter used in Tibetan Buddhism.

*Varuna* (Hinduism)—Vedic keeper of the night sky, and of order, a.k.a. Lord of Consciousness.

*Vedanta* (Hinduism)—The "end of the Vedas." Term used almost interchangeably with Upanishads. Commentary on the Vedas.

*Vedas* (Hinduism)—Sacred scriptures, divine works, that manifest the glorious primal energy of both creation and eternity.

*Venidad* (Zoroastrianism)—Part of the Avesta devoted to spells against demons.

*Vishnu* (Hinduism)—God of preservation and sustenance.

*Vohu Manah* (Zoroastrianism)—The divine aspect of Good Mind.

*Wen* (Confucianism)—Cultural refinement; civilized behavior.

*Wu wei* (Taoism)—Principle of "actionless action;" being spontaneous.

*Yang* (Confucianism, Taoism)—The light, dry, hot force. The masculine force.

*Yasna* (Zoroastrianism)—Liturgical scripture. Includes the Gathas.

*Yellow Hat* (Buddhism)—"Reformed" branch (Gelugpa) of Tibetan Buddhism of which the Dalai Lama is the head.

*Yin* (Confucianism, Taoism)—The dark, moist, mysterious force. The feminine force.

*Yoga* (Hinduism)—Spiritual discipline.

*Yogacara* (Buddhism)—Mind-only school of Mahayana Buddhism.

*Yoni* (Hinduism)—Vaginal symbol.

*Zazen* (Buddhism)—Seated meditation.

*Zen* (Buddhism)—A type of Buddhism that traces its founding to Bodhidharma. Known as Chan in China.

*Zendo* (Buddhism)—A Zen meditation hall.

*Zurvan* (Zoroastrianism)—Eternal time, a concept accepted by a subgroup of Zoroastrians.

# INDEX

## ABOUT THE AUTHOR

Diane Morgan lives in Williamsport, Maryland, with her human family and collection of pets (seven dogs, two cats, and numerous goldfish). She is an adjunct professor of religion and philosophy at Wilson College, in Chambersburg, Pennsylvania. Morgan is currently working on a book about Taoism and Tarot. In addition to writing about religion, she writes books about dogs. She finds them inspiring.

## Meditations on Tantra
Osho
Cassette edition • ISBN: 1-55927-448-4 • $16.95

## Meditations on Tao
Osho
Cassette edition • ISBN: 1-55927-429-8 • $16.95

## Meditations on Zen
Osho
Cassette edition • ISBN: 1-55927-428-X • $16.95

## Opening the Eye of New Awareness
His Holiness the Dalai Lama
Cassette edition • ISBN: 1-55927-576-6 • $17.95

## The Way of Qigong
Kenneth S. Cohen
Cassette edition • ISBN: 1-55927-464-6 • $16.95

## The Way of Zen
Alan W. Watts
Cassette edition • ISBN: 0-940687-90-9 • $10.95

## Wherever You Go, There You Are
Jon Kabat-Zinn, Ph.D.
Cassette edition • ISBN: 1-55927-262-7 • $16.95
CD edition • ISBN: 1-55927-662-2 • $26.00

## Zen and Japanese Culture
D. T. Suzuki
Cassette edition • ISBN: 1-55927-657-6 • $39.95

## Zen Practice, Zen Art
Alan W. Watts
Cassette edition • ISBN: 1-55927-050-0 • $9.95

**To order please call 1-800-452-5589**